D1794842

MAZOVIA

TRADITION AND THE PRESENT

PUBLICATION UNDER THE PATRONAGE
OF THE SEJMIK AND BOARD
OF MAZOWIECKIE VOIVODESHIP

SCIENTIFIC PUBLISHERS SCHOLAR
WARSAW

Authors

Wojciech Dziemianowicz, Aleksander Herz, Józef Kazimierski,
Krzysztof Kostyrko, Roman Szul, Tomasz Zarycki, Jacek Żurowski

Editor

Grzegorz Kaliński, assisted by Roland Smogór

Translated by Aleksandra Rodzińska-Chojnowska

Graphic design

Andrzej-Ludwik Włoszczyński

Typesetting

Jerzy Łazarski

Proofreading

Roland Smogór

Photographs by Maciej and Mirosław Ciunowicz (p. 7, 20, 22, 33, 36, 37, 38,
40, 42, 44, 50, 53, 59, 62, 79, 97, 121, 126 bottom, 129, 135, 138, 140,
147, 148, 149, 150, 151, 152, 153, 154, 156, 158, 159, 160, 162, 163, 166,
168, 169, 170, 173, 174, 176, 177), Michał Sobótka (p. 45, 62 bottom, 68),
Filip Raciborski (p. 65, 71, 92, 139, 143), Krzysztof Wojciewski (p. 136), Marek
Kołaszewski (p. 51), Andrzej Karwowski (p. 93), Marek Kalinowski (126 top)

Copyright © 1999 by Scientific Publishers Scholar, Warsaw

ISBN: 83-87367-83-4

Distribution: Scientific Publishers „Scholar"
ul. Krakowskie Przedmieście 62, 00-322 Warsaw
tel./fax 828-93-91, 635-74-04 w. 218;
sales: 635-74-04 w. 219
e-mail: info@scholar.com.pl
http://www.scholar.com.pl

Printing and binding: Drukarnia Naukowo-Techniczna, Warszawa.

Publication financed by
the Board of Mazowieckie Voivodeship
and Scientific Publishers SCHOLAR.

The publishers would like to express their
gratitude to all those institutions and persons
that assisted in the completion of this work.
Particular thanks are due
to the sponsors of the book:

GRUPA
ComputerLand

BANK HANDLOWY W WARSZAWIE SA
ROK ZAŁOŻENIA 1870

MAZOVIA

■

TRADITION AND THE PRESENT

TABLE OF CONTENTS

AN OUTLINE
OF MAZOVIAN HISTORY

■

In the twelfth century, Płock and its environs came second only to Wrocław and Krakow, both as regards the size and significance. Romanesque architecture developed in numerous concentrations of settlements and castle-towns: in Płock (palatium, Romanesque rotunda and cathedral), Czerwińsk (the Romanesque monastery of the Benedictines and, from 1155, of the canons regular) and, possibly, in Ciechanów and Szreńsk. The interest in Mazovia shown by the first Piast rulers, and the inclusion of this region into the state of the Polanie were not accidental. The terrains on the Vistula, the Bug, the Narew, the Wkra and the Drwęca in the north, and the Pilica and the Bzura in the south were crossed by crucial communication routes and possessed enormous political and economic significance. They constituted the key to the consolidation of the new Gniezno state.

THE EARLY PIAST ERA

In the opinion of the outstanding Polish historian, Aleksander Gieysztor: "Mazovia, its name, territorial range and inclusion into the first Polish monarchy are shrouded by a veil of oblivion"; only investigations pursued by historians and archeologists endeavour to lift this cloak. The very name of Mazovia (Polish: Mazowsze) poses a long unsolved puzzle.

Mazovia was never a uniform land, but contained several regions: Old (Płock) Mazovia, Field Mazovia (left-bank) and Woodland Mazovia (Kurpie). Certain areas – Kurpie, Łowicz and Kołbiela have retained their characteristic image as well as a cultural and even dialect distinction. Ultimately, the name of Mazowsze was accepted for this large land, although it frequently changed its administrative and even Church borders. In the Middle Ages, its inhabitants, known as Mazurzy, settled a considerable part of the borderland part of Prussia, all the way to the Mazury lake district and further on (the later Warmia and Mazuria).

In Mazovia itself, the settlement movement became stable at the end of the seventh century, in the wake of the migration of the peoples and the crisis suffered by Europe after the fall of the Roman Empire at the end of the fifth century. The following period saw rapid development, predominantly in the Płock-Ciechanów part of Mazovia. Here, the tribal system entered the phase of stability during the ninth century. Larger settlement concentrations erected strongholds, particularly in the environs of Płock and Drohiczyn. The fundamental political unit was the tribe, in time followed probably by the multi-tribal union.

To the north, the frontier of Mazovia in the Piast monarchy followed the unsettled stretches of land along the Mazury lakes and reached the Galindzka and Sasińska forests. This border proved to be the most stable and, with slight deviations (in the region of Działdów and along the upper Orzyc), it survived up to the second world war as the northern boundary of the former voivodeship of Warsaw. Further on, it followed the upper Wkra and the woodland valley of the Skrwa to the Vistula. Next, it encompassed Goszynińska Forest and headed south-east. After reaching the Bzura above Łowicz, it followed the river Mroga, embraced the entire basin of the Rawa, and reached the Pilica above Łęgonice. Having crossed the Pilica, it encircled Stromiecka Forest (the late mediaeval Zapilice area) and met the Vistula by following the river Radomka. Subsequently, the frontier arrived at the outlet of the Prądnik and then once again transversed forests situated to the north-east to run along the watershed of the Wilga towards the upper Liwiec. The line on the banks of the Liwiec ended in Brok, having left behind the Kamieniecka and Kamieńczyk Forests in Mazovia, and went up the Bug to the outlet of the Nurzyc. By adhering to the upward current of the latter river, it crossed wooded terrains, partially bogs, and finally reached Sudovia near Grajewo. From here, the boundary turned south-west and ended in the Mazury lake district, which constituted the northern frontier of Mazovia.

Apart from the unwavering northern frontier, also the western and southern parts guaranteed a permanent range owing to dense settlements on the Kujawy, Łęczyca, Radom and Sieciechów side. On the other hand, sparse settlements scattered among immense marshes and forests along the eastern border on the right bank of the Vistula, along the Narew, the Bug, the Liwiec and the Nurzec, became an easy target of the attacks launched by the Balt peoples, the Sudovians, Rus' and, later, the Lithuanians.

Was this unevenly settled area a fragment of a tribal entity known as Mazovia? There is no unambiguous answer to this inquiry. It is known that primal Mazovia was composed of a land to the north of the Vistula and to the west of the Orzyc, with few territorial additions. Gallus Anonymous, the renowned chronicler from the reign of Bolesław the Wrymouth (beginning of the twelfth century), wrote that arrivals from the West "crossed the Vistula towards Mazovia". A recently published article by Prof. Henryk Samsonowicz bears the provocative title: *Czy Warszawa leży na Mazowszu?* (Does Warsaw Lie in Mazovia?).

The distinctness of both regions to the north and to the south of the Vistula became marked particularly in their Church organization, patterned on the administrative-state counterpart. It is clear that the boundaries of the state of Mieszko I at the time of his baptism were delineated by the borders of the Poznań diocese. After the establishment of the Gniezno diocese in 1000, part of the Poznań diocese encompassed the archdeaconry in Grójec (later, in Czersk and, from the fourteenth century, in Warsaw). The Płock diocese, established for the right bank of the Vistula, was created in 1075.

Northern Mazovia was a point of departure for the attempted Christianisation and conquest of Prussia. Here probably lay the first trail followed by St. Wojciech (Adalbert) towards northern Mazovia and further on to Prussia. In 1009, St. Brunon of Querfurt led a mission to the Sudovians, the neighbours of the Pruthenians. This undertaking also ended in failure and the martyrdom of its organizer. Both ventures were conducted with the knowledge and support of Bolesław the Brave.

After the defeat of the two Church missions Bolesław decided to embark upon an armed conquest and conversion of Prussia. With this goal in mind, he resorted to his rights to Prussian lands, granted by Emperor Otto III at the Gniezno convention held in 1000. The first armed expedition from Mazovia set off in 1015. Ultimately, it was stalled by the Mazury lakes and ended in a fiasco. In its wake, relative peace reigned along the Prussian borderland for more than a hundred years.

Bolesław the Brave perceived the protection of the Mazovian-Prussian and Mazovian-Sudovian borderland as an extremely important political issue. This attitude is testified by the erection of a Romanesque rotunda and palatium in the Płock castle-town where Bolesław was a frequent visitor and from which he reinforced the position of his state. Moreover, the Polish ruler intended to influence the extremely slow progress of Christianisation in Mazovia. The first Benedictine abbey was built in Płock probably during his reign.

Upon the death of Bolesław in 1025 and Mieszko II in 1034, power was seized by Kazimierz, later known as the Restorer, whose authority was never recognised by Duke Miecław, the founder of the separate state of Mazovia (1034–1047).

At the beginning of 1038, Duke Kazimierz fled the country in order to seek foreign assistance for his struggle against the rebellious Miecław. Several months later, a Bohemian invasion was accompanied by peasant unrest, known as the pagan reaction, aimed against the rule of the clergy and the castle-towns. A disintegration of the Polish state followed. Peace was preserved only in Mazovia, which offered refuge to members of the clergy and affluent lords from the localities affected by the revolt and apostasy. The newcomers reinforced the apparatus of power at the disposal of Duke Miecław and Mazowsze turned into a populous and rich land. In his capacity as a truly sovereign ruler the duke could afford to conduct his own foreign policy. He entered into an alliance with Sudovia, Lithuania and the Pomeranians, and organized expeditions against Rus'. Furthermore, Miecław decided to regain the left bank of Mazovia and to seize power in the state. Kazimierz proved to be a better politician, and with the assistance of Rus' dispersed the forces of the Mazovian duke in 1047.

The events of those years must have made an indelible imprint upon the character of the Mazovian warriors who were to become members of the extremely numerous local petty gentry: bellicose, proud, self-assured and outright swashbuckling.

After the death of Kazimierz the Restorer in 1054 power was assumed by his two sons: Bolesław (later known as the Bold) in Poland and Władysław Herman in Mazovia. The latter referred to the times of his great predecessor, Bolesław the Brave, and situated his residence in Płock, the main town of Płock Mazovia. During his ducal and regal reign (1054–1079) Władysław Herman proved to be an excellent administrator who created an entire system of castle-towns, strongholds and fortifications along the border with Prussia and throughout northern Mazovia. They are mentioned in the so-called Mogilno forgery – a document issued in 1065 by Bolesław the Bold for the Benedictine monastery in Mogilno, describing the endowment of the monks. Social stability was accompanied by the development of the local economy. The population derived considerable benefits from trade and mediation in commercial exchange, mainly with the residents of Prussian castle-towns. Borderland forests were inhabited by hunters, bee-keepers and pitch burners. Expansion from overpopulated Mazovia to Prussia dates back to the reign of Władysław Herman when the name of Mazovia was given also to the left bank of the Vistula, i.e. the region of Czersk. In this manner, it pertained to the entire historical region.

Płock was also the residence of Bolesław the Wrymouth (1102–1138) who intended to conquer and Christianise Prussia by means of three armed expeditions which set off from northern Mazovia across the Zawkrze region in 1107–1108, 1110–1111 and 1115. Their outcome, however, assumed the form of pillage and the devastation of the lands inhabited by the Prussian, Sasin and Galind tribes. Furthermore, such clashes resulted in Prussian military reprisal, which came to the fore during the feudal disintegration of Poland after 1138.

Władysław Herman and Bolesław the Wrymouth were buried in Płock cathedral where their ashes remain up to this day. The period of their residence in Płock could be described without undue exaggeration as a Golden Age in the history of northern Mazovia.

Mazovian eastward expansion generated rivalry with Rus' for Podlasie and predominantly, the castle-town of Drohiczyn; after the Lithuanian conquest of Rus' at the close of the thirteenth century and in the fourteenth century Drohiczyn found itself under Lithuanian rule.

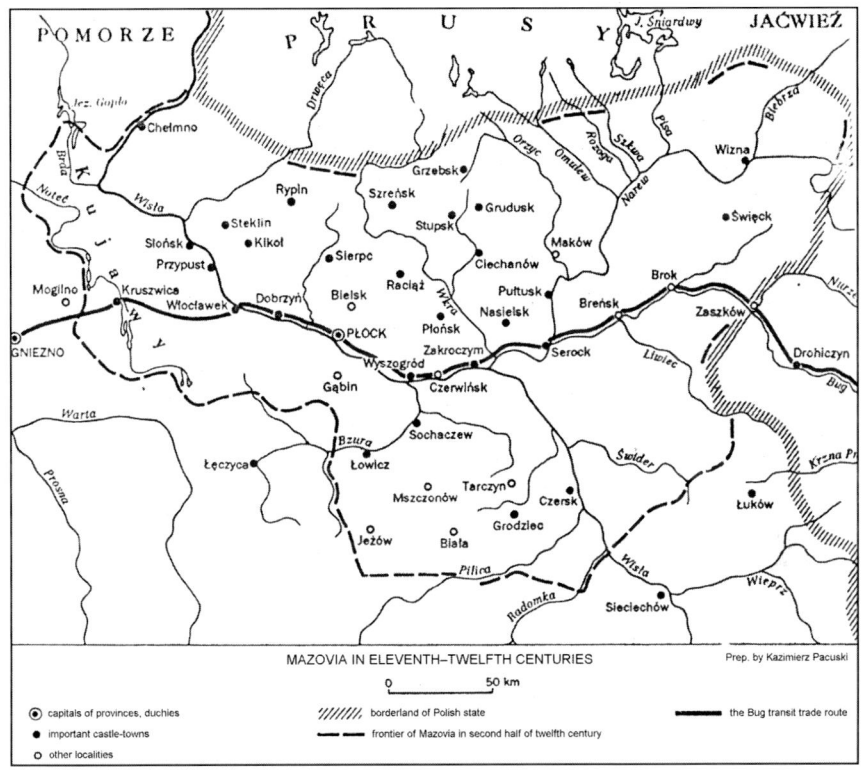

MAZOVIA IN ELEVENTH–TWELFTH CENTURIES

Prep. by Kazimierz Pacuski

0   50 km

⊙ capitals of provinces, duchies   ░░░░ borderland of Polish state   ▬▬ the Bug transit trade route

● important castle-towns   ▬ ▬ frontier of Mazovia in second half of twelfth century

○ other localities

From the 1120s, the military activity of the Prussians grew in intensity. At the beginning of the thirteenth century, they were joined by the Lithuanians and the Sudovians. The ensuing situation became menacing. Invasions destroyed the settlement network in northern Mazovia. The heretofore "land of milk and honey" became depopulated to such an extent that the borderline of Slav settlements receded by about 100 kilometres, rendering the northern and north-eastern (Mazovian) frontier of the Polish state highly vulnerable.

■

THE INDEPENDENT DUCHY OF MAZOVIA

In 1200, power in Mazovia was seized by Konrad I, then under-age, later known as Konrad of Mazovia. The young duke was compelled to tackle two issues: the Prussian question and, after the death of Leszek the White in 1227, the rivalry for the Krakow throne. Ultimately, Konrad decided to invite the Teutonic Order from Hungary, and to assign it the land of Chełmno in return for assistance in overcoming Prussia. In 1226, the Order secured a protection document issued by Emperor Friedrich II (known as the "Golden Bull"), confirming the resolution of the Mazovian duke and granting the Teutonic Knights all the lands which they were to capture in the future.

Freed from all restraints, Knights of the German Order of the Holy Virgin Mary rapidly built a whole system of defensive castles on the vanquished terrains of

11

Prussia, stifled local rebellions held in the thirteenth century and organized a state according to the best European models of the period. The Order also intended to seize Mazovia by establishing trade outposts. Finally, it assumed control over trade on the Vistula by taking over Gdańsk and certain towns in western Pomerania (e.g. Bytów).

In 1228, having ensured peace in the north and in the east, Konrad of Mazovia embarked upon a struggle for the throne in Krakow, but suffered defeat at the battle of Skałka. In 1229, he incorporated the regions of Łęczyca and Sieradz into his duchy.

An outstanding role at the court of Konrad I in Płock and Łęczyca was played by his wife, the ambitious and proud Duchess Agathia, daughter of Svetoslav Andrei, the Duke of Novgorod. The ducal court was composed of educated and worldly counsellors as well as a chancery employing a chancellor, a vice-chancellor and scribes. The scriptorium of Płock cathedral was employed for copying liturgical books.

In the years 1207–1247, Konrad used the title of Duke of Mazovia and Kujawy, and from 1241 – of the Duke of Krakow and Łęczyca as well. The inscription on one of his seals declares: *Sigillum Conradi ducis Poloniae*, expressing the monarchic ambitions cherished by Konrad. The ducal majestic seal depicts "the Mazovian Pogoń" – a likeness of the ruler brandishing a cross and a spear and shown astride a galloping mount.

Equestrian seal of Duke Konrad I from 1223

Under Konrad, the Mazovian duchy stretched from Bydgoszcz to Wizna, and from Szreńsk to Sieradz, the Pilica and the Liwiec. Nonetheless, it remained inferior to numerous other provinces, especially Lower Silesia, both as regards the size of the population and economic potential.

The duke was a forceful ruler, capable of coming to terms with the emancipatory plans of the Church. He multiplied the ranks of the local knights and erected settlement fortifications around certain castle-towns, such as Czersk, which he turned into one of his residences. Finally, he developed landed estates in Błonie-Rokitno and Jazdów, and built the castle-town in Unierzył between Mława and Raciąż. New, vigorous groups of traders appeared in Mazovia. A document issued by the local bishop in 1237 announced the first *locatio civitatis* of Płock: newcomers acquired privileges equal to those enjoyed by the Mazovian knights.

Historical literature assumes that the first half of the thirteenth century was a favourable time for Mazovia. Economic development was associated with the functioning of the old Ruthenian route from Włodzimierz *via* Volhynia and Drohiczyn, along the Bug and the Vistula to Płock and further on across Pomerania to the Baltic coast. On the way, it probably branched off in Serock or Zakroczym.

Upon the death of Konrad, the Łęczyca-Sieradz region joined Kujawy. Mazovia bore the brunt of particularism and economic regression caused primarily by the second Lithuanian onslaught of 1262. On St. John's Eve (23 June 1262) the Lithuanians surprised the unprepared Duke Siemowit I in Jazdów – the Mazovian ruler was beheaded on the spot and his son Konrad was taken captive. The outcome of the invasion is compared to the Tartar raids which overran Little Poland and Silesia in 1241. Jazdów, Czersk and Płock were destroyed, and a considerable number of the population was captured. The entire apparatus of ducal authority and the military potential of Mazovia were shattered. Settlements on the Bug, including parish centres, simply disappeared.

An enormous role in the reconstruction of the duchy was performed by Duchess Perejesława, the wife of Siemowit. In the middle of the 1270s, Mazovia was divided between her two sons: Bolesław II acquired the province of Płock together with five castellan castle-towns (Płock, Wyszogród, Gostynin, Sochaczew and Biała) as well as the title of the Duke of Mazovia and the *dominus* of Płock. Konrad II was granted the province of Czersk together with Ciechanów, Zakroczym, Wizna, Jazdów and the earth-wooden castle-town in Czersk (a brick castle was not built until the mid-fourteenth century) as well as the title of the Duke of Mazovia and Czersk. Perejesława kept Sochaczew, where she probably died in 1283.

Bolesław II, the ruler representing the widest ambitions amongst all the Mazovian dukes at the turn of the fourteenth century (he died in 1313), decided to oppose the Teutonic Order. With this purpose in mind, he concluded an agreement

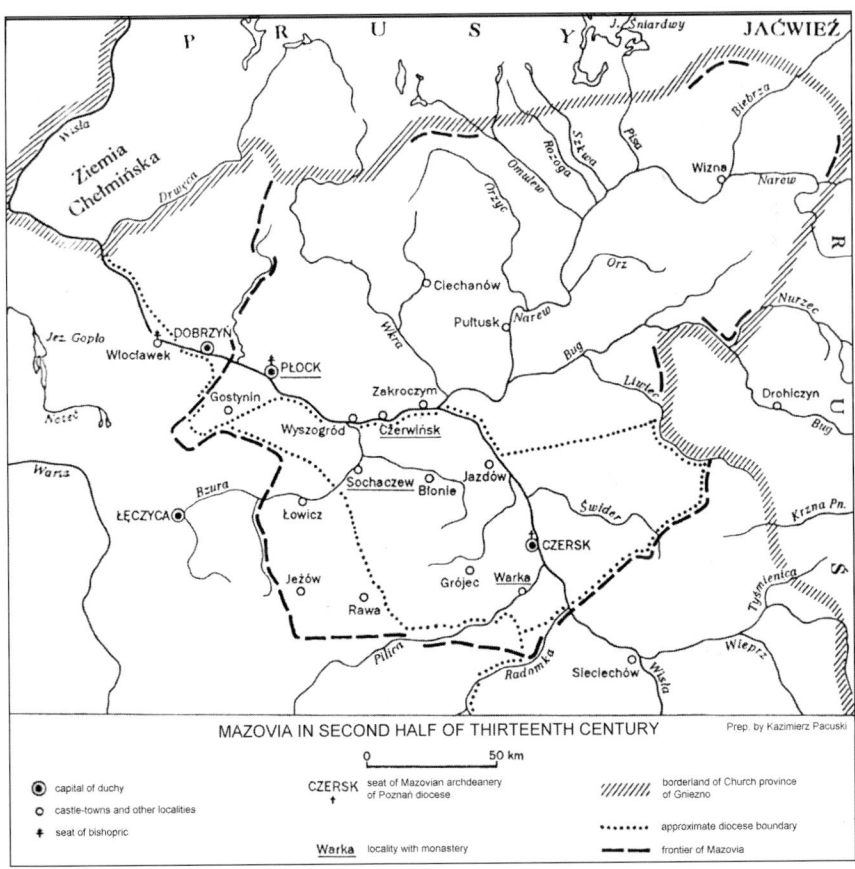

MAZOVIA IN SECOND HALF OF THIRTEENTH CENTURY   Prep. by Kazimierz Pacuski

0   50 km

⊙ capital of duchy

○ castle-towns and other localities

✦ seat of bishopric

CZERSK seat of Mazovian archdeanery of Poznań diocese
✝

Warka locality with monastery

/////// borderland of Church province of Gniezno

••••••••• approximate diocese boundary

▬ ▬ ▬ frontier of Mazovia

with the Lithuanians and Władysław Łokietek (the Short), a policy which, unfortunately, was discontinued by his sons. Once again, foreign armies appeared in Mazovia – first the troops of John of Luxembourg in 1329 (in the Duchy of Płock) and then the Lithuanians.

In 1313, after the death of Bolesław II, Mazovia was divided into three parts. The rank of Płock diminished and was supplanted for a short period of time by Czersk and then by Rawa and Warsaw. A greater part was played by Wizno and Sochaczew which Siemowit II turned into the ducal seat. In his capacity as the senior, he coordinated the foreign policy pursued by Mazovia.

Trojden was granted the province of Czersk, but after the raids neither Czersk nor the wooden manor house in Jazdów were suitable residences. The duke decided to elevate Warsaw to the rank of a town, to surround it with a defence wall, and to built his residence there. Already in 1339, the Polish-Teutonic trial took place in Warsaw (in the House of the Mazovian Dukes, today situated in the Old Town Market Square). Trojden also expanded Czersk, Warka and other towns. He introduced new settlers on the wastelands produced by the hostilities. The peace which prevailed along the borders up to the 1330s was conducive for trade: the importance of the Vistula as a commercial route continued to rise. Trojden himself used the title of *dux Mazoviae ac Varsaviensis dominus*.

The third duchy was received by Wacław, the youngest heir, known as Wańko, the Duke of Mazovia and the *dominus* of Płock, whose turbulent policy sought a political compromise with the Teutonic Order. When in 1329 John of Luxembourg, the King of Bohemia, invaded Płock, the vanquished Wańko recognised his rights to the Polish throne and obligated himself to render assistance in the struggle against Władysław the Short. The Luxembourg-Teutonic alliance posed a threat not only to Mazovia but Poland as a whole. Fortunately, Kazimierz the Great recognised this hazard in time, and bought off the Bohemian claims to the Polish throne in return for considerable sums; nonetheless, for years to come he was forced to acknowledge the feudal dependence of the Płock duchy upon Bohemia.

In 1344, a few months after a Polish-Teutonic treaty was signed in Kalisz, Bolesław III, the son of Wacław of Płock, concluded, together with his uncle Bolesław II, an agreement with the Order regulating the northern border of Mazovia which with certain slight alterations survived until 1939.

The century spanning from the mid-thirteenth century to the mid-fourteenth century signified a veritable breakthrough for Mazovia which remained outside the frontiers of the emergent Polish Kingdom created by Kazimierz the Great. To the north-east, the area of Mazovia increased after the recapture of Wizna and the conquests made in Prussia and Sudovia. The role of Płock diminished, and the capitals of the new provinces: Czersk and Rawa became increasingly important; Warsaw was founded and subsequently developed. Those changes, however, did not affect the backwardness of Mazovia, which it proved impossible to eliminate also in the following centuries.

The mid-fourteenth century marked the commencement of a more advantageous period for Mazovia. Europe went through an economic-social crisis, caused primarily by Black Death, whose victims totalled one-third of the population of

Europe. Western knights willingly participated in expeditions organized by the Teutonic Order against Lithuania, hoping for loot, glory and salvation for their souls. Merchants from Flanders, Germany and Italy as well as residents of assorted Western towns and villages drifted to Mazovia, accelerating the urbanisation of the land on the Vistula. The Mazovian dukes accomplished a re-orientation of their policy, and drew closer to Kazimierz the Great, who was concerned also with protecting the northern frontier of the Polish state. This tendency was skillfully exploited by Duke Siemowit III who in 1355 obtained the whole of Mazovia as a fief. Moreover, the king exempted him from all obligations towards his successors in case he died without leaving a male descendant.

Provincial divisions of Mazovia from 1381

In 1381, after the forty year long reign of Siemowit III, who was buried in Płock cathedral, Mazovia was divided. Janusz I received Czersk, Warsaw, Liw, Nur, Łomża, Ciechanów, Różan, Zakroczyn and Wyszogród, while the younger duke Siemowit IV was granted Płock, Płońsk, Zawkrze, Rawa, Gostynin, Sochaczew and Wizna. The state governed by Janusz was extensive but poorer than the Rawa or Płock regions. Furthermore, it was situated in the very centre of conflicts between the Teutonic Knights and Lithuania, and Lithuania and Poland, respectively. Janusz I focused his attention on the economic development of his state, and Siemowit IV continued the plans of his predecessor – to ascend the throne in Krakow – for which he required considerable funds. He began to draw debts, predominantly in the state of the Teutonic Order, and in 1382 and 1384 signed an alliance with the Knights. Ultimately, the situation was clarified by the election of Jagiełło as the King of Poland. Siemowit IV married the sister of Jagiełło, and Janusz I – the sister of Witold, the Grand Duke of Lithuania and the brother of the newly crowned monarch.

At the turn of the fourteenth century, the Teutonic state imported Mazovian timber, pitch, birch tar, wax, calx, honey and food (grain and oxen). Trade enabled further development of Hanseatic towns, headed by Toruń, Gdańsk and Królewiec (Königsberg).

This state of affairs did not, however, denote peace along the frontiers. In 1393, Teutonic detachments demolished the castle in Złotoria, built at the outlet of the Supraśl to the Narew, and abducted from Opinogóra Duke Janusz together with his family and guards. Teutonic raids reached central Mazovia. Not a single month passed without assault and plunder. Even after the battle of Grunwald and the ensuing first peace of Toruń, signed in 1412, the boundary with the state of the Teutonic Knights remained ablaze.

Let us now take a closer look at the development of the administration and socioeconomic relations in Mazovia up to the end of the fifteenth century. The complete Christianisation of this terrain was determined by the expansion of the parish network, initiated during the twelfth century and linked with rural and castle-town settlement and, subsequently, with the urbanisation of Mazovia. Completed at the close of the fourteenth century and during the fifteenth century, only in the eastern terrains did this process take place as late as the sixteenth century.

15

The fourteenth and fifteenth centuries saw the formation of territorial self-government and the emergence of town and land courts. The administrative structure was composed of counties, lands and voivodeships. Towns founded according to the German (Środa or Chełmno) law enjoyed economic and court immunities.

Extensive transformations became possible only after the Polish-Lithuanian union, signed at the end of the fourteenth century. Armed hostilities along the borderland came to an end, and the eastern frontier of Mazovia ceased acting as the eastern border of the state. A transition from a natural to a commodity-money economy freed the existing and newly founded villages and settlements from the burdens of ducal law and led to grants of the Chełmno law. The settlement movement in Biała Forest and Zagajnica, later known as Zielona Forest, grew in intensity. These terrains were the destination of settlers from Płock Mazovia and regions situated to the west of the Vistula that gained advantage from particularly favourable conditions – they made payments, necessary for the retention of castle-towns and the maintenance of the ducal court. The settlers were also obligated to render military services, i.e. to participate in the defence of threatened frontiers. The Mazovian dukes were interested in a rapid colonisation of the forests. At the end of the fifteenth century and during the sixteenth century demand for Polish timber continued to grow in Western Europe, especially in the Netherlands and Portugal. Geographic discoveries entailed the further development of ship building, and Polish pines and yews provided excellent material.

A large role in shaping the settlement movement was performed by trade routes which, after the Polish-Lithuanian union, now ran across Mazovia. Lithuania, the largest fur exporter in the region, became a partner in international trade. Already at the beginning of the fifteenth century, the important route leading from Brześć to Wrocław, *via* Liw, Warsaw, Piotrków, Wieluń and Bolesławiec was used for transporting Oriental commodities. Another significant route joined the two capitals: Krakow and Wilno.

Urbanisation in Mazovia was inaugurated relatively late, undoubtedly due to the low material standing of local society. This situation remained unchanged until the development of transit trade, the attainment of stability along the borders, and the development of commerce on the Vistula during the fourteenth and fifteenth century. The Mazovian dukes now required towns, conceived as centres of trade and sources of revenue.

Up to 1374, only ten towns in Mazovia, including Warsaw, were granted *locatio civitatis*. In 1429, there were already 66 urban centres, providing considerable profits used by Siemowit IV for competing for the throne in Krakow and by Duke Janusz I for building castles and residences in eastern Mazovia. Janusz I also erected manors in Opinogóra, Nowe Miasto, Maków, Różan, Ostrołęka, Łomża and Nowogród. The Duke travelled from locality to locality, controlling the economic life of the country and performing judicial functions. The regular nature of those visits contributed to enlivening the economic and cultural activity of the towns and ensured larger and regular revenues for the ducal treasury. During this period (to 1525), 56 towns were founded in northern Mazovia and 50 in the southern part – the largest number of *locationes* took place under Siemowit IV and Janusz I.

In the fifteenth century, the dependence of Mazovia on Poland assumed a feudal form. The extinction of ducal lines in particular districts at the end of the fifteenth century and the beginning of the sixteenth century liquidated the distinctness of Mazovia (with its own court system, coinage and independent foreign policy which consisted maintaining an equilibrium between Poland, Lithuania and the Teutonic Order). The newly established voivodeships of Rawa and Płock were incorporated into the Crown (in 1462 and 1495, respectively), and in 1526 King Zygmunt the Old finally put an end to the independence of the Duchy of Mazovia by creating the voivodeship of Mazovia. For a certain time, Mazovia managed to retain a separate Sejm, own courts (to 1540) and law (to 1577). The Polish monarch even consented to the publication of a collection of local laws known as the Goryński Code.

In this way, an independent Duchy of Mazovia ceased to exist within the powerful Commonwealth. In its time, it was a phenomenon in Europe, compared by certain historians with Burgundy, situated between the Loire and the Rhône. Not until the reign of Louis XIV did Burgundy, whose golden age took place in the fifteenth century, did it ultimately return to France.

■

In the Commonwealth of Two Nations

The incorporation of Mazovia into the Crown wsas followed by the emergence of three new voivodeships: the largest voivodeship of Mazovia (capital in Warsaw, 22 572 square kilometres, a population of 415 000, including 83 000 townspeople), more than four times as small voivodeship of Rawa (5 075 square kilometres, and a population of 110 000, including 19 000 in towns) and five times smaller voivodeship of Płock (4 200 square kilometres, a population totalling 115 000, including 18 000 city dwellers). The greatest population density occurred in the voivodeship of Płock (27,4 persons per 1 square kilometre), and a lesser one in the voivodeship of Rawa (21,7 persons per 1 square kilometre) and the voivodeship of Mazovia (18,4 persons per 1 square kilometre). These are extremely large figures in comparison with other provinces of the Commonwealth, where 1 square kilometre in Royal Prussia was inhabited by 15,1 persons, in Great Poland – by 14 persons, in Little Poland – by 12 persons, in the Pomeranian voivodeships – by 11,4 persons, in Red Rus' – by 8 persons, in Volhynia and Podolia – by 7 persons, and in Ukraine – by as few as 3 persons. Overpopulation spurred emigration to Podlasie, Prussia and Lithuania, and primarily to sparsely populated Rus', Podolia, Volhynia and Ukraine. The inhabitants of Mazuria made their way as far as the Crimea and the regions on the Dnieper, and settled the entire southern part of Prussia.

In the sixteenth century and up to the mid-seventeenth century Mazovia basked in yet another Golden Age. Peace ruled along the borders of the voivodeship, now situated in the very centre of the mighty Commonwealth. From 1596, Warsaw was the seat of the monarchic court, and from 1612 it held the rank of the royal residential town. The decision to transfer the royal court to Warsaw, made by

Zygmunt III, was undoubtedly inspired by its localisation in the centre of Poland and greater proximity to the king's native Sweden. Development was on the rise also in other towns: Płock (which from the beginning of the sixteenth century lost its economic significance in favour of dynamically expanding Warsaw), Pułtusk, Rawa, Sochaczew, Łowicz, Łomża, Przasnycz, Mława, Ostrów, Wyszogród, Zakroczym, Nur, Warka, Liw, Ostrołęka, Garwolin, Gąbin, Brok, and Wyszków. Jewish settlers arrived in Mazovian urban centres; the first mention of a Jewish community in Płock dates back to 1237, and in Mława 1512. At the beginning of the fourteenth century, Warsaw Jews lived in Żydowska Street in the Old Town. Jewish Kahals functioned in sixteenth-century Płock, Łomża, Sochaczew, Wyszogród, Zakroczym, Mława, Rawa, Czersk, Maków and Ciechanów.

In 1564, Warsaw became the site of conventions held by the Sejm of the Commonwealth; from 1572 elections of Polish monarchs were determined to a considerable degree by the votes of the numerous petty gentry of Mazovia. Sizable profit was gained from trade on the Vistula and the export of timber and grain to

M. Allessandrini, *Election of Augustus II in Wola (Warsaw) 26 June 1697* (fragment of painting)

Gdańsk. Warsaw became a salient centre of intellectual and artistic life (the expansion of the Royal Castle, the establishment of a royal orchestra, the staging of *Odprawa posłów greckich / The Dismissal of Greek Envoys/* by Jan Kochanowski in Ujazdowski Castle).

Mazovia was regarded as the prime bastion of Catholicism in the struggle against the Reformation. During the sixteenth century, the papal nuntio Juliusz Rygier informed his Roman superiors that "Mazovia is as Catholic as Italy itself." The famous Pułtusk school was founded by Jesuits brought over from Braniewo in 1565. Its lecturers included Rev. Piotr Skarga and Rev. Jakub Wujek, the first translator of the Holy Scripture into Polish and an outstanding Hebrew scholar. *Geometria*, the first Polish textbook on surveyance, was written in Pułtusk by Stanisław Grzebski, who took part in the famous "włóka measurement" conducted by Zygmunt August in the royal landed estates in Lithuania. The collection of coins and medallions amassed by Grzebski as well as part of his library enriched the collections of the Krakow Academy.

The magnificent castles in Łowicz and Pułtusk – the residences of the Primate and the bishop – were built during the sixteenth century; the collegiate churches

18

in both those localities were granted a Baroque form, admired up to this day. New constructions included the cathedral in Łomża and numerous parish churches, for example, in Brochowo, Krasne, Gołymin, Piaseczno and Brok.

The Swedish invasion of 1655–1657 put an end to the Golden Age. Mazovia became the main theatre of war (the battle of Nowy Dwór, the three day-long battle of Warsaw, the siege of Warsaw, the battle of Warka, the Rakoczy invasion and the destruction and burning down of Mława). Plunder of cultural property reached an unprecedented scale. It is worth accentuating that the entire area of Mazovia to the north-east of the Wkra never subjugated itself to the Swedes. From October 1655, it became the scene of partisan warfare, the first on such a large scale in the history of Poland. Partisan detachments, supported by scattered regular army units and composed of up to several hundred persons, forced the Swedes to concentrate considerable forces in Mazovia (about 40 00–50 00 men), paralysed transport and supplies, and compelled the enemy to seek refuge in local castles.

The consequences of the Swedish invasion proved to be outright catastrophic for Mazovia. One-third of royal towns was completely devastated or razed by fire, and the number of houses fell to one-fifth of the prewar state. For the next several decades, the equally ruined Mazovian village was incapable of overcoming its decline. This state of affairs stirred migration movements and the settlement of, among other, Kurpiowska Forest.

The Swedish invasion ended with the peace of Oliwa, signed in 1660. The following years of reconstruction were relatively favourable only for royal and magnate estates, a situation which, however, proved to be short-lived. We may hazard the opinion that Mazovia developed by leaps and bounds – from defeat to progress and vice versa. A war between Sweden and Russia, both embroiled in a competition for influence over the Baltic and Eastern Europe, broke out in 1700. The dethronement of August II and the election of Stanisław Leszczyński as the King of Poland, announced in 1703, initiated the struggle between "Sas" and "Las", the latter enjoying the support of Mazovia and Great Poland. During the Northern War, Mazovia bore the dire consequences of a bubonic plague (1707–1712). The devastation wrought by wartime hostilities and pestilence was enormous. Roaming, unpaid mercenary soldiers committed violations and robberies, especially in the voivodeship of Płock, where the local gentry was compelled to organize self-defence detachments composed of peasants, an issue debated by the Sejm in 1712.

By way of a digression, let us mention that in 1705 the Russian armies, under the command of Tsar Peter the Great, entered Mazovia, occupied Płock, and moved further on. From that time, they remained in Poland, with certain intervals, i.a. in 1807–1812 and 1816–1839, up to 1992.

Up to 1768, the Russians were engaged in reinforcing their position in Poland. Having encountered the opposition of the patriotic gentry, they imprisoned and deported its best-known leaders (Hetman Wacław Rzewuski, Bishop Kajetan Sołtyk, Bishop Jędrzej Załuski and Deputy Seweryn Rzewuski). In 1768 this policy led to an anti-Russian confederation organized in Bar (Podolia). In

Statue of
Kazimierz Pułaski
in Warka

1768–1772 the confederate tide swept across the whole country. One of its most celebrated commanders was Kazimierz Pułaski, born in Warka and later a hero of the American War of Independence. The confederates intended to seize Warsaw and even abducted King Stanisław August Poniatowski, whom they released several hours later. In 1770, northern Mazovia became the battlefield of Sawa Caliński, whose person and armed clashes soon became legendary. Caliński adopted confederates from the Wyszogród division, and reorganized them in Zielona Forest. Nominated the Marshall of Wyszogród, he commanded a cavalry detachment numbering 1 000. After the confederates were defeated at the battle of Rachów (23 April 1771), waged against regular Russian troops led by Alexander Suvorov, Sawa Caliński retreated to Mazovia together with the remnants of his detachment. Here, he was soon surrounded by the enemy – the detachment was routed, and its commander died of wounds or perished in Szreńsk Castle.

After the fall of the Confederation of Bar, Prussia, Russia and Austria carried out the first partition of Poland (1772), confirmed by the Sejm, which gathered in Warsaw under the duress of Russian bayonets. Mazovia continued to be part of the Commonwealth, but its further fate appeared to be predestined.

The 1740s initiated a period of economic prosperity both for Mazovia and the entire Commonwealth. New towns were founded, while others were relocated. Royal towns were swelled by special private districts (*jurydyki*). Warsaw was now the largest urban centre in Poland; its population grew rapidly: from 30 000 in 1764 to 115 000 in 1792. Internal order was introduced (the Pavement Commission), and the town was enclosed within ramparts (1770) protecting it against the plague; new investments included the Saxon Axis and Marszałkowska Street. Warsaw attracted residents of Mazovian villages, towns and boroughs. Other arrivals included numerous Jews who bypassed the formal ban on settlement, and resided in the *jurydyki*, where, at the end of the eighteenth century, they totalled 6 750. Industry expanded beyond the ramparts of the Wola district (mills, breweries, brickyards). Newly opened manufactories (carriages, bells) and banks (Tepper, Blank, Prot Potocki) encouraged the most affluent merchants to live there. The school system flourished (*Collegium Nobilium* founded by Stanisław Konarski, the Knights' School) and the Commission for National Education assumed the role of the first "Ministry of Education". Warsaw saw the opening of the Załuski Library and the National Theatre, the erection of numerous palaces (Łazienki), and the redesigning of the Royal and Ujazdowski castles. The Infant Jesus hospital became the first modern institution of its sort. Famous painters (Marcello Bacciarelli)

Bernardo Bellotto, known as Canaletto, *Krakowskie Przedmieście Street towards Zamkowy Square*

and architects (Jakub Fontana, Dominik Merlini) pursued their branches of the arts. Warsaw drew not only the most talented and enterprising inhabitants of Mazovia, but also exerted an impact on the nearest environs. The palace built in Otwock by Marshal Bieliński was followed by the palace in Jabłonna and the Romantic-sentimental park in Arkadia near Łowicz. Manufactories appeared in landed estates belonging to the Primate in Łowicz and Skierniewice. The development of Warsaw had a great impact on the situation in Mazovia – a tendency discernible also in the following centuries.

In 1788–1792, the Four Years' Sejm embarked upon attempts at salvaging the Commonwealth and passed, i.a. in statute on royal towns (21 April 1791). Systemic reforms were crowned by the Third May Constitution. The confederation organized in Targowica, and instigated by Russia, led to the Polish-Russian war of 1792 and the second partition of Poland (1793), confirmed at the partition Sejm convoked in Grodno. Deputies from Mazovia were elected in Mława, which was unoccupied by the Prussian army, but their protest proved to be in vain.

The spoils of second partition of Poland enabled Prussia to acquire a large part of the Płock and Rawa voivodeships. The borderline delineated in Mazovia ran from Działdowo to Wyszogród and then along the Bzura to Łowicz, situated on the Prussian side; from here, it led towards the Pilica in the region of Inowłodz. Part of the Zawkrze region (together with Szreńsk and Radzanów) was incorporated by Prussia.

The dismembered Commonwealth was given a new administrative division, defined at the Sejm in Grodno. The Crown was now composed of ten voivodeships. That part of the Mazovia which remained in Poland was divided into three voivodeships: Mazovian (the lands of Wisk, Łomża and Mur), Warsaw (the lands of Czersk, Warsaw and Liw) and Ciechanów (the lands of Ciechanów, Zakroczyn and Różan). The remaining fragment of the Zawkrze region found itself within the

21

land of Ciechanów and the new voivodeship of Ciechanów. In its extremely reduced state the Commonwealth became a protectorate of Russia. The actual ruler of vanquished Poland was the Russian ambassador O. Igelström who resided in Warsaw. His authority was based on an extensive espionage and information system, and his governance was ruthless and harsh. This situation was regarded as insufferable by all Poles, particularly by the gentry and the townspeople who remembered well the time of the Confederation of Bar, whose ranks totalled more than 100 000 men, and whose heroic sacrifices gave rise to another generation intent on battling for liberty and independence. The radicals, known as the Jacobins, counted on the support of the French Revolution.

Maciejowice
– monument
of the Kościuszko
Insurrection

The Kościuszko Insurrection constituted a consecutive attempt at defending the sovereignty and independence of the Commonwealth. Mazovia, including Warsaw, became one of the main scenes of armed clashes (the several month long siege of Warsaw, ending with a victory of the insurgents, struggles along the front on the Narew, battles waged by partisan detachments and preparations for an uprising in northern Mazovia). Ultimately, the Insurrection ended with defeat at Maciejowice (10 October 1794) and the capitulation of the remnants of the Polish forces at Radoszczyce (18 November 1794). The price was extremely high: devastated and plundered towns and villages, a massacre of the population and the conflagration of Praga (4 November 1794), as well as general breakdown and depression after Tadeusz Kościuszko was taken prisoner.

The collapse of the Insurrection denoted the end of the Commonwealth, although we must agree with the opinion expressed by Prof. Andrzej Zahorski, an expert on the period, that "although Kościuszko suffered defeat, he showed the path for further struggle for freedom, waged by collective efforts ofr the whole nation, which was his political testament."

■

AFTER THE THIRD PARTITION

Owing to the third partition of Poland (1795) a larger part of Mazovia, together with Warsaw, found itself under Prussian rule. A small area to the east of the Vistula and to the south of the Bug was occupied by Austria. In south-eastern Mazovia, a narrow strip of land from Serock to Karczew was governed by the Prussians.

Prussian rule proved to be extremely onerous. The population of Warsaw declined from 115 000 to about 65 000. The Prussian partition area included newly established New-Eastern Prussia and Southern Prussia. The former was composed of two departments with capitals in Płock and Białystok. This former terrain of northern Mazovia was envisaged as a region of rapid Germanisation.

Southern Prussia was subdivided into the Poznań, Kalisz and Warsaw departments. Southern Mazovia became part of the Warsaw department (together with the suburban fragment of Mazovia on the right bank of the Vistula). The departments, in turn, were made up of counties, whose number in the Warsaw department totalled 10 (Gostynin, Sochaczew, Błonie, Warszawa, Łęczyca, Zgierz, Brzeziny, Rawa, Czersk and Orłów). Here, the Prussians pursued a different policy towards the Polish population. The partitioning authorities were well aware of the fstrong attachment to Polishness so that all Germanisation plans had to be deferred for years. Foremost Prussian decisions in the subjugated country pertained to the confiscation of Church and royal estates (in order to weaken the financial standing of the Polish clergy and to create a powerful and prosperous group of junkers), a wide-spread colonisation campaign (by way of example, in the landed estate of Tomasz Łubieński in Guzowo the Prussian authorities settled 300 families of German colonists – a much commented case), and the subjugation of private towns to state control. The introduction of an oppressive bureaucracy was accompanied by methodic financial exploitation. The Polish gentry faced bankruptcy, and joyously welcomed the defeat of the Prussian army and the advance of the Napoleonic forces.

■

In the Duchy of Warsaw

French troops reached Warsaw on 27 November 1806, an event which marked the beginning of the first Polish war waged by Napoleon against Russia in northern Mazovia, ending with the capture of Mława and Działdowo (26 December 1806). During his stay in Warsaw in January 1807 Napoleon proclaimed the establishment of authorities known as the Government Committee. The director of the War Department was Prince Józef Poniatowski, who quickly raised a Polish army. At the end of January 1807, the Russians initiated hostilities in Prussia, which culminated in the battle of Iława Pruska (Eylau) and a severe defeat of Tsarist troops. The following battle of Frydland (Friedland, 14 June) signified the final catastrophe of the Russian armies, and resulted in the peace of Tylża (Tilsit, 9 July) and the creation of the Duchy of Warsaw. Armed campaigns were conducted primarily in northern Mazovia and Prussia. Supplies for the French army, numbering 100 000, and more than 10 000 strong Polish forces were supervised by Józef Wybicki, whose organizational skills and self-sacrifices protected the soldiers from hunger and the local population from death caused by starvation and the plague.

The Duchy consisted of six departments, including the departments of Warsaw, Płock and Łomża. After the victorious war with Austria, the Podlasie region, situated on the Bug, acquired the department of Siedlce, with the regions of Liw and Garwolin (1809). The department of Płock embraced almost all of Mazovia to the north of the Vistula and the Bug, together with the land of Dobrzyń, and the Warsaw department consisted of practically the whole of Mazovia to the south of the Vistula and the Bug, together with the land of Łęczyca; the department of Łomża was made up of Mazovian terrains on the central Narew and the Biebrza.

The crisis apparent in the Duchy of Warsaw was the outcome of its inclusion into the Continental System blockade, which impeded the export of grain. The country ruffered and it was only slightly better in towns where the crafts and local trade continued to grow. Prominent changes included the abolishment of serfdom, the reorganization of the court system, a restriction of the Church influence, modernisation of the army, and the introduction of the Napoleonic Code. Education flourished in Warsaw, Płock, Łomża, and Łowicz. Amazingly, all those transformations took place in the course of merely a few years (1808–1812), the last of which coincided with a war against Russia, with the Poles on the Napoleonic side and with the hope for the reconstruction of the Polish state.

The defeat of the Napoleonic Grande Armée at the end of 1812 entailed Russian military occupation of the whole of Mazovia (to the end of February 1813). Only the Modlin fortress did not capitulate until 25 February 1813. Once again, Mazovia was turned into a wasteland; this time, devastation was incurred by the retreating French army, groups of marauders, and Russian soldiers. Anarchy did not come to an end until the beginning of 1814.

■

In the Russian Partition Area

In 1815, Mazovia found itself within the autonomous Kingdom of Poland, frequently known as the Congress Kingdom, devised at the Congress of Vienna, and granted a constitution in November 1815. In January 1816, the governor confirmed a new administrative division which remained in force, basically unaltered, until 1845. The Kingdom was divided into eight voivodeships. The borders of Płock voivodeship in Mazovia corresponded to those of the former department. The Warsaw department was now known as the Mazovian voivodeship, composed of the land of Łęczyca and Kujawy. The department of Łomża became Augustów voivodeship, with the capital in Łomża (to 1818) and then in Suwałki. The lands of Garwolin and Liw were incorporated into Siedlce voivodeship, and Zapilice into Radom voivodeship. The districts within the voivodeships were equal to one or even several counties.

The 1815–1830 period marked the reconstruction and growth of Mazovia, best testified by the growth of inhabitants by one-third in fifteen years. At the end of 1830, the population of Mazovia totalled almost 1,2 million, of which 72% lived in the country. The Russian authorities introduced order into the spatial configuration, prepared regulation plans, and made historical-topographic-statistical descriptions (1820–1821) and copies of privileges. Work was initiated on the so-called great town planning charter. The main task of the Town Commission, created by the Government Commission of the Interior in 1820, was to conduct "regulations", i.e. to introduce order into town planning. This policy evolved into a ban on erecting new buildings without approved projects. Spatial configuration and municipal developments underwent enormous changes. New investments included residential housing and public utility buildings, mainly town halls (Płock, Gostynin, Łomża, Ciechanów, Piaseczno, Góra Kalwaria, Ostrołęka, Łowicz, Kutno, Sochaczew, Skierniewice and others). Streets and market squares were given hard surfaces and thatched roofs were forbidden. Streets became lined with trees and lit with lanterns. Slaughterhouses and public baths were built. However, certain towns still had only a few brick houses (three in Ciechanów) or none (Garwolin, Latowicz, Serock, Różan, Nowogród). Trade and crafts thrived, and numerous fairs and markets were held. An essential role was played by the Jewish population, in the majority of Mazovian and Podlasie towns and boroughs that autnumbered the Polish. The construction of the town of Żyrardów was initiated in 1830; at the end of the nineteenth century, the large local textile enterprise, completed in 1833, employed up to 10 000 workers.

The Warsaw-Terespol hard-surface road, the first in Poland, was built in 1820 mainly.

Education and culture continued to flourish: Warsaw University was opened in 1816, a National Theatre was established in Płock, and the Płock Scientific Society, which inaugurated its work in 1820, was the third such institution in the Kingdom, preceded by societies in Warsaw (1800) and Lublin (1818).

The pro-independence strivings of Polish society were expressed by numerous clandestine youth societies as well as the National Freemasonry and the Patriotic Society, both founded by Walerian Łukasiński. One of such conspiracy organizations was the secret "society" formed by second lieutenant Piotr Wysocki in the Warsaw Infantry Officers School. An uprising broke out on 29 November 1830, and once again Mazovia became the main theatre of war (i.a. the battles of Iganie, Stoczek, Dębe, Ostrołęka and Grochów near Warsaw). The Mazovian nobility and burghers, even the local peasants and Jews, supported this successive pro-independence national upheaval. The Uprising is sometimes known as a Polish-Russian war, since the hostilities engaged regular detachments of the Polish army. Led by many generals who remained at odds with each other, and outnumbered by the Russian forces, the November Uprising ended in failure. After capitulation, Polish detachments left Warsaw and, marching across Modlin, Płock and Rypin, reached Świedziebno near Brodnica, on the Prussian frontier, where they laid down their arms (5 October 1831). Many officers and rank-and-file men decided to emigrate, mainly to Switzerland and France, in the hope of embarking upon a new struggle, assisted by the West.

Meanwhile, ruined Mazovia succumbed to Russian repressions. Landed estates were confiscated, and the members of the gentry were deported to Siberia. The autonomy of the Kingdom was curtailed, and the Polish army and Sejm were abolished. Local Polish offices were maintained, but Russian superiors, gendarmerie and secret police were installed. Russian troops were stationed throughout the Kingdom, a Citadel was being erected in Warsaw, and the fortress in Modlin was expanded. The new administrative system emulated the Russian model. In 1837, voivodeships were replaced by gubernias, and civilian governors were appointed. Districts became known as counties, and counties – as circuits (the *ukase* from October 1842). Further changes were announced on 5 January 1845. The gubernia of Podlasie was liquidated, and its terrains became part of the gubernia of

Lublin. In 1846, the gubernias of Mazovia and Kalisz were supplanted by the large gubernia of Warsaw, and the Zapilice region, up to the river Radomka, was incorporated into the gubernia of Radom.

The years between the November and the January uprisings are known as the Paskevich period, from the name of the Russian Field Marshal Ivan Paskevich, who stifled the former insurrection and then was appointed Viceroy of the Kingdom of Poland (1832–1856). This ruthless ruler became infamous for the implementation of the hostile policy pursued by Tsar Nicholas I towards the Polish nation.

A gradual enfranchisement of the peasants was introduced in 1846–1859. The customs border was abolished, and uniform tariffs were introduced in 1851. The Kingdom was drawn into the economic range of the Russian Empire. Mass-scale peasant unrest directed against serfdom broke out in 1862. The legal emancipation of the Jewish community stated. Despite severe reprisals, Warsaw and Mazovia underwent economic development (the metallurgical industry, distilleries, sugar plants, the textile industry and mills). The railway network was enlarged. The population of 97 towns in Mazovia and Warsaw grew by 28% and achieved a total of 362 000 (1827–1857). The number of the inhabitants of Warsaw rose to 205 000.

Conspiracy societies and secret patriotic organizations continued to emerge. A compulsory conscription announced by Margrave Aleksander Wielopolski spurred the outbreak of an uprising on 23 January 1863. Deprived of European support, it had no chances for success, and could only assume the form of a political demonstration enacted by an oppressed nation. The January Uprising spread across the whole of Mazovia: 253 out of about 1100 skirmishes fought in the country took place in the region. Thousands of insurgents fell in battle, were hanged or deported to Siberia.

Post-uprising repercussions included the liquidation of the distinct status of the Kingdom. Once again, Mazovia was divided, this time into three gubernias (Płock, Łomża and Warsaw). Some of the counties in the Lublin gubernia – Garwolin, Łuków, Biała Podlaska, Siedlce, Sokołów and Węgrów – were joined to become the gubernia of Siedlce.

In 1868, the partitioning authorities introduced the Russian language in all public offices, and in 1876 in courts of law. Russian became the language of instruction even for teaching religion. In 1864, all Church property was confiscated, and numerous monasteries were liquidated. As many as 66 towns and boroughs were deprived of municipal rights, and only 33 towns remained in Mazovia. In the suburbs of Warsaw, such towns as Piaseczno, Góra Kalwaria, Stanisławów, Dobra, Wyszków, Nowy Dwór, Radzymin, Serock, Wyszków, Mogielnica and Zambrów were reduced to the status of settlements.

Despite extensive repressions, Polish society managed to dismiss the effects of defeat and embarked upon so-called organic work, as evidenced by the emergence of the Warsaw Industrial Region and the Warsaw Municipal Complex, which maintained their significance up to 1914. In the years 1868–1908, the population of Mazovia climbed from 1,8 million to 3,7 million, and that of Warsaw – from 206 000 to 896 000.

The Revolution of 1905–1907 secured an alleviation of Tsarist repressions. The Polish language was reinstated in schools and offices. Reactivated institutions included the Scientific Society of Płock. The "silence of the graves" – a term describing the situation after the collapse of the January Uprising – was broken.

■

THE FIRST WORLD WAR

During the first year of World War I, declared on 1 August 1914, armed hostilities took place along the eastern front, primarily in the Austrian and Russian partition areas, including northern Mazovia and areas to the west of Warsaw. For the very first time, poison gas was used by the Germans at the battle of the river Rawka near Bolimowo.

On 5 August 1915, German troops seized Warsaw and the entire left-bank Mazovia where war operations lasted until the middle of August, accompanied by the resettlement of tens of thousands of local inhabitants. All larger Mazovian enterprises, offices and courts were evacuated into the depths of Russia; those which remained were systematically devastated – this was the fate of the Textile Mill in Żyrardów. The Tsarist Warsaw University was also evacuated, together with its Russian staff, to Rostov on the Don. The Russians resorted to the "burnt earth" policy wherever possible (bridges, train stations, more important industrial enterprises, etc.). Some 300 000 persons were deported to Russia.

Borman, Szwede and Co. Mechanical Works in Warsaw, beginning of twentieth century

Meanwhile, in the occupied terrains German authorities tried to enlist Polish support in the hope of gaining about 1 million recruits. The act of 5 November 1916, issued by the emperors of Germany and Austria, proclaimed the establishment of a Polish Kingdom, dependent on the two signatories. The Germans agreed to the creation of a Provisional Council of State, which during the initial period was even backed by the Polish Military Organization (POW). At the beginning of 1917 the German authorities demanded that the Polish Legion pledge an oath of allegiance to the Polish Kingdom and the future monarch. The text of the oath also mentioned a brotherhood of arms with German and Austrian troops. On 9 July 1917, the Legions were split into opposing factions when men from the former Kingdom of Poland, inspired by Józef Piłsudski, refused to take the oath. Disarmed, they were interned in special camps in Bieniaminowo (officers) and Szczypiorno (soldiers). On 21 and 22 July 1917, J. Piłsudski and K. Sosnkowski were arrested and imprisoned in a military fortress in Magdeburg. POW members were repressed and arrested. Ultimately, the Organization announced its disobedience towards the Council of State and, in accordance with a previously made plan, resorted to conspiracy.

■

In the Reborn Polish State

The independence of Poland – the motif of dreams harboured by generations – was regained on 11 XI 1918. It became mandatory to seek swift cures for the wartime wounds incurred by the enemy. Numerous towns such as Sochaczew, Przasnysz, Serock, Ostrołęka, Różan, Nowy Dwór, Bolimów as well as innumerable villages were reduced to ruins, communication was paralysed, thousands of hectares of land lay waste, and hundreds of thousands of deportees were returning to Poland. It was necessary to build everything anew, and to organize state and self-government authorities, the judiciary, the police and, finally, the Polish army. The first test faced by the reborn state was the Bolshevik onslaught of 1920 – battles were waged for Łomża, Ostrołęka, Mława, Płońsk and Płock; the most important battle of Warsaw took place at Radzymin and Ossów. The society of Mazovia interpreted correctly the propaganda contents of tempting Bolshevik slogans, and took an extremely active part in the hostilities.

The effects of the Bolshevik invasion merged with the devastation wrought by World War I. The war waged for the sake of sovereign Poland played a highly positive role by shaping the national consciousness of the population of Mazovia, integrated in the struggle for independence.

Now was the time for a consecutive reconstruction of Mazovia. Renascent Poland restored the old names of administrative units – the voivodeship and the county. The voivodeship of Warsaw, established after 1918, encompassed a major part of the lands of historical Mazovia, and included 23 counties: Nieszawa, Lipnów, Rypin, Włocławek, Płock, Kutno, Gostynin, Łowicz, Sochaczew, Błonie, Skierniewice, Rawa, Grójec, Warszawa, Mińsk, Radzymin, Pułtusk, Maków, Przasnysz, Ciechanów, Mława, Płońsk and Sierpc. Only the counties of Ostrołęka and Ostrów were not incorporated.

A law altering the voivodeship boundaries was issued on 12 June 1937. As a result, the voivodeship of Warsaw lost the counties of Lipnów, Nieszawa, Rypin and Włocławek, which were acquired by the voivodeship of Pomerania; in turn, the county of Działdowo, formerly in the voivodeship of Pomerania, was gained by the voivodeship of Warsaw. The statute of 9 April 1938 introduced succesive changes – the voivodeship of Łódź took over the formerly Warsaw counties of Kutno, Łowicz, Skierniewice and Rawa, while the voivodeship of Warsaw got the counties of Ostrów, Ostrołęka and Łomża (previously in the voivodeship of Białystok), the counties of Sokołów, Węgrów and Garwolin (formerly in the voivodeship of Lublin) as well as the commune of Irena, together with Dęblin (earlier in the county of Puławy).

In 1918–1939, a tremendous effort was directed at the reconstruction and expansion of towns and buroughs. Much invention and entrepreneurship was disclosed by the reborn self-government authorities. Płock and Włocławek increased their area threefold, Mińsk Mazowiecki – fourfold, Nasielsk and Sochaczew – twentyfold and Kutno and Kałuszyn – more than thirtyfold. Considerable changes occurred in suburban towns of the Warsaw region. The setting up of a town-planning project enabled the expansion of Otwock (the Soplicowo civil servants' residential estate, train station, town hall, two synagogues, and even a casino). The "dormitory" town of Wołomin continued to grow. The Machine Tool Works, opened in Pruszków in 1919 together with a Construction Office, was the first modern enterprise of this type in Poland. The S. Majewski pencil factory, a faience factory, and the large Railway Rolling Stock Repair Works were enlarged. The EKD commuter railway solved the communication problem along the Warsaw–Milanówek–Grodzisk Mazowiecki line. In 1937, Pruszków had 22 industrial enterprises, employing 5 799 workers, and as many as 663 commercial and crafts enterprises. In 1939, this town, the best developing urban centre in Mazovia, boasted a population of almost 29 000.

Warsaw, Marszałkowska Street

Great changes place in Żyrardów, Skierniewice, Siedlce (the Nowe Siedlce district), Ostrowia Mazowiecka (town hall), Łowicz, Gostynin, Gąbin, Brok (a summer resort) and Mława, which from the close of the nineteenth century was one of the most rapidly developing towns in Mazovia (next to Płock, Łomża and Pruszków). Despite frequently striking differences in living conditions, each town and borough had its own climate and unique ambience, and was known or distinct for certain accomplishments: excellent local products, famous markets or fairs, renowned secondary schools or even celebrated firemen's brass bands or good beer (Warka).

Warsaw comprised the largest concentration of Jews in Poland, Europe and even beyond (400 000 in 1939). Other noteworthy Mazovian towns with sizable Jewish communities included Nowy Dwór Mazowiecki (36%), Sokołów (50,7%), Węgrów (55,7%) and Siedlce (40,1%).

■

THE SECOND WORLD WAR

When on 1 September 1939 German armies crossed the borders of the Republic of Poland, Mazovia became an important battlefield (the battle of Mława: 1–4 September, and on the Bzura: 14–16 September). The resultant material and human losses were enormous but the gravest repercussion was the general

29

breakdown generated by the defeat. Administrative changes in the occupied terrains included the liquidation of Warsaw voivodeship; part of its lands, incorporated into the General Gouvernement, became the district of Warsaw and the Regency of Ciechanów, now included into Eastern Prussia. Western Mazovia (the counties of Gostynin and Kutno) was annexed by Reichsgau Wartheland.

Poles reacted to Nazi occupation by organizing an underground state, partisan detachments and sabotage. An extensive clandestine secondary school system was set up in Mazovia. The Germans carried out a planned extermination of the Jewish population (approx. 500 000 concentrated in the Warsaw ghetto). Some members of the Jewish community managed to flee to the Soviet Union (1939–1940), find refuge among the Poles or join partisan detachments, mainly in the region of Wyszków. A death camp in Treblinka (the district of Warsaw) was created both for the Jews and Poles; Soviet prisoners of war were detained and killed in Grądy–Komorów near Ostrowia Mazowiecka and Suchożebry near Siedlce.

The culminating point of the heroic struggle conducted by the population of Warsaw and Mazovia against the Nazi occupant was the Warsaw Uprising, which lasted for 63 days (1 August–2 October 1944). The toll of lives totalled about 250 000 inhabitants of Warsaw, including 22 000 insurgents (killed, gravely wounded and missing in action). The German losses are estimated at about 10 000 killed, 6 000 missing in action and 9 000 wounded.

After the capitulation of the Uprising the entire civilian population of Warsaw was deported to the General Gouvernement (ca. 400 000) and the Third Reich (approx. 250 000). The insurgents were interned in the concentration camp in Auschwitz and, after the capitulation of Warsaw, imprisoned in camps throughout Germany.

■

THE PEOPLE'S REPUBLIC OF POLAND

In 1944–1945, liberation came to Mazovia in two stages. From July to October 1944, Soviet troops, together with the First Polish Army, advanced across terrains between the Bug and the Vistula, all the way to the Narew in the north. The remaining part of Mazovia was liberated in January 1945. The seats of the authorities of Warsaw voivodeship were consecutively Otwock and Mińsk Mazowiecki (during the so-called Lublin Poland period from August 1944 to February 1945), and then Pruszków and Płock (from February 1945).

A session of the voivodeship national councils and offices, held on 25 February 1945, established a single voivodeship office in Warsaw. On 7 July 1945, the county of Łomża was extracted from the voivodeship of Warsaw, now composed of 22 counties, and incorporated into the voivodeship of Białystok. The place of the county of Błonie, liquidated on 23 February 1948, was taken by the newly established county of Grodzisk Mazowiecki. In 1949, the voivodeship of Warsaw gained the county of Siedlce, transferred from the voivodeship of Lublin, while in 1950 the county of Działdowo was assigned to the voivodeship of Olsztyn. The creation of Greater Warsaw on 1 July 1952 denoted the end of the large county of Warsaw, supplanted by the counties of Nowy Dwór, Piaseczno, Pruszków, Otwock and Wołomin (in place of the county of Radzymin). This veritable carousel of changes came to a halt on 1 January 1956 due to the delineation of the counties of Łosice, Ryki, Wyszków and Żuromin.

The first period of the People's Republic of Poland brought a land reform, a liquidation of the stratum of the landowners, at times carried out in an extremely brutal manner, and an elimination of large peasant farms (owned by the so-called kulaks). The nationalisation of the industry resulted in the closure of certain enterprises and even mills, brickyards, etc. Mazovia and Podlasie became the scene of bloody political clashes, known as a civil war. This region concentrated the largest number of partisan detachments; the last was crushed at the beginning of 1950s. It is assumed that about 100 000 people fell on both sides – a toll which could have totalled 30 000 in Mazovia and Podlasie alone.

Warsaw 1945

The armed struggle conducted by the Polish Underground was a reaction to the murders, repressions and deportations to Russia of members of the Home Army, the National Armed Forces, and other organizations, which during the war fought against the Germans and now were combatted by the NKVD and the Polish security police.

Polish society faced the task of rebuilding the entire country. Some 85% of Warsaw lay in ruins. The rebirth of the capital was an enormous accomplishment of its residents, Mazovia, and the whole of Poland. The following years brought the construction of, i.a. the Automobile Works in Żerań and the Warsaw Steel Plant as well as the expansion of the municipal infrastructure. Other new industrial enterprises in Mazovia included the Petrochemical Works in Płock, the cellulose-paper enterprise in Ostrołęka, the meat plant in Sokołów Podlaski, and the dairy works in Węgrów and Mława. Dams and electrical plants were built on the Bug–Narów in Dębe, and the Zegrzyński Reservoir was created.

Reconstruction of the capital

The dual role – both positive and negative – played by Warsaw *vis a vis* Mazovia came to the fore. The capital, which dominates over the entire region as an economic, scientific and cultural centre, functioned according to the principles of

31

Voivodeships
established
in present-day
Mazowieckie
voivodeship
after the 1975
reform

a "suction pump", seriously restricting chances for the development of the voivodeship, although, after all, it was the whole population of Mazovia and Podlasie which, to a significant degree, contributed to the reconstruction of Warsaw. Not until the mid-60s was it decided to open branches of assorted Warsaw-based industrial enterprises throughout the rest of the Mazovia. This policy was an attempt at an activisation of the region, the creation of a working class subservient to the authorities, and halting the further growth of Warsaw itself.

Changes introduced into the administrative division of Poland in 1975 established within Mazovia, the voivodeships with seats in Warsaw, Płock, Ciechanów, Ostrołęka, Siedlce and Skierniewice.

■

IN THE NEW MAZOWIECKIE VOIVODESHIP

The new Mazowieckie voivodeship, with authorities in Warsaw, dates back to 1 January 1999. It embraces the former voivodeship of Radom (with the counties of Radom, Kozienice, Białobrzegi, Przysucha, Szydłowiec, Skaryszew, Lipsko and Zwoleń), but not such historical Mazovian lands as the counties of Rawa, Skierniewice, Łowicz and Kutno in the western part of the voivodeship, the Łomża, Kolno and Grajewo counties in the north-eastern part, and the county of Ryki in the south-eastern part of the voivodeship.

Today, the voivodeship of Mazovia is once again the largest in Poland. Its relatively uniform character, central location at the crossing of communicational routes, and large economic, technical, cultural and intellectual potential offer great opportunities for favourable development and moulding the regional identity of its inhabitants.

Józef Kazimierski

32

AREA AND LOCATION

Mazowieckie voivodeship is the largest in Poland. With an area totalling 35 600 square kilometres, i.e. 11,4% of the country, it is larger than Belgium and Luxemberg put together. In the north, the voivodeship borders with Warmińsko-Mazurskie voivodeship, in the north-east – with Podlaskie voivodeship, in the south-east – with Lubelskie voivodeship, in the south – with Świętokrzyskie voivodeship, in the south-west – with Łódzkie voivodeship, and in the north-west – with Kujawsko-Pomorskie voivodeship. Its entire area is situated to the east of the geometric centre of Poland. Nonetheless, since the most important communication routes of the country converge in Warsaw, the location of the Mazovian voivodeship is, actually, more central than would follow from its geographic site.

POMORSKIE

WARMIŃSKO-MAZURSKIE

ZACHODNIOPOMORSKIE

KUJAWSKO-POMORSKIE

PODLASKIE

MAZOWIECKIE

WIELKOPOLSKIE

LUBUSKIE

ŁÓDZKIE

DOLNOŚLĄSKIE

LUBELSKIE

ŚWIĘTOKRZYSKIE

OPOLSKIE   ŚLĄSKIE

PODKARPACKIE

MAŁOPOLSKIE

Division of Poland into voivodeships in force since 1 January 1999

The present-day Mazowieckie voivodeship, established within the administrative division reform introduced in 1998, is composed of the following former "small" voivodeships: Płock, Ciechanów, Ostrołęka and Warsaw. With the exception of two gminas, it includes the entire former Radom voivodeship, a large part of Siedlce voivodeship (without the south-eastern part), the western fragment of Skierniewice voivodeship, and small (western) parts of the Łomża and Biała Podlaska voivodeships.

Natural Conditions

From the viewpoint of the relief of the terrain, Mazovia comprises a *sui generis* concave basin – drained in the east by the Płock breach while its peripheries gather water from the entire southern and eastern part of the country. The general relief outline of the voivodeship is justified by the geological construction of the deeper strata. It is here that the axes of the two main tectonic depressions of Central Europe cross. In Mazovia, the crystalline base is 2 000–3 000 metres deep. Nevertheless, not far from the Mazovian boundaries, namely, in the adjacent parts of Podlasie and in the Lublin and Radom regions there appear outcrops of chalk marl, while Jurassic rocks reach the surface near Nowe Miasto on the Pilica and Tomaszów Mazowiecki as well as in the area of Koluszki. The centre of the horseshoe-shaped arch of the outcrops of Mesozoic rocks flanking Mazovia contains a depression known as the Mazovian Basin, filled with Tertiary drift. Together with an analogous Great Poland Basin, the Mazovian Basin forms the Polish Central Depression, from which the sea withdrew for the last time during the Oligocene period, i.e. almost 20 million years ago. This period left traces in the form of extremely characteristic, water-resistant sand deposits, known as the glauconite formation. Its considerable significance for the economy of Mazovia consists in yielding in the Mazovian Basin a level of Artesian water supplies which, in drilling 150–250 metres deep, produces water under pressure. From the time of their discovery (1898), Artesian water supplies were used intensively in industry. At present, they are being increasingly appreciated as a source of pure drinking water, made available in increasingly numerous wells at the disposal of town populations. Remnants of lush vegetation from the later Tertiary period, when tropical conditions prevailed in Poland, produced brown coal deposits of considerable thickness. Prime accumulation emerged predominantly in the submerged, deeply intersected river valleys from the previous period and the peripheries of the Central Depression. This is the reason why in Mazovia, located in the central part of the Depression, they are less imposing or situated at levels inconvenient for exploitation.

The following period witnessed a cooling of the climate. Changes in vegetation were accompanied by a transformation of types of deposit in the rivers, which carried silty material originating in the Little Poland Upland. The Mazovian Basin was filled by a characteristic multi-hued silty build-up, the so-called formation of coloured clay, a ceramic raw material used in the production of construction material. At the onset of the Quaternary period, the climate continued to grow colder. The impact of tectonic movements also reversed the river configuration in the region. The water run-off towards the Black Sea was supplanted by a flow from the Little Poland Uplands to the north, *via* the Mazovian Basin, which changed into a marshland filled in by gravel and sand. The first glaciation did not reach Mazovia. On the other hand, consecutive glaciation, with the exception of the last one, covered its surface, a process associated with moraine drift and a great changeability of the river network, supplied by water from the melting glaciers. The retreating glaciers left behind characteristic forms of frontal moraines – elongated hillocks built up in front of the glacier. Depressions of the terrain contained large water basins. Consequently, a typical feature of the regional relief were long, latitudinal bands, composed interchangeably of moraine rises and outlet valleys or non-outlet depressions. The best known mineral raw material connected with the Ice Age is the so-called varved clay, which at the time settled in water basins, and which comprises excellent material for brick production. Such clay provides better ceramic material than the coloured variety of silt, but it occurs more rarely and creates strata of an extremely complicated construction. Other mineral raw material – remnants of the Ice Age – are clay and gravel.

The glacier left behind numerous so-called erratic boulders, brought over from Scandinavia and additionally accentuated by aeolian processes occurring in the wake of the withdrawal of the continental glacier, when the wind removed the slighter fractions of sand and dust, that, in turn, assumed the form of dunes. The last glaciation blocked the outflow of water towards the north. Seeking new courses, the waters joined the basin of the Łaba and the drainage basin of the North Sea. Rivers formed a latitudinal system of antecedent valleys which altered their configurations depending on the location of the continental glacier, closing or opening assorted drainage routes to the west. Copious water in those valleys, produced by melting and encumbered by large amounts of material carried out from the glacier, was conducive for the emergence of expansive accumulation terraces, linked with sizable detrital fans created by water. The latter composed a large arch fringing Mazovia to the north, and joined conical spheres in the region of Serpiec and Kurpiowska Forest. At the same time, drier areas of the fans, the valley ter-

Erratic boulder in front of the Earth Museum in Warsaw

races and the sandy rises developed dunes, which drifted from the west to the east and produced whole systems of parabolically arched mounds, so typical for this part of Mazovia. Today, the best known dunes are those of Kampinoska Forest, arranged in two parallel strips divided by a marshy depression. They are all of parabolic shape, and the tallest are 30 metres high.

Progressing deglaciation was followed by the retreat of the tundra and the appearance of increasingly numerous forests, interspersed with open meadows. A further growth of warming yielded pine forests, which gradually included trees with greater climactic requirements. Peat-land started to expand, while dunes ceased shifting and became covered by woods. Further progress of a warm and humid Atlantic climatic tide, which took place only several thousand years ago, produced conditions for the development of deciduous woodlands. In the successive period, some of the marshes changed into meadows. The rather early discovery of morass ore meant that iron could be obtained relatively easily. Such iron was brittle, of course, but it could replace bronze, which was much less accessible and imported from afar. Generally speaking, Mazovia is a land lacking traditional resources, its prime natural assets being Artesian and surface water. Noteworthy fossil raw material include ceramic clay and sand, used for the production of silicate brick. Mention should be made also of brown coal deposits, rather inaccessibly located near Gostynin, in the region of Płock, or in Głowaczów on the Radomka. The largest amount of useful fossils is to be found in the southern part of the former Radom Voivodeship – phosphorite near Iłża and iron ore in the commune of Przytyk near Radom.

Archaeological excavations in Brwinów – a two thousand years-old mill

Pruszków – Potulicki Palace – Metallurgy Museum

37

RELIEF

For all practical purposes, the entire Mazowieckie voivodeship is situated within the range of the central Polish lowlands. The sole exception is the southern "non-Mazovian" extremity of the voivodeship, which is part of the Little Poland Upland, or more exactly, the Iłżeckie Foothills. As has been mentioned, an overwhelming part of the landscape of the region was shaped under the impact of glaciation, and in particular – Central Polish glaciation. The fundamental types of relief forms in Mazovia are rises, plains and river valleys.

Rises are the product of the continental glacier, which, moving along the surface of the Earth, carried assorted material in the form of clay, sand, gravel, and erratic boulders. As a rule, they possess the form of levelled and, in places, folded areas of the ground moraine, sometimes variegated by uplifted areas. The rises encircle the centre of Mazovia with the Warsaw Basin. To the north, they include the rises of Płońsk and Ciechanów, to the south – of Rawa, and to the east – of Kałuszyn and Siedlce, as well as the western part of the Żelechów Rise.

Plains cover a relatively small area of Mazovia. In most cases, they comprise denuded areas of glacier accumulation, built of sandy and clay material. Sometimes, they are overlaid by excellent soil, as in the instance of the Łowicz–Błońsk Plain whose eastern fragment is part of Mazowieckie voivodeship. The other plains are: the Raciąska, the Kurpiowska, the Warszawska, the Kozienicka, the Wołomińska, the Garwolińska and the Radomska.

Vistula near Warsaw. Characteristic escarpment of left bank

River valleys, at times very wide, are a characteristic element of the relief of Mazowieckie voivodeship. Almost all their latitudinal fragments were moulded by water produced by the melting continental glacier, flowing westwards in accordance with the inclination of the terrain.

Within, the river valleys usually contain several terraces, remnants of former river-bed levels, whose edges are, as a rule, distinctly marked. The terraces can be of a meadow, woodland, sand or dune character; they can also be divided into inundation and supra-inundation terraces and, therefore, reached by water in the conditions of high level, as well as those outside its range.

■

Mezo-regions

The voivodeship in question has the following mezo-regions bearing the features of a valley: the Central Vistula Valley, the Lower Bug and the Lower Narew valleys, and the eastern part of the Białobrzeska Valley.

An important physical-geographic mezo-region of the voivodeship is the centrally placed Warsaw Basin, composed of a widening of the Vistula valley at the convergence of the valleys of the central Vistula, the Bug, the Narew and the Bzura. The dunes and marshes along the left bank of the Vistula preserved Kampinoska Forest, which has been turned into the largest national park in Poland. A typical feature of the Warsaw Basin is its unsymmetrical shape. While the right bank consists of broads without an unambiguously delineated boundary, the left bank ends in a steep and picturesque escarpment running, i.a. from the south to the north, across the whole of Warsaw.

The remaining mezo-regions of the voivodeship are the Łomżyńskie inter-river region, which is a moraine rise situated between the valleys of the lower Narew and the lower Bug, the left-bank part of the Podlaskie Breach on the Bug, the Mławskie Heights – distinct kame and moraine forms rising up to 235 metres above sea level – and the Węgrowskie Depression.

The Iłżeckie Foothills, the sole mezo-region in the voivodeship which is part of the Little Poland Upland, disclose different features, with Quaternary period sand and clay in the depressions. Other forms include gravel hillocks, which are remnants of the glacier. Inselbergs of forms associated with glaciation occur, i.a. in the environs of Szydłowiec, with distinct rock bands of not very resilient lower Jurassic, so-called Szydłowiec sandstone, used in the building industry. At the same time, this is the highest region of the voivodeship, with the Altana rise, near Skarżysko Kamienna, being the largest in the entire Mazowieckie voivodeship (408 metres above sea level).

■

Soil

The major part of the soil in the voivodeship is usually of medium or lower quality, originating on post-glacier forms or even younger deposits. It occupies more than three-quarters of the area of the voivodeship, and usually emerged on sand and boulder clay. Those types of soil which came into being on the rises are, as a rule, the richest, and belong to the third and fourth classification classes. Soil in the lower areas, the valleys and the plains, originated on loose sands; it is of inferior quality and classified as the fifth and sixth class. Moreover, it coincides with the important wooded complexes of the voivodeship. The relatively rare podzol, appearing on dust forms and thus much more fertile, appears on rises and is, for all practical purposes, totally cultivated. Small areas are occupied by bog soil of average richness. Better types of soil: brown, black-earth and fen, are sporadic in Mazowieckie voivodeship.

■

CLIMATE

The climate of Mazovia is transitory, between marine and continental, with a typical variability of the weather, and thus resembling the climate of the whole of the remaining Polish lowlands. The major part of the voivodeship belongs to the Mazovian–Podlasie climatic region, and the smaller part is located within the range of the Kujawy and Mazury regions. The boundary between the central and eastern climatic areas runs to the east of the capital; the latter region is slightly colder. The more to the east, the stronger the impact of the continental climate, associated with greater temperature amplitudes, a longer summer (85–95 days, the shortest being in Mazury – to 75 days), and a long, cold winter (80–90 days in the western part; 90–100 days in the east). Average temperature in January reaches about – 3°C, and in July – approx. 19°C. In the spring and the autumn mean temperature differences between the northern and the south-western parts reach three degrees, and are lesser in the summer and the winter.

Mazovian landscape near Brok

Warsaw is a markedly warm island on climatic maps, with a discernible warming effect produced by compact settlement. In the autumn, the earliest ground frost takes place in October, and is usually several days earlier in the eastern part of the region. As a rule, the last ground frost in the spring occurs at the end of April, although sometimes as late as the middle of May. The average rainfall is lower than that of the country as a whole, and oscillates between 450 and 500 mm. On the average, snow lasts unmelted for 50 days, and up to 80 days in the eastern parts of the voivodeship. Differences concerning the duration of the vegetation period (200–220 days) span three weeks. Throughout the year, the dominating winds are westerly. Generally speaking, the climatic conditions of the voivodeship should be assessed as rather mild, both from the viewpoint of agriculture and settlement.

■

RIVERS

Rivers. The entire voivodeship is situated in the basin of the Vistula, the dominating river of the region. The Warsaw Basin is the site of an important hydrographic junction of the country; here, the Bug, the Narew, the Wkra, the Bzura and several lesser rivers join the Vistula. The remaining larger tributaries of the Vistula, flowing across the voivodeship, are the Pilica, the Radomka and the Świder. The local rivers do not reveal such considerable stage oscillations as their mountain counterparts. Nonetheless, they pose a flood threat owing to wide valleys and the lowland character of the terrain. As a rule, the Mazovian rivers are not regulated, a feature which grants them extremely picturesque and natural qualities but increases the flood hazard. The great width of the Vistula bed is the remnant of its former function of an antecedent valley, draining the glacier waters. In places, the river is composed of several arms embracing sandy islands, and shifts the current from bank to bank. A serious problem is created by ice embacles. Nonetheless, the Vistula freezes over increasingly rarely, a tendency associated not so much with the warming of the climate as the introduction into its waters of a considerable amount of sewage.

Lakes. The number of lakes in Mazovia is relatively slight. Their greatest concentration is the Gostynińskie Lake District, whose part is a fragment of the voivodeship (the counties of Gostynin and Płock). The majority of the lakes are post-glacial. The region has also a number of meander lakes, which originated in old river beds. A large man-made lake – the Zegrzyński Reservoir – was created in 1962 by swelling the Narew near Dębe. Now, it plays the role of a water reservoir for the capital, protects against floods, and, predominantly, remains an important leisure and tourism object. Part of the artificial Włocławek reservoir on the Vistula is located in the voivodeship. Mention should be made of a rather large number of man-made fish ponds.

41

The considerable pollution of the local rivers is regarded as a grave problem. The number of sewage-treatment plants is decidedly much too small. This holds true even for Warsaw, where only right-bank sewage undergoes treatment, a situation calling for urgent, large-scale investments. The quality of the water supplied by the city mains also requires improvement.

Navigation on the Vistula and other rivers has become almost non-existent, although in the past it was very intensive. Canals are scarce, and navigation is feasible only along the Żerański Canal, linking the Vistula and the Narew; others fulfil drainage functions.

Fragment of Kampinoska Forest

42

Woods

Woods. A major part of Mazovia was overgrown with woods, whose elimination was initiated extremely early on. Intensive stubbing dates back to the Middle Ages, but fragments of forests have survived up to this day, usually on poorest soil.

Mazovian woodlands have succumbed to considerable evolution. Once dominated by mixed and deciduous trees, they are now composed chiefly of pine. The prevailing tree is the common pine, usually grown in mono-cultures. On sand dunes, such pines frequently assume a stunted form. Richer types of soil, albeit also on sandy dunes covered with a layer of humus, are the site of new and mixed woods, with a well-developed and multi-storey composition, variegated vegetation and lush undergrowth. Waterlogged terrains are the site of deciduous woods; here, the dominating trees are the black alder, the white and black poplar, and the European white birch. The ground cover is, as a rule, composed of juniper, hazel and young trees. The Mazovian woods occupy the area of 188 000 has., which makes up 22% of the voivodeship area. 55% are state owned forests.

A characteristic feature of Mazovian woods is the absence of the beech, the fir and the great maple (sometimes introduced by man). On the other hand, there are natural concentrations of the Polish larch and spruce. Another typical property of the Mazovian region is the universal presence of peat-bog and sand vegetation. Analogously to the transitory character of the local climate, vegetation displays a temporary character that changes along the east-west axis. Moving towards the east of the voivodeship, we witness a gradual disappearance of Atlantic vegetation and the increased presence of north-eastern plants.

Wood growing on moraine hillock. The Uroczysko Reservation in Florianów, near Kałuszyn

The best-known and largest woodland complex in the voivodeship is Kampinoska Forest, mentioned earlier upon several occasions. In 1959, it was granted the status of a national park, the second largest in Poland. About two-thirds of its area are reservations, whose number today totals more than twenty. The park includes not only woods, but also meadows and fields belonging to the villages situated in the Forest, gradually bought up and afforested.

Alongside the aforementioned and celebrated parabolic dunes, other attention-worthy features are the local peat bogs. The Forest is a home to numerous rare plants as well as individual specimen of old trees. A large forested complex of this variety, granted the rank of a national park and situated in the direct vicinity of a capital, is unique on a European scale. Warsaw can boast of other wooded areas within its municipal region or directly adjoining it, especially the Młociński Wood

43

Oak
in Rembertów

and the Kabacki Wood, which is a landscape park. The complex of the mixed Chojnowskie Woods in the south, encompassing the resort of Konstancin and the vacation spots of Zalesie Górne and Dolne, are protected as part of the Chojnowski Landscape Park. The strip of Otwockie Woods, stretching into Warsaw from the southeast in the form of the Olszynka Grochowska and the Sobieskiego Wood reservations, is safeguarded as the Mazowiecki Landscape Park. The remaining landscape parks of the voivodeship include the Nadbużański (the largest in Poland), the Gostynińsko--Włocławski, the Brudzeński, the Górznieńsko-Lidzbarski, the Bolimowski and the Kozienicki.

Apart from Kampinoska Forest, Mazovia is the site of many other wooded complexes also known as forests, i.a. Biała, Bolimowska, Kamieniecka, Kurpiowska, Mariańska, Wiślicka and Zielona. Although the area of some of them exceeds that of Kampinoska Forest, none possesses such a well-preserved compact forest stand, diverse vegetation and natural conditions. In the majority of cases, they are rather remnants of forests, divided into numerous small sections.

Wild animals can be encountered in Mazovia primarily in the above listed larger woodland complexes. The mammals include moose, lynx, beavers (all three species were restituted), red deer, fallow deer, roe deer, wild boars, foxes, badgers, woodland and beech marten, hares, rabbits, bats, wolves and assorted small rodents. Noteworthy birds include the extremely rare black stork and numerous white storks. Attention is due also to cranes, herons, buzzards, and kestrels. Rare species include eagle owls, columbines, sea eagles, the grey heron, ospreys and kites. Water and marsh fowl as well as songbirds are numerous and diverse. Large numbers of reptiles and amphibians occur especially in plant concentrations on waterlogged terrains and along water-courses. Various examples of fish and lamprey abound. The examination of the imposing insect world still awaits completion.

Tomasz Zarycki

SOCIETY

Mazowieckie voivodeship is inhabited by more than 5 million residents, making it the most populated voivodeship in Poland. The largest town is Warsaw, with a population of about 1,6 million, while the whole agglomeration totals ca. 2,5 million dwellers, concentrating half of the population of the entire voivodeship; the cities comprise 64% of the overall populace. The voivodeship has 83 towns and 9 137 rural localities.

Warsaw predominates not only among the remaining towns of the voivodeship but is the largest city in Poland. The dimension of the social differentiation of the voivodeship depends to a considerable degree on the relation between the capital and its surroundings. Other sizable cities are Radom (population of 230 000) and Płock (population of 130 000), the remaining urban centres being much smaller. This marked contrast between the capital and its surroundings is a characteristic Mazovian trait, additionally intensified by the agrarian nature of a large part of the voivodeship. Historical references indicate that such a structure of the settlement space is typical for all those Polish territories which in the past were part of the Russian partition area. In Mazovia, municipal functions were concentrated in the capital city and several larger towns.

The capital-peripheries differentiation is seen best on a map depicting population density (map 1). The centre of the voivodeship is marked with a red spot denoting the Warsaw agglomeration. Its characteristic branches point to several directions – these are suburban localities, densely distributed along communication routes, primarily railway lines. The longest "arms" of this kind occur along those lines which were built earliest, the first being the route to Skierniewice, part of the Warsaw-Vienna line, and opened in 1845.

Map 1. Population density in Mazowieckie voivodeship in 1998
(no. of persons/sq. km.)

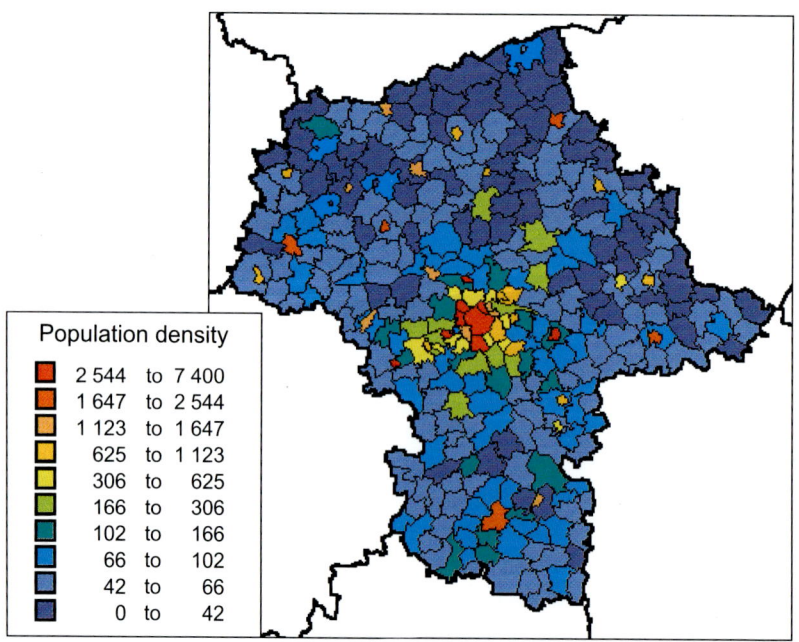

Population density

■	2 544 to	7 400
■	1 647 to	2 544
■	1 123 to	1 647
■	625 to	1 123
■	306 to	625
■	166 to	306
■	102 to	166
■	66 to	102
■	42 to	66
■	0 to	42

The localities which developed along this particular line are Piastów, Pruszków, Brwinów, Milanówek and Grodzisk Mazowiecki. The next line, at the time wide-gauge, led to Białystok. Inaugurated in 1862, it was part of the route towards St. Petersburg, then the capital, with such localities as Ząbki, Kobyłka, Wołomin and Tłuszcz along the way. Other "branches" of the Warsaw agglomeration progressed along the Lublin line, opened in 1877 (i.a. Otwock and Józefów), and the Działdowo line, dating from the same year (Legionowo, Nowy Dwór Mazowiecki). The greater the distance from Warsaw, the more rapid the decline of the population density which frequently drops below 50 persons per square km. (without, however, reaching the lowest level in the country, i.e. less than 15 persons per square km., as in the case of Western Pomerania). The characteristic feature of the countryside is a relatively level population density index, usually oscillating from 50 to 70 persons per square km. Next to Warsaw, the most distinguished centres in Mazovia are those of former voivodeships – Radom, Płock, Siedlce, Ciechanów and Ostrołęka. Work on a territorial administration reform, conducted in 1998, was accompanied by debates concerning its effects on chances for development, available for heretofore voivodeship towns. The adherents of the reform defended the view that even if such cities were to lose some of the assets (by no means certain in market economy), the opportunities to be enjoyed by dozens of poviat centres would grow.

■

Demographic Structure

Women comprise 51,8% of the population of the voivodeship, which in January 1999 totalled 5 063 917 persons. The age structure is illustrated in fig. 1.

Fig. 1. Demographic structure of Mazovia compared to the demographic structure of Poland

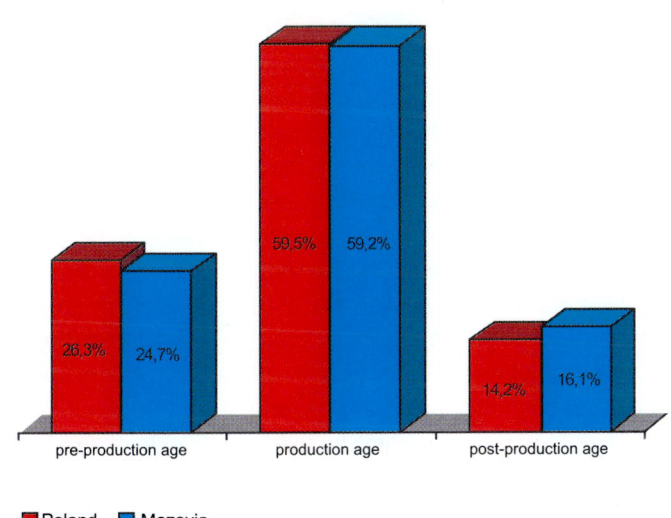

| pre-production age | production age | post-production age |

■ Poland ■ Mazovia

This is a structure slightly less favourable against the backdrop of national indices, but more favourable as contrasted with the situation prevailing in Western Europe. The percentage of the post-production age population is relatively slight. Importance is also attached to inner differentiation. In the Warsaw agglomeration and in Radom and Płock we observe a markedly higher percentage of the production-age population and a lower percentage of persons younger than 14 years of age in comparison to the national mean. This feature is associated with an influx of people seeking employment in the capital and a reduced natural birth rate. The same factors explain why in the capital we encounter a larger number of women per 100 men and the lowest number of births. The size of those indices is comparable solely with Łódź. Nonetheless, only in Mazovia are the indices of birth and childbearing slightly lower than in the case of the entire population of Poland. The natural birth rate in Mazowieckie Voivodeship is negative, and totals -0,8 per 1 000 inhabitants. The positive migration balance reaches 1,1 per 1 000 inhabitants. Great significance is ascribed to inner migration differentiations. Furthermore, it is interesting to note that the migration balance attains the highest positive level not only in the capital itself but also in the gminas surrounding it. It is here that the largest number of arrivals settle down. The balance is negative in the rural regions – the most in the northern part of the voivodeship. The centre of the voivodeship has the highest percentage of inhabitants born outside their place of residence.

■

The Differentiation of Functions Fulfilled by Rural Areas in the Voivodeship

The dependence of the titular differentiation on the distance from the capital and the communication routes leading to it constitutes yet another important factor. Gminas directly adjoining the capital (e.g. Piaseczno, Ożarów Mazowiecki) are dominated by residential functions and services, with a slight participation of the industry and agriculture. Some of the gminas in the region of Warsaw perform the function of "suburban" agriculture, connected with the proximity of municipal sales markets. This tendency is perceptible in particular in the case of orcharding (e.g. Tarczyn, Grójec, Góra Kalwaria). Gminas situated along the Zegrzyński Reservoir are characterised by prevailing tourist functions which enjoy a prominent rank also in the gminas of Kampinoska Forest. Not a single gmina in which a fundamental role would be played by traditional private farms is to be found within the boundaries of the former Warsaw voivodeship. The socioeconomic functions of the entire region depend on the proximity to the capital. Wide strips of non-farming gminas (mainly with predominant residential or industrial functions) stretch from Warsaw towards the boundaries of the voivodeship, in the direction of Łódź, Białystok, Lublin and Siedlce. Non-agrarian functions prevail also in the gminas situated in the direct proximity of Radom and to the south of that town, in the area of Iłża and Szydłowiec, or near the remaining cities in this part of the voivodeship. This is the northern edge of the Old Polish Industrial Region. The prevalence of farming is to be seen in almost the whole of the former Ciechanów voivodeship, the major part of the former Płock voivodeship (excluding the environs of Płock and Gostynin), the northern part of the former Radom voivodeship and the sizable areas in the former Siedlce voivodeship (with the exception of communication "corridors" leading to Lublin, Białystok and Brześć). In the case of the former Ostrołęka voivodeship, agriculture performs a role practically equal to non-agrarian functions.

It seems worth drawing attention to the fact that until recently both Warsaw and, to a lesser degree, other largest cities in the present-day voivodeship were the destinations of long-distance commuting. Yet another factor conducive to the development of this phenomenon were residence restrictions binding in towns in the direct vicinity of Warsaw. The local labour force proved insufficient for the numerous industrial enterprises located in the agglomeration, and low ticket prices facilitated commuting. The consequence was two-stage commuting: numerous residents of suburban towns worked in the capital, while workplaces situated in those cities were manned by employees from nearby small towns and villages. During the post-1989 period, the scale of commuting diminished essentially.

■

UNEMPLOYMENT

The socially significant problem of unemployment emerged together with the socioeconomic transformations of the last decade. In the middle of 1999, the unemployment rate in Mazowieckie voivodeship totalled 8,5% (as compared to the national average of 11,6%). Its spatial differentiation corresponds to a large degree to the centre-peripheries structure. The level of unemployment is the lowest in the Warsaw agglomeration where, for all practical purposes, it does not constitute a grave issue. It is here that people from all over Poland and even abroad (especially the former Soviet Union) search for jobs. The further the distance from the capital, the higher the level of unemployment, especially in the countryside (mainly in the former Płock, Ciechanów and Ostrołęka voivodeships). Relatively high unemployment exists in the southern fragments of the voivodeship, and thus in the urbanised part of the former Radom voivodeship, reaching 25% in the county of Szydłowiec (the highest index in the voivodeship). This tendency is linked mainly with the restructurization of the tool and armament industry, developed in this region during the era of the Polish People's Republic; those two branches could not rely on the impact of an extensive influx of foreign investment that alleviated socioeconomic problems and proved so beneficial for Warsaw.

■

EDUCATION

About 500 000 children attend 2 250 primary schools. The school reform introduced in 1999 created in the voivodeship 666 junior-high public schools and 107 private schools, attended by more than 65 000 pupils and employing about 39 000 teachers.

Secondary level schooling discloses a favourable trend: there are more pupils in comprehensive schools and less in vocational schools. The percentage of young people attending 301 comprehensive schools is higher than the national mean. They attract 37% of secondary school pupils, while this index for the whole of Poland totals 31%. On the other hand, the percentage of young people in vocational schools is smaller than the national mean (by about 3,5%). The staff of all the secondary schools amounts to some 15 000 teachers.

Recent years noted an extremely dynamic development of higher education institutions in Poland. This situation prevails also in Mazovia where 63 such schools are attended by more than 200 000 students. Some of them are the best higher-level schools in Poland and widely renowned throughout the world. The most important higher education institutions in Warsaw include Warsaw University, the Warsaw University of Technology, the Main Trade Academy, the Main Agricultural Academy, the Medical Academy, the Cardinal Stefan Wyszyński University (established in 1999), the Frederic Chopin Music Academy and the Aleksander Zelwerowicz Theatrical Academy.

In recent years, the appearance of numerous private schools has considerably intensified the development of academic education. Numerous such institutions are situated outside the capital city – a highly favourable tendency. There are four institutions of higher learning in Radom – three business schools and the state Radom Polytechnic with 12 000 students. Siedlce has the newly opened state Podlaska Academy, attended by about 7 000 students, and a private school. Płock boasts of a branch of the Warsaw University of Technology and the vigorous Paweł Włodkowic Academy. A true phenomenon among private academies is the Higher School in the Humanities in Pułtusk which in the course of several years, and

New building of Warsaw University Library, containing up-to-date equipment and regarded as a leading current investment in higher education

thanks to resorting to the scientific potential of Warsaw, has become an expansive institution (with about 10 000 students) and gained excellent reputation as regards the level of offered education.

Fig. 2. Students in Mazowieckie voivodeship

Warsaw University
of Technology – 25 thous.

Podlaska Academy – 7 thous.

Radom
Polytechnic – 12 thous.

Warsaw
University – 50 thous.

other schools – 86 thous.

Main School
of Agriculture – 10 thous.

Main School
of Commerce – 10 thous.

HEALTH SERVICE

The structure of the health service in the voivodeship is based on 87 hospitals with about 27 000 beds, 225 clinics and 395 centres in smaller localities. Moreover, there are several private hospitals and hundreds of private doctor offices. The

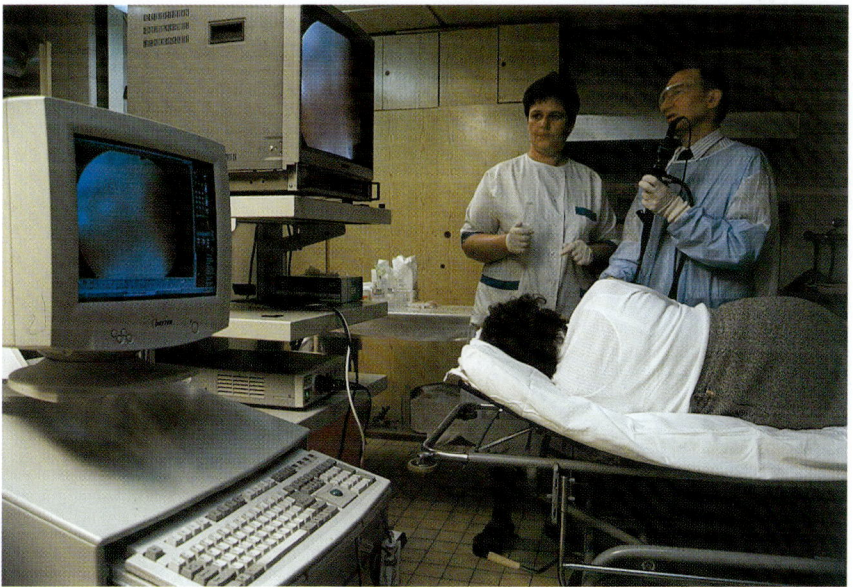

Endoscopic blocking of an oesophagus verices hemorrhage. General Surgery and Liver Diseases Chair and Clinic at the Medical Academy in Warsaw

public health service employs almost 13 000 doctors (including approximately 1 800 dentists), around 26 000 nurses and more than 2 500 midwives. The voivodeship has 750 pharmacies of which an overwhelming majority are privately owned. The standard of medical care varies, and the largest number of highly skilled doctors is to be found in Warsaw where they have at their disposal modern diagnostic apparatus. Nevertheless, good doctors and well-organised hospital wards can be found in numerous county towns.

The situation in the health service has changed basically after the announcement of the health care system reform (1 January 1999). The entire sphere of financing the health service has been assumed by patients' funds; the entire voivodeship is included within the range of the Mazovian Patients' Fund .

■

ADMINISTRATION AND POLITICAL LIFE

The territorial organisation of Poland changed on 24 July 1998 when a newly-passed law introduced a three-stage territorial division of the state, establishing 16 voivodeships and 308 land and 65 municipal poviats. Mazowieckie voivodeship became the largest of all Polish voivodeships. The reform became binding as of 1 January 1999.

Today, the voivodeship embraces 325 gminas, 38 counties, and four towns with the status of a poviat. Gminas and poviats are conceived as units of territorial self-government, and the voivodeship is of a dual character: it holds the rank of a government administration unit and of a regional self-government community.

The Constitution of the Republic of Poland grants a high position to all organs of territorial self-government. Alongside extensive statutory competence, their role is reinforced by the principle of the presumption of a territorial self-government features as regards the execution of those public tasks, which neither the Constitution nor the law reserves for other agencies of public authorities.

Particular rungs of the territorial self-government are formally independent; this is not to say that in practice their organs refrain from coordinating their activity.

The most important competence of the communes include communal and housing economy, the protection of natural environment and territorial administration, education within the range of primary schools and kindergartens, social services, communal roads and streets, culture and registers of economic activity. Furthermore, the gminas are entrusted with the realisation of tasks concerning government administration. Authority is yielded by a gmina council, elected for a four-year term, and a Board. The tasks of the Board are supervised by a mayor (in municipal gminas), a *wójt* (an elder, in rural communes), or a President (in large cities).

Poviats are new units of territorial self-government which, as a rule, encompass several gminas. Their most important competence pertains to communication and transport, county roads, secondary schools, construction supervision, water management and the protection of the natural environment, land management and surveying, culture and the labour market. Authority in the poviat belongs to a council elected for a four-year term. Its work is directed by a chairman. The council also elects a poviat board, headed by the *staroste* of the given poviat.

The competence of a voivodeship, conceived as a unit of territorial self-government, entails regional policy, higher and post-secondary schools, social care and specialist health care, voivodeship roads, regional culture institutions, the protection of the natural environment, and spatial planning. Authority in the voivodeship belongs to a dietine (sejmik), elected every four years. The work of the sejmik is supervised by a chairman, and includes electing a voivodeship board, headed by a marshal. Self-government administration on the voivodeship level is concentrated in the Office of the Marshal.

As a unit of government administration, the voivodeship is ruled by a voivode, appointed by the Prime Minister. The voivode is held responsible for the implementation of government policies throughout the voivodeship; in particular, he exercises control over the work conducted by joint government administration organs, supervises the performance of tasks commissioned by the government and carried out by self-government organs, is burdened with numerous tasks concerning state defence and security and, finally, acts as a representative of the State Treasury in reference to entrusted property.

The system prevailing in Warsaw differs in essential respects. The fundamental unit of the city's self-government are also gminas, which, however, are components of an obligatory union. Among the eleven gminas comprising Warsaw, the largest and most important is Warsaw-Centre. The Warsaw Council is chosen in direct elections. The executive organ is composed of a board headed by the municipal President, who also oversees the management of the Warsaw-Centre gmina. The borders of the city coincide with those of the county of Warsaw. The prevailing system remains rather fluid and will probably change in the foreseeable future.

Bankowy Square. This historical complex of buildings is the seat of the authorities of Mazowieckie voivodeship and the capital city of Warsaw

53

POLITICAL LIFE. Political life in Mazovia cannot be described separately owing to the fact that Warsaw remains the centre of Polish political life.

One of the most synthetic and, simultaneously, extremely complex ways of portraying the political scene is an analysis of the regional differentiation of election results. We shall restrict our description of the "political scene" in the voivodeship to two basic dimensions and attendance. The first is the dominating "right-left" axis, known also as the "value axis". In the parliamentary elections of 1997, the left and right wings were represented by the Democratic Left Alliance (SLD) and the Solidarity Election Campaign (AWS). The second axis involves predominantly a conflict concerning economic questions, and is thus known as the "interest axis". Here, the foremost opponents were the Polish Peasant Party (PSL) and the Freedom Union (UW). In the self-government election held in 1998, the place formerly occupied by PSL was taken by the "Social Alliance" Coalition (made up of PSL, UP [the Labour Party], and KPEiR [the National Pensioners Party]), in which the main force continued to be PSL. In order to illustrate the differentiated nature of the political scene in Mazowieckie Voivodeship it was necessary to resort to data concerning elections to the voivodeship dietine (sejmik), with a poviat as an analysis unit. Pertinent maps demonstrate the difference between the percentage of voices supporting SLD and AWS. The higher the positive values, the more left-wing the given county. A map of this size makes it easy to notice a general diversity between the eastern and western parts of the voivodeship. Areas of the former Ostrołęka, Siedlce and Łomża voivodeships are distinctly more right-wing. We are dealing primarily with traditions of parts of the region of Podlasie, well-known for their pro-right sympathies and today constituting Mazowieckie voivodeship. Certain analysts associated the contemporary profile of Podlasie with its historical past, drawing attention to such factors as the extremely high percentage of the petty gentry in this region. A second distinct area of support for the right-wing are the environs of Warsaw on the right-hand bank of the Vistula – the Otwock line from Garwolin to Wołomin. Traditionally, support for the right-wing is rather considerable in the vicinity of Warsaw and usually remains higher than in the city itself. This contrast was even greater in preceding years. Emphasis must be placed on the absence of a discernible dependence of political preferences upon the level of urbanisation. Apparently, in the suburbs of the capital we are dealing primarily with working-class voters, symbolised by the workers of the Ursus Enterprises, known for a predominating right-wing orientation. The main left-wing regions of Mazovia include the north-west (the former voivodeship of Płock and the northern part of the voivodeship of Ciechanów, with the Żuromin poviat in the forefront). The second pro-left area is the south-eastern edge of the voivodeship (the poviat of Lipsko), a fragment of a larger region with extremely durable left-wing traditions whose centre is Ostrowiec Świętokrzyski. It seems worth drawing attention that according to sociological studies support for the right-wing option is rather strongly linked with religious activity. Presumably, a map of this factor to a certain degree depicts spatial differentiation in the level of religiousness in the voivodeship.

The "interest axis" map of electoral preferences (map 3) resembles extremely closely the above discussed differentiation between the town and the countryside. The dominating centre of the "liberal" option, i.e. a source of support for UW, is Warsaw and gminas in its immediate vicinity. The enclosed map illustrates some of the capital's "arms", primarily the Skierniewice route. The Otwock and Białystok lines are much less vivid. Naturally, the map distinguishes all the cities, as a rule proportionately to their size. Just as distinct are areas of large support for UW within the former Radom voivodeship, and primarily in Radom itself, Kozienice and Szydłowiec.

Meanwhile, strong backing for PSL occurs in the southern part of the former voivodeship of Płock. The second most important region of support for this party in Mazowieckie voivodeship are the eastern poviats of Sokołów and Siedlce. Within this context, mention should be made also of the poviats of Lipsko and Zwoleń in the former voivodeship of Radom. Apparently, although UW is supported chiefly in the cities, farming regions do not disclose an analogous connection between the size of the rural population and an increase in support for PSL.

Map 2. Voting preference differentiations in the SLD–AWS dimension in elections to the voivodeship sejmik in 1998 (vote percentage differences)

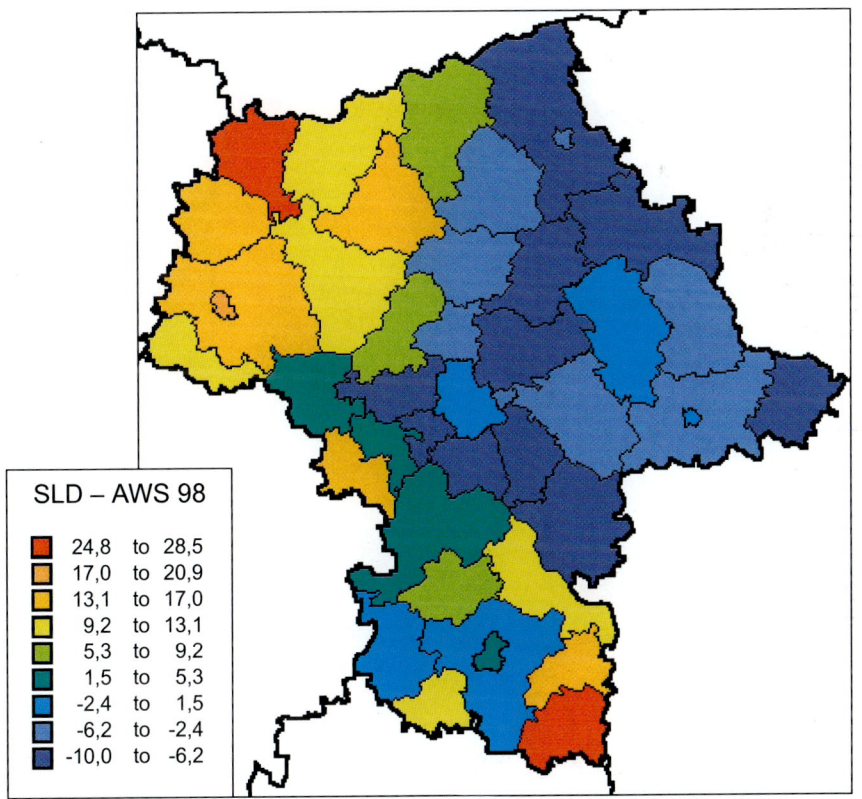

SLD – AWS 98

24,8 to 28,5
17,0 to 20,9
13,1 to 17,0
9,2 to 13,1
5,3 to 9,2
1,5 to 5,3
-2,4 to 1,5
-6,2 to -2,4
-10,0 to -6,2

A map of attendance in the self-government elections held in 1998 (map 4) introduced a certain dose of surprise, since it differs from the attendance pattern in parliamentary elections. Warsaw, in which attendance achieved the highest level, is now situated within the range of the voivodeship mean. Other larger cities – Płock, Radom, Siedlce, Sochaczew or Mińsk Mazowiecki – have the lowest attendance in the voivodeship. During parliamentary elections, attendance in those towns achieved a decidedly higher level. On the other hand, the highest attendance level in self-government elections is noted more frequently in rural poviats, where local elections pertain to the daily issues of the population in a much more direct manner. A decidedly ascending election attendance is found along the eastern edges of the voivodeship, and in particular in the eastern part of the former voivodeship of Siedlce, i.e. southern Podlasie. Other regions with similar attendance include the poviats of Żuromin, Szydłowiec, Przysucha and Sokołów Podlaski.

ELECTION RESULTS. In 1998, elections to the dietine of Mazowieckie voivodeship were won by AWS which received 33,4% votes and 32 seats in the 80-mandate dietine. SLD won 31,2% votes and 30 seats, the Social Alliance (a coalition

Map 3. Voting preference differentiations in the Social Alliance–UW dimension in elections to the voivodeship sejmik in 1998 (vote percentage differences)

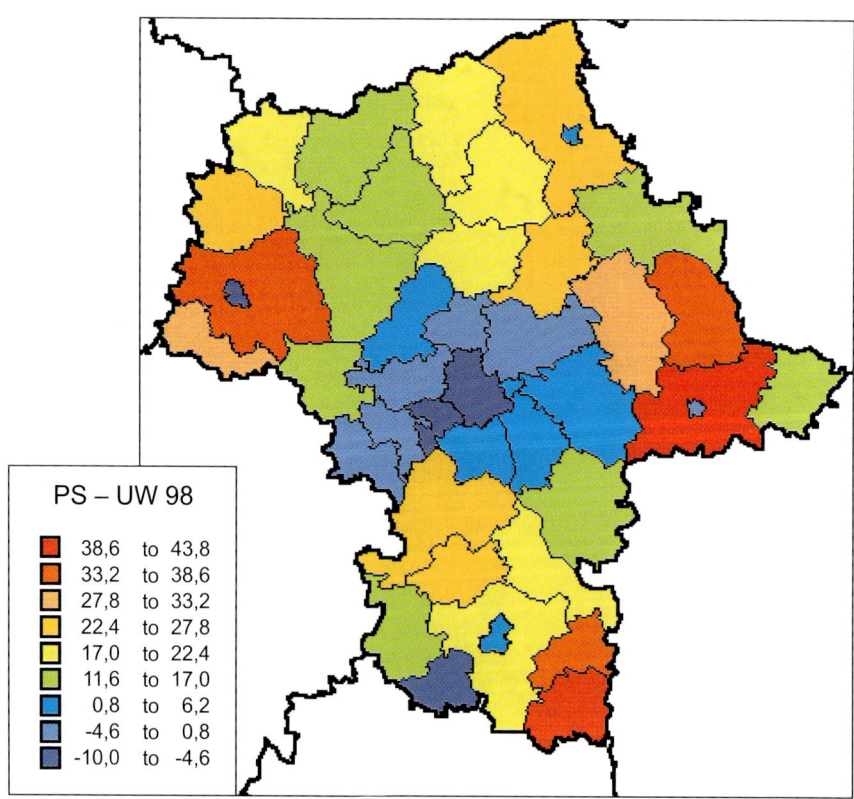

PS – UW 98

38,6 to 43,8
33,2 to 38,6
27,8 to 33,2
22,4 to 27,8
17,0 to 22,4
11,6 to 17,0
0,8 to 6,2
-4,6 to 0,8
-10,0 to -4,6

composed of PSL, UP and KPEiR) – 14,8% and 11 seats, UW – 11,3% and 6 seats, the Polish Family (associated with "Radio Maryja") – 5,6% and 1 seat (the only one in Poland) in the dietine. Ruch Patriotyczny – "Ojczyzna" (the "Motherland" Patriotic Movement, under Jan Olszewski) received 2,7% votes – too little to obtain a seat.

Elections to the authorities of the dietine, the marshal of the voivodeship and the remaining members of the board denoted a success for the SLD-PSL coalition. The chairman of the Voivodeship Dietine is Włodzimierz Nieporęt, recommended by SLD, the marshal of the voivodeship is Zbigniew Kuźmiuk, recommended by PSL, and the Voivodeship Board is composed of Jerzy Dobek, Leszek Mizieliński, Henryk Kisielewski and Leszek Kwiatek.

The party-designated composition of the county boards is a simple consequence of the election results presented in maps 2 and 3. In those areas where victory was won by AWS, the latter usually established poviat boards either by itself or in a coalition with UW (sporadically with other groups). Analogously, SLD usually creates "ruling" coalitions with PSL. All told, AWS has 489 seats in the poviat councils, SLD – 284, the Social Alliance (chiefly PSL) – 259, and UW – 48, while the remaining groups and unaffiliated representatives hold 190 mandates.

Map 4. Voting attendance differentiations in self-government elections in 1998 (elections to the voivodeship sejmik, data in %)

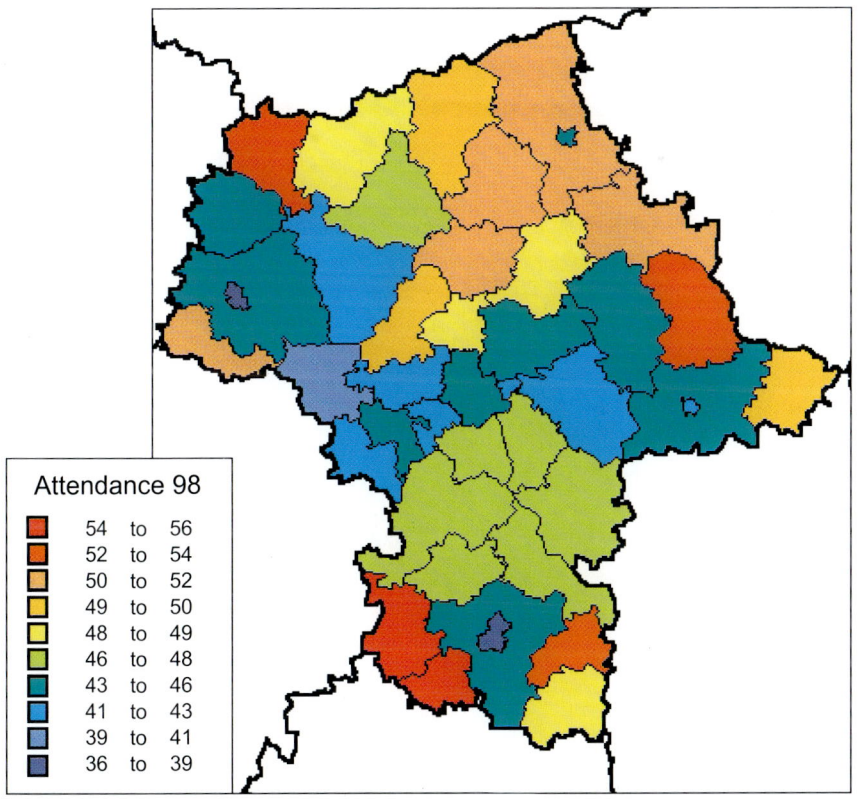

Attendance 98		
54	to	56
52	to	54
50	to	52
49	to	50
48	to	49
46	to	48
43	to	46
41	to	43
39	to	41
36	to	39

The Council of Warsaw is composed of 68 members – 29 mandates are controlled by AWS, 25 – by SLD, 13 – by UW and 1 – by Ruch Patriotyczny – "Ojczyzna". The election of the President of Warsaw encountered considerable obstacles owing to specific statutory solutions referring to the course of his appointment. Ultimately, lengthy negotiations led to the emergence of a coalition composed of AWS and UW which obtained the support of SLD at the cost of including a representative of this party into the boards of the capital city and all Warsaw gminas.

Political life in Mazovia does not veer from democratic standards. During the first year of the administrative reform – an extremely difficult period for the local authorities – we have observed a gradual alleviation of party rivalry, the consolidation of the administrative bodies of the voivodeship and the poviats and increased professionalism in their activity.

ECONOMY

Mazowieckie voivodeship yields 20% of the gross national product (GNP) of Poland. Warsaw comprises the financial centre of the country. Mazovian industry contributes about 19% of the sold production of the Polish industry. Milk and fruit orchards are the symbol of Mazovian agriculture and the poviat of Grójec could be described as an extensive orchard; 35 000 hectares of apple and other fruit trees comprise the largest area of this type in Europe.

In 1997, Mazowieckie voivodeship yielded 19,7% of the gross national product, i.e. 0,06% higher than in 1996, and 1,6% more than in 1995. Calculated per capita, the GNP amounts to 17 300 PLN, which is the best result in the country (table 1). In Śląskie voivodeship, which comes second in the ranking, this sum totals 13 300 PLN.

Table 1. GNP estimate according to voivodeships

Voivodeship	1995	1997	1995	1997
	mln. PLN		thous. PLN per capita	
Dolnośląskie	21 999	32 434	7,4	10,9
Kujawsko-Pomorskie	14 247	20 289	6,8	9,7
Lubelskie	12 309	18 880	5,5	8,4
Lubuskie	6 929	10 053	6,8	9,9
Łódzkie	19 724	28 933	7,4	10,8
Małopolskie	21 377	32 892	6,7	10,3
Mazowieckie	**51 266**	**87 588**	**10,2**	**17,3**
Opolskie	7 225	10 801	6,6	9,9
Podkarpackie	12 150	18 346	5,7	8,6
Podlaskie	6 954	10 211	5,7	8,3
Pomorskie	16 669	25 020	7,7	11,5
Śląskie	43 224	64 888	8,8	13,3
Świętokrzyskie	7 365	10 726	5,5	8,0
Warmińsko-Mazurskie	8 398	12 949	5,7	8,8
Wielkopolskie	26 233	41 570	7,9	12,5
Zachodniopomorskie	12 632	19 169	7,3	11,1

Source: W.M. Orłowski, E. Saganowska, L. Zienkowski (1998), *Szacunek produktu krajowego brutto według 19 województw za 1996 i 1997 rok (Metoda uproszczona)* (Estimated GNP in Nineteen Voivodeships in 1996 and 1997 [Simplified Method]), Zakład Badań Statystyczno-Ekonomicznych GUS i PAN, series: *Z prac Zakładu Badań Statystyczno-Ekonomicznych*, fasc. 262.

The structure of added value in Mazowieckie voivodeship against the backdrop of other voivodeships is presented in table 2.

Table 2. Estimated structure of gross added value in 1996

Voivodeship = 100%

Voivodeship	Agriculture, forestry and fishery	Industry	Construction	Market services	Non--market services
Dolnośląskie	5,9	32,2	7,0	39,4	15,4
Kujawsko-Pomorskie	9,5	30,8	5,3	38,8	15,6
Lubelskie	14,0	24,4	5,2	38,7	17,7
Lubuskie	6,5	29,3	5,0	39,6	19,7
Łódzkie	7,1	35,9	5,0	37,3	14,6
Małopolskie	4,5	29,9	8,1	41,6	16,0
Mazowieckie	**6,0**	**26,0**	**5,6**	**48,5**	**14,0**
Opolskie	11,6	30,6	6,7	37,4	13,7
Podkarpackie	6,6	33,9	5,9	36,7	16,8
Podlaskie	13,7	21,8	5,6	40,9	18,0
Pomorskie	4,7	28,1	6,7	46,3	14,3
Śląskie	1,5	44,4	6,9	36,4	10,8
Świętokrzyskie	9,5	28,1	5,8	40,7	16,0
Warmińsko-Mazurskie	11,3	27,9	5,7	37,2	17,9
Wielkopolskie	11,8	31,9	6,7	36,5	13,1
Zachodniopomorskie	7,4	24,4	6,3	46,2	15,8

Source: W.M. Orłowski, E. Saganowska, L. Zienkowski, *op. cit.*

ENTERPRISES

At the end of 1998 there were 400 464 enterprises in the voivodeship, i.e. one registered firm per 12 inhabitants. In practice, the number of enterprises is much smaller, since some of them do not pursue any sort of activity. An overwhelming number, as many as 358 89, belong to self-employment persons.

Within the KRUPGN-REGON system, which encompasses natural persons and independent organisational units without legal personality, there were 41 575 registered subjects, with a predominating participation in the economy of Mazovia. Their structure, according to the type of ownership, is presented in diagram 1.

61

Diagram 1. Structure of enterprises according to the type of ownership (legal persons)

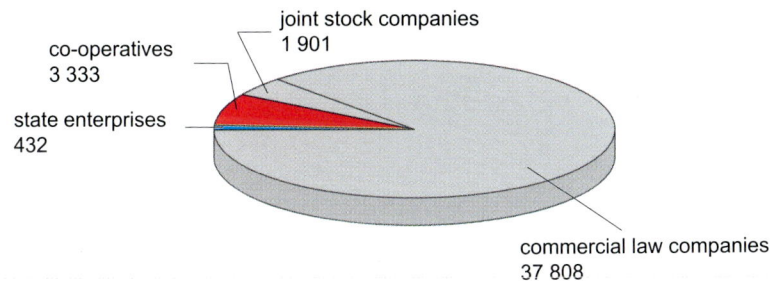

joint stock companies
1 901

co-operatives
3 333

state enterprises
432

commercial law companies
37 808

Source: "Biuletyn Statystyczny woj. mazowieckiego", September 1999.

BANKS AND BUSINESS SURROUNDINGS INSTITUTIONS

A characteristic trait of Mazowieckie voivodeship is the highest participation of market services in the country in gross added value, totalling almost 50%. This is the outcome of the activity pursued in the voivodeship – primarily in Warsaw – by the majority of bank head offices and the largest foreign trust and investment funds, particularly essential from the viewpoint of enterprises, especially foreign ones.

The overall number of bank central offices and branches per 100 000 inhabitants is 7,9, which is the fourth best result in the country (better indices are to be found in Dolnośląskie, Podlaskie and Lubuskie voivodeships). Mazowieckie voivodeship decidedly outdistances all other voivodeships as regards the presence of bank central offices – 12 per 1 mln. inhabitants; in the second ranking Dolnośląskie Voivodeship this index totals four. Warsaw is the site of all the central offices of foreign banks active in Poland, including Commerzbank AG, Citibank, J. P. Morgan, Bayerische Hypo und Vereinsbank AG, ING Group, Deutsche Bank AG, Westdeutsche Landesbank (WestLB), Bank of America, Creditanstalt Bankverein, ABN-AMRO Bank, DG Bank, Dresdner Bank, Banco Commercial Portugues, Centro Internationale Handelsbank AG, Banca Commerciale Italiana, Societe Generale, Berliner Bank AG, Kredietbank N. V., Credit Lyonnais, Rabobank, Investentbank Austria AG, Cassa di Risparmio di Padova, Bank of New York, Giro-Credit Bank AG and the majority of the central offices of domestic banks as well as those in which shares belong to foreign banks.

The list of the largest enterprises in Mazowieckie voivodeship includes numerous banks in "the first fifty", i.a. PKO BP (with a revenue of 9 571 mln. zlotys in 1998), Bank Pekao SA-Grupa Pekao SA (7 906 mln. zlotys), BGŻ SA (3 221 mln. zlotys), Bank Handlowy w Warszawie SA (3 087 mln. zlotys), and PBK SA (2 156 mln. zlotys). A more detailed image of the banking sector may be obtained by analysing data contained in table 3.

One of the effects of economic transformation is the growing importance of services, especially those supporting economic development. In 1998, the 44 business surroundings institutions located in Mazowieckie voivodeship included training-advisory centres, local law and guarantee funds, entrepreneurship incubators, technological centres as well as venture capital funds.

INDUSTRY

In Mazowieckie voivodeship 26% of gross added value is associated with industry. An even greater participation of industry is a characteristic feature of the following voivodeships: Śląskie (44,4%), Łódzkie (35,9%), Podkarpackie (33,9%), Dolnośląskie (32,2%) and Wielkopolskie (31,9%). Lower indices occur only in Podlaskie (21,8%), Lubelskie and Zachodnio-Pomorskie voivodeships (24,4% each). The low participation of industry in the structure of gross added value does not signify that local industry is weak in comparison with the rest of the country, but is a simple consequence of the domination of market services. In 1997, Mazowieckie voivodeship employed 12,3% of all workers in domestic industry, and concentrated 15% of permanent means value in industry. Even higher was the participation of the voivodeship in the domestic investment input in industry (15,9%) and in the total sold value of industry (18,9% in 1998).

Participation in domestic industry grants the voivodeship second place after Śląskie Voivodeship.

A general picture of the character of Mazovian industry may be obtained by observing the structure of sold production within the range of the statistical category of "production activity". The largest participation in sold industrial products was characteristic for the following branches:

- food and beverages — 27,55%
- chemicals and chemical products — 9,15%
- publishing and printing — 8,94%
- machinery and equipment — 5,80%
- radio, television and communication equipment and apparatus production — 5,30%
- clothing and fur — 2,61%
- metal articles (without machinery and equipment) — 2,42%
- other branches of production — 32,23%

The largest production firms in Mazowieckie voivodeship are Petrochemia Płocka SA, which in 1999 became part of Polski Koncern Naftowy, Daewoo-FSO Motor, Thomson Polklor sp. z o. o., ZPTR SA, Zasada SA, Polski Tytoń SA, and Alcatel Polska. The biggest employer in Mazovia is Daewoo-FSO Motor, which has about 15 000 workers. For other large production firms see table 3.

From the viewpoint of the future, essential significance is ascribed to the size of investments. The investments of several firms representing seemingly traditional branches of the industry appear to be impressive. By way of example, only in 1998 Petrochemia Płock spent 1 242 mln. zlotys, and Daewoo-FSO company – 783 mln. zlotys; in the case of the latter, 1998 was a consecutive year of high investments. Other considerable investments were made by Intercell SA in Ostrołęka (see table 3).

The building industry participates in the gross added value structure to a relatively small extent. The voivodeship has such large firms as Mostostal Warszawa or Mostostal Siedlce. Among foreign firms we come across Bau Holding Aktiengesellschaft, Epstein, Chelverton Properties, Lend Lease Central Europa, Bilfinger und Berger Bau AG, Bouygues, Hochtief and Fluor Daniel B. V. Progress of the building industry is favoured by a veritable boom in Warsaw, especially as regards modern office buildings and hotels, as well as investments in communication infrastructure: the construction of the underground in Warsaw, the Świętokrzyski Bridge and the Toruńska Route. A bridge on the Vistula was completed in Wy-szogród in 1999, and an expressway ring road in Radzymin – a year earlier.

The underground is a leading Warsaw investment. The first functioning section is Kabaty–City (15 km)

Housing construction continues to develop satisfactorily, especially in the Warsaw agglomeration. In 1998, the number of flats completed in Mazowieckie voivodeship totalled 17 160 – the largest number in the country. Mazowieckie voivodeship also holds first place (*ex aequo* with Podlaskie voivodeship) as regards the number (3,5) of completed flats per 1 000 inhabitants; on the average, these flats are more spacious than the ones built in other parts of Poland. Nonetheless, the growth rate of housing resources is much too low in relation to enormous requirements, as shown by demographic factors (the large number of young people starting families and the positive migration balance) as well as historical factors (enormous destruction dating from World War II).

In 1998, the sold production of the construction industry achieved the value of 15 823 mln. zlotys and continued to grow dynamically in 1999. A comparison of

Table 3. List of largest enterprises in Mazowieckie voivodeship in 1998

Specification	Form of owner-ship	Income from total activity in thous. zł	Revenue changes since 1997 in thous. zł	Gross financial outcome in thous. zł	Net financial outcome in thous. zł**	Profitability index in %	Employ-ment in posts	Investment input in thous. zł
1. PSE SA, Warszawa	100	13 483 365	1 680 706	85 592	31 082	0,63	732	356 280
2. Petrochemia Płock SA, Płock	241	12 614 252	19 139	774 063	607 331	6,14	7 402	1 242 662
3. TP SA, Warszawa	100	10 611 919	2 031 371	1 967 982	1 046 045	18,55	72 807	3 983 859
4. PKP, Warszawa	100	9 603 800	62 400	-1 370 100	-1 370 100	-12,50	11 679	2 014 800
5. PKO BP, Warszawa*	200	9 571 963	1 268 030	-498 686	-1 300 120	-5,21	40 807	no data
6. Bank Pekao SA – Gr. Pekao SA, Warszawa	120	7 906 551	no data	965 504	521 274	12,21	11 149	no data
7. Daewoo-FSO Motor sp. z o.o., Warszawa	510	7 388 175	3 101 463	201 195	137 853	2,72	14 695	783 468
8. PZU SA, Warszawa	100	6 791 289	no data	540 033	258 523	7,95	12 299	no data
9. CPN SA, Warszawa	100	6 530 696	-1 169 047	171 923	92 175	2,63	6 578	219 824
10. Makro Cash and Carry SA, Warszawa	500	5 480 133	no data	115 681	60 462	2,11	5 138	143 594
11. PZU Życie SA, Warszawa	100	4 415 675	no data	233 470	150 910	5,29	no data	no data
12. Centrum Daewoo sp. z o.o., Warszawa	500	4 210 339	1 316 723	5 462	3 653	0,13	585	7 630
13. Poczta Polska PPUP, Warszawa	200	3 917 054	457 910	39 086	9 441	1,00	97 702	101 148
14. Ruch SA, Warszawa	100	3 441 396	498 680	38 287	20 406	1,11	9 938	24 387
15. BGŻ SA Centrala, Warszawa	140	3 221 632	no data	404 567	338 559	12,56	820	no data
16. Bartimpex SA, Mariew	400	3 200 907	581 303	183 531	120 703	5,73	47	12 864
17. Bank Handlowy SA, Warszawa*	451	3 087 068	399 669	465 046	301 550	9,77	4 031	no data
18. PBK SA, Warszawa*	415	2 156 182	351 490	422 518	280 505	19,60	no data	no data
19. PLL LOT SA, Warszawa	100	2 089 917	241 853	-26 358	-26 358	-1,26	3 999	14 588
20. Kredyt Bank PBI SA, Warszawa*	425	2 035 564	1 140 354	220 494	153 034	7,52	5 615	no data
21. BIG Bank Gdański SA, Warszawa*	540	1 923 544	1 278 458	221 850	146 504	7,62	4 757	no data
22. Totalizator Sportowy sp. z o.o., Warszawa	100	1 885 581	no data	237 418	129 892	12,59	593	no data
23. BRE SA, Warszawa*	450	1 779 839	790 084	345 123	205 087	11,52	1 820	no data
24. Polkomtel SA, Warszawa	450	1 722 926	976 895	-58 968	-58 968	-3,42	no data	689 648
25. PTC sp. z o.o., Warszawa	452	1 643 081	945 282	105 207	26 386	6,40	no data	986 144
26. Porty Lotnicze, Warszawa	200	1 639 974	708 167	206 736	120 281	12,61	2 343	124 192
27. TVP SA, Warszawa	100	1 630 804	307 277	150 853	92 748	9,25	6 734	109 447
28. Impexmetal SA, Warszawa	410	1 585 985	-1 131 290	4 414	4 306	0,28	no data	7 368
29. TU i R. Warta SA Centrala, Warszawa	412	1 428 320	no data	44 265	44 265	3,10	no data	no data
30. Ciech SA, Warszawa	140	1 336 756	-299 623	9 082	8 424	0,68	547	4 571
31. Thomson Polkolor sp. z o.o., Piaseczno	510	1 228 551	426 546	-23 208	-23 208	-1,89	5 327	119 487
32. Elektrim SA, Warszawa	410	1 226 890	-143 665	2 180	-82 313	0,18	273	40 849
33. Rolimpex SA, Warszawa	410	1 215 630	-270 147	-9 849	-9 849	-0,81	213	13 755
34. Elektrociepłownie Warszawskie SA, Warszawa	100	1 187 056	179 851	56 682	22 399	4,78	4 376	96 427
35. Commercial Union Polska, Warszawa	500	1 166 260	no data	151 520	95 860	12,99	no data	no data
36. Polimex-Cekop SA, Warszawa	125	1 090 799	460 015	23 140	13 784	2,12	264	5 309
37. ZEWT SA, Warszawa	100	1 085 097	169 755	33 011	28 059	3,04	no data	65 095
38. Stoen SA, Warszawa	100	1 034 484	146 221	32 092	15 512	3,10	1 682	71 376
39. Milo sp. z o.o., Warszawa	540	902 916	no data	1 329	769	0,15	no data	3 905
40. ZPTR SA, Radom	150	900 008	190 669	27 557	8 518	3,06	1 511	43 227
41. Zasada SA, Warszawa	540	895 843	no data	30 058	27 593	3,36	211	1 379
42. Polski Tytoń SA, Radom	410	890 033	121 179	6 056	3 422	0,68	766	2 281
43. Alcatel Polska SA, Warszawa	510	847 251	83 109	62 721	22 106	7,40	no data	14 564
44. Statoil Polska sp. z o.o., Warszawa	500	827 103	144 558	-18 571	-18 571	-2,25	1 045	137 800
45. Orfe SA, Warszawa	500	813 309	no data	48 728	30 368	5,99	206	2 636
46. BIG Bank SA (Millenium), Warszawa*	540	788 652	420 796	22 505	10 636	2,85	981	no data
47. Orbis SA, Warszawa	145	786 173	91 561	108 992	69 759	13,86	no data	134 388
48. Citibank Poland, Warszawa	500	758 540	no data	253 268	157 688	33,39	645	no data
49. Daewoo E. Manuf. Pol. sp. z o.o., Gęsin	500	735 163	196 579	-5 595	-5 595	-0,76	no data	9 142
50. Animex SA, Warszawa	412	726 444	29 480	18 132	5 842	2,50	215	8 983
51. Agora SA, Warszawa	450	713 714	-380 251	86 313	54 734	12,09	no data	39 402
52. Master Foods sp. z o.o., Sochaczew	500	672 642	no data	2 571	2 571	0,38	1 246	54 579
53. Budimex SA, Warszawa	420	647 845	-48 318	34 289	20 808	5,29	381	29 781
54. Cormay Poland SA, Warszawa	400	640 451	283 904	8 383	4 324	1,31	531	32 257
55. Cefarm Centr. Farm., Warszawa	200	620 368	-5 952	17 644	9 489	2,84	510	5 806

Table 3. (cont.)

Specification	Form of owner-ship	Income from total activity in thous. zł	Revenue changes since 1997 in thous. zł	Gross financial outcome in thous. zł	Net financial outcome in thous. zł**	Profitability index in %	Employ-ment in posts	Investment input in thous. zł
56. ZWUT SA, Warszawa	540	613 663	no data	72 722	37 488	11,85	no data	no data
57. Kraft Jacobs Suchard sp. z o.o., Warszawa	500	605 795	91 485	21 685	10 065	3,58	no data	16 943
58. Amplico Life SA, Warszawa	500	605 420	no data	64 530	38 930	10,66	no data	no data
59. Pażur SA, Warszawa	400	540 583	169 920	5 623	5 134	1,04	165	11 694
60. BOŚ SA, Warszawa*	245	531 917	351 308	148 136	101 573	27,85	no data	no data
61. Peugeot Polska sp. z o.o., Warszawa	500	517 019	467 694	-2 296	-3 072	-0,44	90	1 500
62. Przyjaźń Pern, Płock	200	512 479	131 908	208 309	115 137	40,65	798	163 240
63. Tchibo Warszawa sp. z o.o., Warszawa	500	507 105	70 849	25 820	15 533	5,09	463	9 344
64. Henkel Polska SA, Warszawa	510	500 982	94 192	8 616	1 929	1,72	633	17 792
65. Huta LW sp. z o.o., Warszawa	510	489 622	50 909	-44 044	-44 044	-9,00	2 220	35 439
66. Prosper Bank SA, Warszawa*	540	488 869	362 433	15 195	10 298	3,10	621	no data
67. GO-MAN sp. z o.o., Warszawa	540	457448	111 675	12 746	7 021	2,79	390	3 775
68. Polisa Tur SA, Warszawa	400	438 300	no data	-152 170	-152 540	-34,72	1 616	no data
69. Nationale-Nederlanden Polska SA, Warszawa	500	410 450	no data	32 780	22 170	7,99	b.d.	b.d.
70. Intercell SA, Ostrołęka	524	407 129	-8 362	-14 720	-14 720	-3,62	2 308	93 640
71. Casinos-Poland sp. z o.o., Warszawa	100	403 193	22 240	10 749	5 359	2,67	688	1 315
72. Billa Polen sp. z o.o., Warszawa	540	402 717	84 673	-7 700	-8 354	-1,91	1 054	8 201
73. Inco-Veritas SA, Warszawa	400	402 532	-2 989	26 302	23 202	6,53	3 676	20 391
74. Prokom Software SA, Warszawa	450	390 021	no data	98 817	61 949	25,34	no data	15 577
75. Nissan Poland sp. z o.o., Warszawa	540	389 437	139 505	3 115	1 437	0,80	48	2 811
76. SZMS SA, Sokołów Podlaski	400	388 364	84 537	7 980	5 571	2,05	1 709	13 985
77. Iberia Motor Company SA, Warszawa	540	382 449	-3 828	16 375	10 572	4,28	60	4 011
78. Ferrero Polska sp. z o.o., Warszawa	500	378 423	50 988	-26 004	-26 004	-6,87	484	no data
79. Pekaes Multi-Sped. sp. z o.o., Warszawa	410	377 157	no data	16 133	9 400	4,28	no data	6 333
80. Zespół Elektrowni, Ostrołęka	200	370 978	41 136	7 272	3 128	1,96	1 385	7 719
81. Mostostal Warszawa SA, Warszawa	400	352 477	51 881	20 848	13 612	5,91	611	8 294
82. RCB SA, Warszawa*	500	348 525	99 530	43 503	26 032	12,48	511	no data
83. Neste Polska sp. z o.o., Warszawa	500	342 950	-116 624	4 824	4 824	1,41	275	4 404
84. Polfa Tarchomin SA, Warszawa	100	337 652	-28 472	418	662	0,12	2 622	b.d.
85. Forte SA, Ostrów Maz.	450	336 005	6 592	5 697	3 189	1,70	no data	8 690
86. ABC-Data sp. z o.o., Warszawa	450	334 989	no data	3 051	1 819	0,91	b.d.	1 360
87. BEL Leasing sp. z o.o., Warszawa	400	327 791	77 298	-3 748	1 738	-1,14	107	no data
88. CTL SA, Warszawa	425	325 563	68 100	8 056	4 958	2,47	145	256 967
89. ABN Amro Bank (Polska) SA, Warszawa	400	324 784	158 529	29 147	16 148	8,97	147	no data
90. Electrolux Poland sp. z o.o., Warszawa	500	310 140	no data	2 081	-583	0,67	140	4 759
91. BM sp. z o.o., Warszawa	500	305 962	no data	21 775	9 927	7,12	no data	19 200
92. Warbud SA, Warszawa	540	302 766	141 182	32 075	20 863	10,59	no data	5 632
93. Computerland Poland SA, Warszawa	540	294 717	86 308	24 574	15 571	8,34	493	5 557
94. Bakoma SA, Warszawa	400	294 311	178 474	46 171	30 336	15,69	865	38 148
95. Browary Warka sp. z o.o., Warka	410	291 279	107 757	26 330	15 030	9,04	798	35 703
96. Gaspol SA, Warszawa	513	269 587	34 481	19 709	19 700	7,31	566	75 488
97. Farm Food SA, Warszawa	450	269 577	-3 601	4 384	1 213	1,63	1 070	6 394
98. Carcade Invest SA, Warszawa	540	263 377	no data	13 084	7 902	4,97	27	138 408
99. Alima-Gerber SA, Warszawa	540	263 042	21 977	5 553	5 553	2,11	940	8 309
100. Drosed SZD SA, Siedlce	400	261 127	40 786	6 718	4 104	2,57	1 373	10 118

Source: Institute of Economic Sciences, upon the basis of source documents forwarded by enterprises to the Centre of Economic Information at the Ministry of the Economy.
In the case of banks and insurance institutions the data was obtained from "Monitor Polski", and the remaining data – according to List 500, published in a supplement to "Rzeczpospolita" of 6 May 1999.

the results of this industry during the first nine months of 1999 with the outcome in an analogous period of the previous year indicates an approx. 28% production growth calculated in fixed prices (data supplied by the Statistical Office). This is the greatest dynamics in Poland. In September 1999, the construction industry employed about 105 000 workers.

New residential estates in the Warsaw district of Ursynów

TELECOMMUNICATION AND INFORMATICS BRANCHES

Those two branches of economy are thriving in Mazowieckie voivodeship. Cable telephony, basically monopolised by Telekomunikacja Polska SA, has 1 329 276 subscribers, which is the highest index in Poland – more than 262 subscribers per a thousand inhabitants (1997). Every year, the number of subscribers grows by several percent while the largest increase, more than 10% annually, is observed in areas up to now neglected in this respect.

Cellular phones are flourishing. Among all the Polish operators active in Mazovia the oldest is Polska Telefonia Komórkowa Centertel sp. z. o.o. Since 1992, Centertel has been an operator of an analogue network whose range embraces almost all of Poland and is accessible to 98% of the population living in 96% of the territory of the country. It also operates the GSM 1800 digital network functioning under the name of Idea Centertel, available in larger towns from March 1998 (including the Warsaw agglomeration – see map). Today, the prime and future-orientated domain of activity pursued by this firm is the construction of a GSM 900/1800 dual-range network, also under the Idea trademark. Mazovia will be one of the first regions to be included into the new network whose completion is foreseen in 2000–2001.

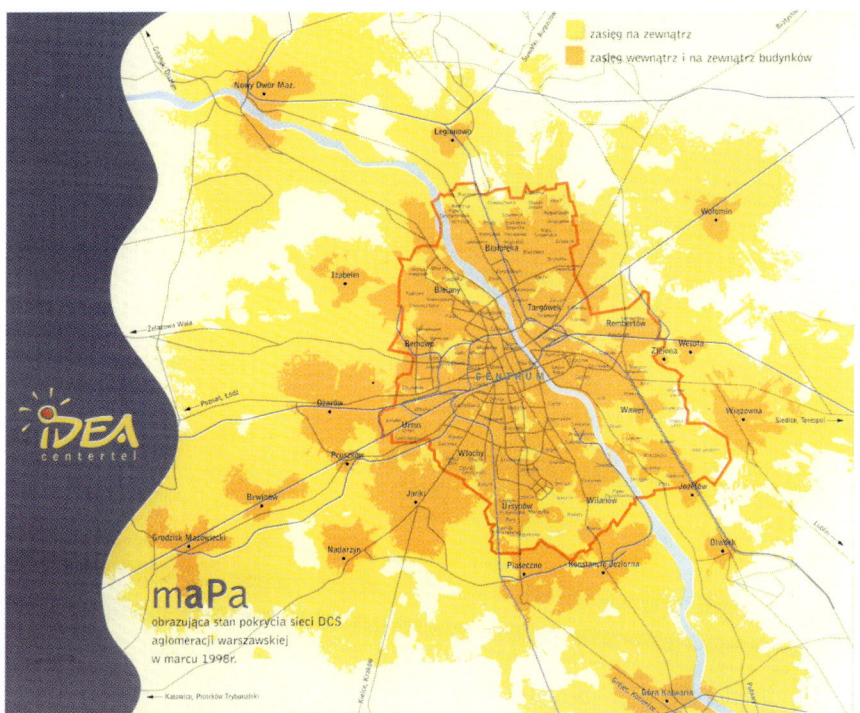

A second cellular telephony company – Polkomtel SA – inaugurated its activity in 1996, and now offers services within a GSM 900 digital network under the name of Plus GSM. In 1999, the firm was granted license for services in the 1800 MHz band. In a short period of time, Polkomtel constructed a network which at present services more than 1,5 mln. subscribers and is accessible to 95% of the population of Poland, living in 90% of the country's territory. Plus GSM services can be enjoyed almost everywhere on Mazovia (see map 2). The firm is also a well-known patron of cultural events.

The third cellular phone operator is Polska Telefonia Cyfrowa, a slightly smaller enterprise offering services in the Era GSM network. Its range resembles that of the Plus GSM network.

Cellular telephone firms comprise one of the greatest investors not only in Mazovia, but also in the country as a whole. Jointly, their investments exceeded 2 billion złotys in 1998 alone. An essential part of this revenue was produced in Mazowieckie voivodeship. Cellular telephone companies created an opportunity for economic activity even in the rather numerous small Mazovian localities deprived of access to stationary telephones.

Map 2. Map of planned Plus GSM ranges. Mazowieckie voivodeship

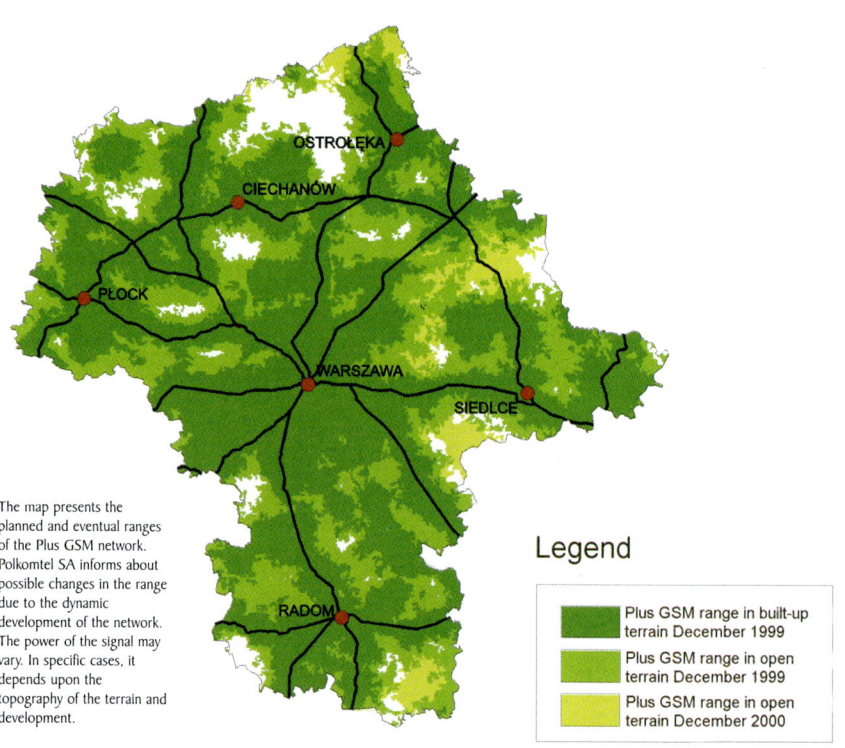

The map presents the planned and eventual ranges of the Plus GSM network. Polkomtel SA informs about possible changes in the range due to the dynamic development of the network. The power of the signal may vary. In specific cases, it depends upon the topography of the terrain and development.

Legend

■ Plus GSM range in built-up terrain December 1999

■ Plus GSM range in open terrain December 1999

■ Plus GSM range in open terrain December 2000

The development of the informatics branch in Mazowieckie voivodeship is a consequence of general civilisational trends as well as a concentration of market services and modern branches of the industry, and the fact that Warsaw constitutes the administrative centre of the country.

According to this year's TELEINFO 500 report the voivodeshipa has a total of 256 tele-informatics firms which last year employed about 30 000 workers and made a profit of more than 7 billion złotys.

The specificity of the region consists in the fact that it is the site of the central offices of the largest domestic firms (ComputerLand, Softbank, Apexim) as well as representatives of leading world concerns (Cisco, Hewlett-Packard, IBM, Microsoft, Oracle). Warsaw also concentrates the largest branches of those domestic firms whose main seats are located in other towns (Prokom, ComArch). Informatics firms in the Mazovia region represent all specialisations: software and equipment production, integration, net services, training, consulting and trade. Another characteristic feature of the region is the fact that it draws both gigantic firms and relatively small ones (Computer 2000 Polska Warszawa, which comes first in the ranking, achieved a turnover of 385 mln. złotys, while the turnover of Soft-tronik Service Warszawa, which comes hundredth, totalled 13 mln. złotys).

Mazowieckie voivodeship is the centre of wholesale trade, employing more than 130 000 workers (September 1999). Nevertheless, retail trade comprises a domain within which the transformations of recent years appear to be most visible. The first reaction to the introduction of the free market was an explosion of bazaars and street trade. Today, the only vestige of this period is probably the largest open-air market in Europe, situated in a sports stadium in Warsaw. The next stage witnessed the emergence of thousands of commercial firms, most frequently single-person, throughout the entire present-day voivodeship, and just as many shops, large and small. The mid-1990s brought an expansion of supermarkets, built chiefly in Warsaw and its environs. This branch attracted large foreign capital. The most extensive network of retail and semi-wholesale trade includes Makro-Cash and Carry, Géant, Billa, Hit, Real, and Globi, all of which make enormous profits. By way of example, Billa Polen declared that in 1998 its profit totalled 395 mln. zlotys. In September 1999, more than 80 000 people worked in retail enterprises, each employing no less than five persons. Taking into consideration smaller firms, still predominant in this sphere of employment, we may assess that retail trade employs about 200 000 workers.

The Géant supermarket in Warsaw. Shopping in such centres has become a very popular pastime

ComputerLand
01-248 Warsaw
Jana Kazimierza 62A
tel. (+48 22) 532 97 77
fax (+48 22) 532 98 88
info@computerland.pl
http:/www.computerland.pl

ComputerLand's mission:
To become the unchallenged strategic partner for our customers by delivering business and organizational benefits deploying proven information systems through the best people.

ComputerLand renders advanced IT services for four sectors of the economy: banking-finance, industry, public and tele-communications. Thanks to the sector specialization, the Company has extensive knowledge of the Customer's market. Experienced specialists, proven products and excellent references guarantee the highest level of services. The IT solutions offered by ComputerLand bring profits and generate savings for customers.

ComputerLand's offer for the public sector:
We have experience in completing individual "turn-key" projects for the central administration, delivering IT products for local administration as well as software for the health care sector.
The most important projects and products:

➤ ALSO: complete computerization of Employment Offices (system PULS) and Social Help Bureaus (system POMOST)
➤ "Internet lab in every municipality" – equipment for 808 labs
➤ GIS – Geographical Information System for cities and municipalities
➤ Command Control Center for the Police
➤ systems for the health care system, including systems supporting health insurance offices

Furthermore, we offer electronic data interchange system (EDI), group work systems, document processing systems and Library Information System.

P R O M O T I O N

ComputerLand's offer for the industrial sector:
Our strategic products for industrial, commercial and transport enterprises are:
➤ Oracle Applications: an ERP-class management system
➤ On Line Analytical Processing: Oracle Financial Analyzer, Oracle Sales Analyzer
➤ PROMIS S/4: Integrated Management System
➤ Pro/FIT: Decision Support System.

ComputerLand's offer for the banking-financial sector:
We offer the following systems:
➤ transaction systems: PROFILE®, FLEXCUBE, BANKER®, SAPOD and others
➤ electronic banking: System ELBA24
➤ management systems: Oracle Financials, IPS-SENDERO, Pro/FIT
➤ systems for investment banks and funds: FLEXCUBE Investment
➤ systems for broker agents and firms: FLEXCUBE Investor Services
➤ systems for pension funds: System ELBA24/OFE, SAT/OFE
➤ reporting systems, including obligatory reporting for the National Bank of Poland: RABA, BAKIS, EWIS, DIS, RGS
➤ systems for leasing firms and financial management: Leasing 2000
➤ data warehouses.

ComputerLand's offer for the telecommunication sector:
The Competence Center for Technical Telecommunication Technologies (TTT) supplies ComputerLand's proprietary systems for telecommunications. We also offer systems of our partner – Ericsson Hewlett-Packard Telecommunications (EHPT).
ComputerLand's systems:
➤ Pas'Tel – inventory system of the telecommunications networks
➤ Fault Service
➤ SITEL – Investment Process Support System for TP SA EHPT's systems (installed in 60 countries, in 450 locations):
➤ EHPT Progressor – a billing system
➤ EHPT Billing Mediation Platform
➤ EHPT Settler – system for account settlements between operators
➤ EHPT Net Turner – network traffic management system.

73

A new idea is the essence of growth.

(Albert Einstein)

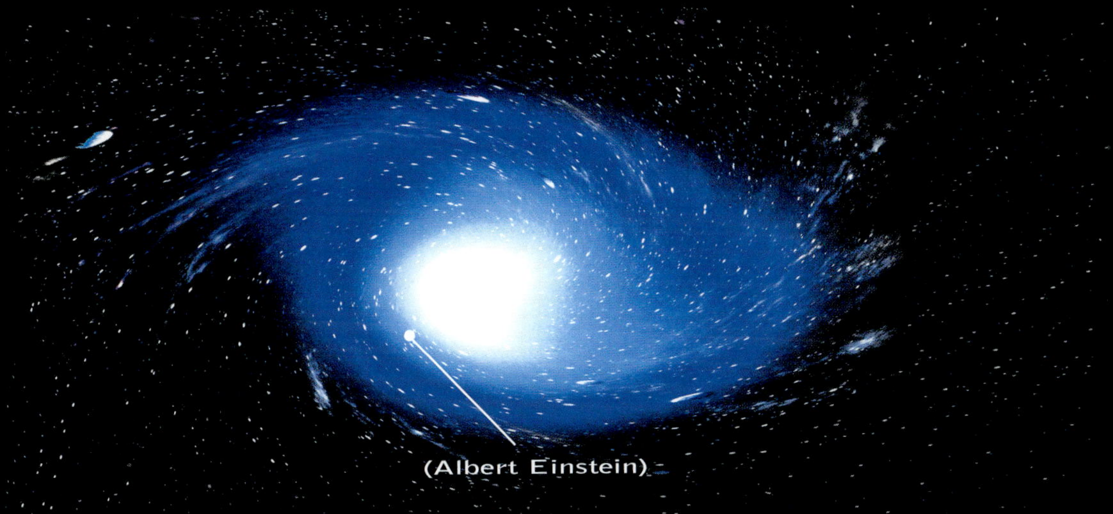

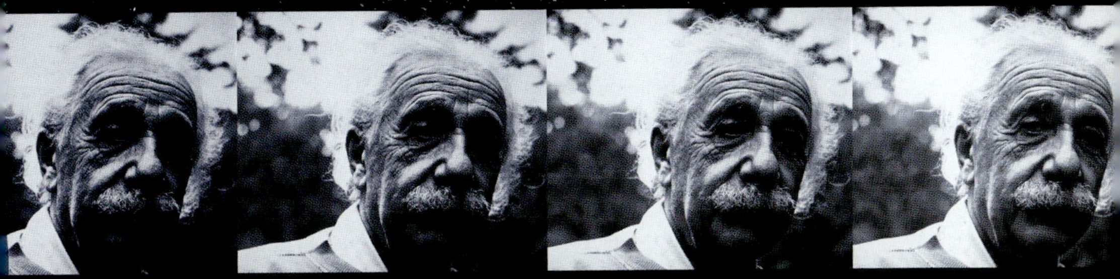

The minds of geniuses are changing the world. They show that a new idea is the essence of growth.
Our Idea is a continuous stream of ideas which you turn into your own.

to have an idea

Plus GSM. A change for the better

A characteristic feature of the voivodeship is the largest area of cropland in the country (2 394,1 thous. hectares). Some 1 757,2 thous. hectares comprise arable land (73,4%) and 74,5 thous. hectares, i.e. 31% of all arable land, is composed of orchards (in Lublin voivodeship, which holds second place in Poland, an analogous area is twice as small); meadows constitute 361,2 thous. hectares (the largest area in Poland). There are about 310 000 farms whose average size is 7,8 hectares.

Orchards in the region of Grójec

The most important traits of agriculture in the Mazowieckie voivodeship include:

■ the participation of commodity farming in the general number of farms, higher by about 10% points from the domestic mean (49%);

■ an inferior outfitting of farms as regards the gas, telephone, water and sewage infrastructure;

■ the average size of a farm, close to the national mean; the highest production of rye, oats, potatoes and vegetables in Poland;

■ specialised fruit production;

■ a level of the yield of the majority of plants lower than the national mean;

■ a high livestock population (with the exception of sheep).

Despite the fact that agriculture in Mazovia demonstrates certain backwardness, it also discloses symptoms of modern development. Emphasis is due to such features as the commodity nature of farming and especially the extremely high production of fruit, vegetables and good quality milk. On the average, about 110 mln. litres of milk are bought up in Mazovia in a single month (the largest amount in the country).

Diagram 2. Soil cultivation in Mazowieckie voivodeship in 1997

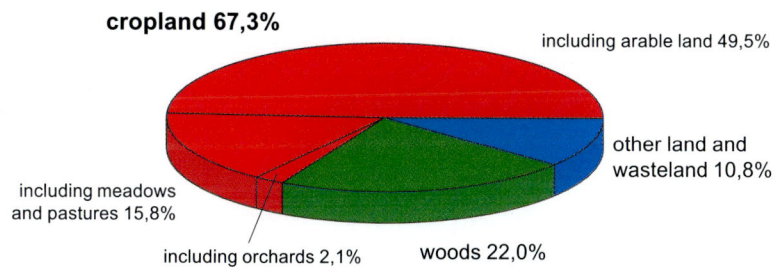

cropland 67,3%

including arable land 49,5%

other land and wasteland 10,8%

woods 22,0%

including meadows and pastures 15,8%

including orchards 2,1%

79

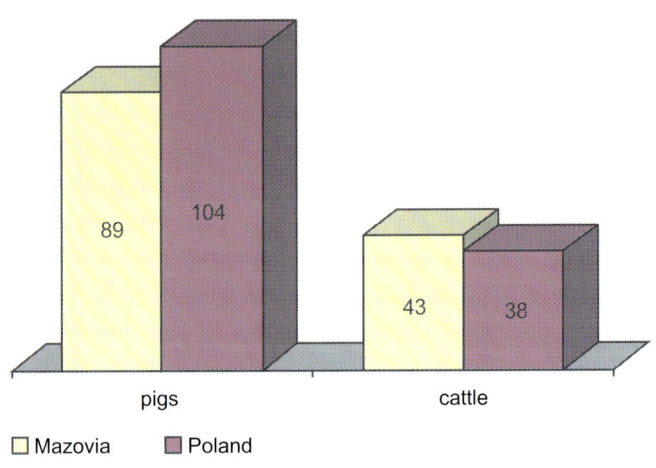

Diagram 3. Cattle and pig population per 100 hectares of cropland (July 1998)

☐ Mazovia   ▧ Poland

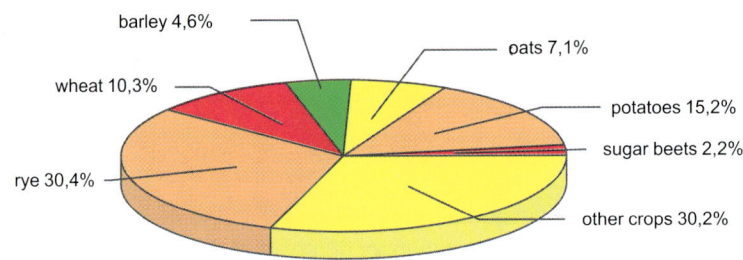

Diagram 4. Crops structure in 1997

barley 4,6%
oats 7,1%
wheat 10,3%
potatoes 15,2%
sugar beets 2,2%
rye 30,4%
other crops 30,2%

THE COMPETITIVENESS OF MAZOWIECKIE VOIVODESHIP

In 1995–1997, the average participation of the voivodeship in Polish export totalled 20,9%. This is the largest index in the country; participation of Śląskie voivodeship, which holds second place, amounts to 16,1%.

The main trade partners of Mazovian firms are Germany (21,2%) of export, Russia (14,9%), France (4,9%), Italy (4,9%), and the United Kingdom (4,6%).

The most significant export commodities include products of the electronic engineering industry, processed fruit products, pharmaceutical products, furniture, cabinetmaking products, clothing and underwear.

Despite considerable inner differentiation, Mazowieckie voivodeship is regarded as the leader of transformation whose rate is the quickest in large cities and most effective in Warsaw itself. The situation in the capital city to a great extent affects the general results obtained in the voivodeship. Below, we present three fundamental indices characterising economic transformation.

Foreign investments. There are more than 12 500 companies with foreign capital (table 4). In this respect the voivodeship in question decisively outdistances the remaining voivodeships. By way of example, the second-ranking Dolnośląskie voivodeship had 3 648 companies of this type. In 1998 alone, 1 283 companies with foreign capital were established in Mazovia.

Table 4. Activity of foreign investors acc. to voivodeships

Voivodeship	Companies with foreign capital registered in the REGON system on 31 Dec. 1998	Investors on the PAIZ List June 1999
Dolnośląskie	3 648	159
Kujawsko-Pomorskie	988	79
Lubelskie	562	52
Lubuskie	1 606	42
Łódzkie	1 551	113
Małopolskie	1 812	106
Mazowieckie	12 564	461
Opolskie	815	36
Podkarpackie	445	49
Podlaskie	283	31
Pomorskie	2 568	144
Śląskie	3 143	264
Świętokrzyskie	354	45
Warmińsko-Mazurskie	599	45
Wielkopolskie	3 346	227
Zachodniopomorskie	2 566	76

Source: GUS, PAIZ.

The voivodeship witnesses the growing activity of great international corporations. In mid-1999, the PAIZ List of all firms which had invested more than 1 mln. USD in Poland included 750 firms, of which 461 pursued activity exclusively or partially in the voivodeship in question. The successive Śląskie and Wielkopolskie voivodeships attracted a much smaller number of large investors (264 and 227 respectively).

It must be kept in mind that foreign companies concentrate primarily in Warsaw where, up to the end of 1998, some 28% of all companies with foreign capital in Poland were registered (table 5). Warsaw drew 26,4% of all companies registered just in 1998.

Table 5. Registered companies with foreign capital

| | Registered companies with foreign capital | | | |
| | to end of 1998 | | in 1998 | |
	no.	%	no.	%
Urban communes	29 276	79,4	2 905	74,3
incl.: Warsaw	10 609	28,8	1 033	26,4
Wrocław	1 671	4,5	161	4,1
Poznań	1 671	4,5	173	4,4
Krakow	1 206	3,3	106	2,7
Łódź	1 034	2,8	86	2,2
Szczecin	1 163	3,2	111	2,8
Gdańsk	944	2,6	77	2,0
Katowice	636	1,7	53	1,4
Urban-rural	4 196	11,4	513	13,1
Rural	3 378	9,2	490	12,5
Poland	36 850	100	3 908	100

Source: Own calculations upon the basis of GUS data.

Enterprises belonging to natural persons. Data for the end of 1998 show that the voivodeship had 351 891 registered enterprises belonging to natural persons. This index of the entrepreneurship of the local population was the highest in Poland: the number of firms of this sort in Śląskie, Wielkopolskie and Dolnośląskie voivodeships was much smaller.

Mazovia enjoys priority also as regards the number of enterprises belonging to natural persons per 1 000 inhabitants. It is outdistanced only by Zachodniopomorskie Voivodeship with an index of 72,6 (Mazovia – 71). In 1998 alone, 30 700 enterprises of this kind were established in Mazowieckie voivodeship.

Employees. The considerable activity of foreign investors and the economic initiatives of the local population contribute to the retention of a favourable situation on the labour market. In 1998, the unemployment rate remained at the level of 7,2% (7,8% in the previous year and 9,8% two years earlier). In 1998, Mazovian enterprises employed more than 1 406 000 persons. In the same year a larger number of workers was found in Śląskie voivodeship which had the highest index of employees per 1 000 inhabitants (289 persons) while Mazowieckie voivodeship held second place (278 persons). Let us note that this labour force is, as a rule, better trained than in the remaining regions of the country.

In the above presented outline of Mazovian economy frequent mention was made of the domination of Warsaw over the rest of the voivodeship and other regions of Poland. Below, we present indices characterising the inner differentiation of the voivodeship.

Table 6. Inner differentiation of voivodeships in 1996

Voivodeship	Gross added value per capita			Variability index
	Average level = 100		Ratio max./min	
	Poorest poviat (min.)	Most prosperous. poviat (max.)		
Dolnośląskie	70	141	2,0	17,9
Kujawsko--Pomorskie	59	140	2,4	22,1
Lubelskie	59	160	2,7	25,1
Lubuskie	81	135	1,7	17,1
Łódzkie	55	151	2,8	26,8
Małopolskie	52	149	2,9	33,0
Mazowieckie	37	155	4,2	43,7
Opolskie	77	143	1,8	18,5
Podkarpackie	65	197	3,0	35,3
Podlaskie	66	143	2,1	20,1
Pomorskie	60	157	2,6	25,5
Śląskie	56	145	2,6	21,1
Świętokrzyskie	65	139	2,2	20,0
Warmińsko--Mazurskie	71	157	2,2	23,9
Wielkopolskie	63	130	2,1	16,9
Zachodnio-pomorskie	61	144	2,4	28,1

Source: W.M. Orłowski, E. Saganowska, L. Zienkowski, *op. cit.*

Table 7. 20% of poviats with the highest and 20% of poviats with the lowest
values of discussed indices in the country

	Dynamics of companies with foreign capital in 1994–1997 per 10 000 inhabitants		No. of enterprises belonging to natural persons in 1997 per 10 000 inhabitants		No. of employees in 1997 r. per 10 000 inhabitants	
	No. of gminas with values					
	max.	min.	max.	min.	max.	min.
Dolnośląskie	13	1	6	0	5	1
Kujawsko-Pomorskie	1	6	3	2	3	6
Lubelskie	1	10	3	16	4	9
Lubuskie	11	0	5	0	2	0
Łódzkie	1	8	6	4	4	5
Małopolskie	1	6	3	6	5	10
Mazowieckie	6	14	11	10	6	19
Opolskie	2	0	1	4	1	0
Podkarpackie	0	9	3	11	5	8
Podlaskie	0	10	2	8	2	7
Pomorskie	8	0	6	1	4	2
Śląskie	5	3	8	1	21	2
Świętokrzyskie	0	5	1	7	2	3
Warmińsko-Mazurskie	2	2	2	4	2	1
Wielkopolskie	7	1	9	1	5	2
Zachodniopomorskie	17	0	6	0	4	0

Source: Own calculations upon the basis of BDL.

Data concerning the differentiation of the economic force of the counties in all the voivodeships are included in table 6. The ratio of gross added value per capita in the most affluent county to the added value in the poorest county totals 4,2. In Warsaw, this index reaches the value 55% higher than the voivodeship mean. In the least prosperous county, gross added value per capita attains barely 37% of the voivodeship mean. There is no other such differentiated voivodeship in Poland, a situation confirmed also by the value of the variability index.

Furthermore, the inner differentiation of the voivodeship is indicated by an analysis of such phenomena as the dynamics of companies with foreign capital per 100 000 inhabitants the number of employees per 100 000 inhabitants, and the number of enterprises belonging to natural persons per 100 000 inhabitants. An analysis, conducted on a national scale, of the configuration of 20% of the best and 20% of the least favourable poviats (from the viewpoint of the above mentioned indices) produced the results pointing both to the assets of the voivodeship and its weaker aspects, discernible in a considerable number of poviats considered as the most backward in the country (table 7).

Map 3. Investment attractiveness of new voivodeships

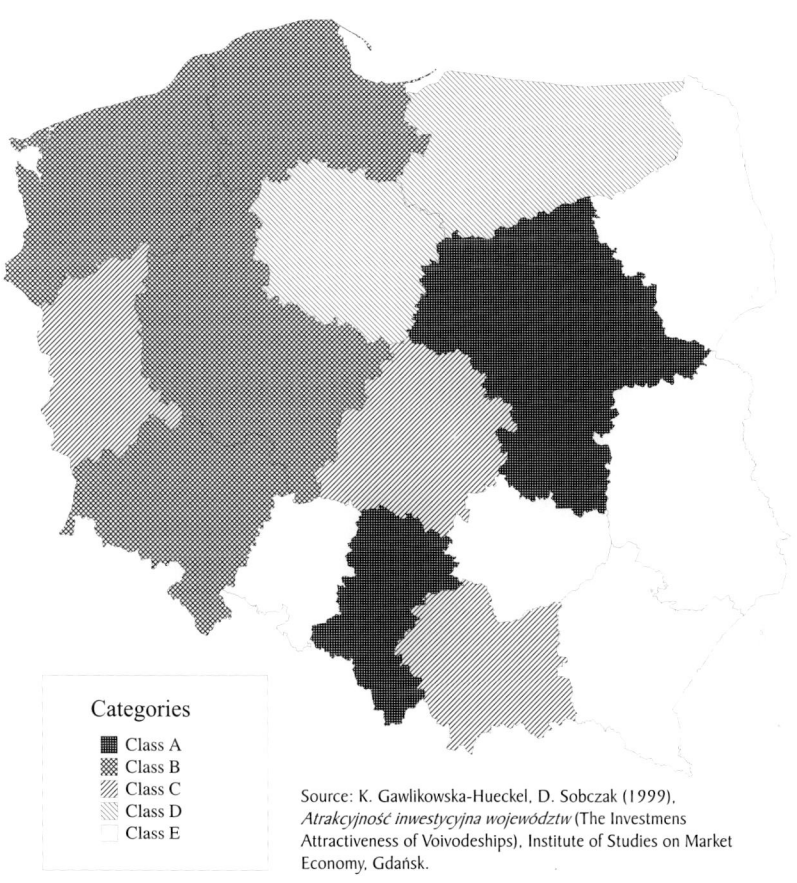

Categories

■ Class A
▨ Class B
▨ Class C
▨ Class D
☐ Class E

Source: K. Gawlikowska-Hueckel, D. Sobczak (1999), *Atrakcyjność inwestycyjna województw* (The Investmens Attractiveness of Voivodeships), Institute of Studies on Market Economy, Gdańsk.

From the viewpoint of foreign capital, the examined voivodeship is the most attractive region of Poland (map 3). This assessment stems from an analysis of seven investment conditions: communication accessibility, the level of the development of industry, the labour market, business surroundings, economic transformation, market absorptivity and tourist attractiveness. In all the aforementioned respects Mazovia proves to be the leader.

The voivodeship offers foreign investors convenient air and railway connections as well as a dense network of international routes.

The previously mentioned conditions draw foreign capital. Another essential factor is market absorptivity; in its capacity as one of the largest and most prosperous regions, Mazovia guarantees the highest level in the country.

Moreover, the voivodeship offers numerous tourist attractions (historical monuments, national and landscape parks) as well as a well – developed hotel network, especially in Warsaw.

INVESTMENT ATTRACTIVENESS OF TOWNS IN MAZOWIECKIE VOIVODESHIP

For the past two years, the Institute of Studies on Market Economy has conducted research concerning the investment attractiveness of Polish towns. The overall attractiveness of a given town is composed of the assessment of ten investment conditions which include the absorptivity of the local market, the quality of the labour market, the social climate, technical infrastructure, business surroundings infrastructure, costs of conducting economic activity, communication accessibility, economic transformation, leisure facilities and the marketing activity of local authorities.

More than 800 analysed towns were divided into four groups, for which an independent ranking was carried out, pertaining to voivodeship towns, municipal gminas, gmina cities and remaining towns. The synthetic results of the analysis are presented in maps 4–7.

Map 4. Investment attractiveness of voivodeship towns

Source: P. Swianiewicz, W. Dziemianowicz, *Atrakcyjność inwestycyjna miast* (Investment Attractiveness of Towns), Institute of Studies on Market Economy.

Map 5. Investment attractiveness of municipal gminas
(without towns included in class E, F and G)

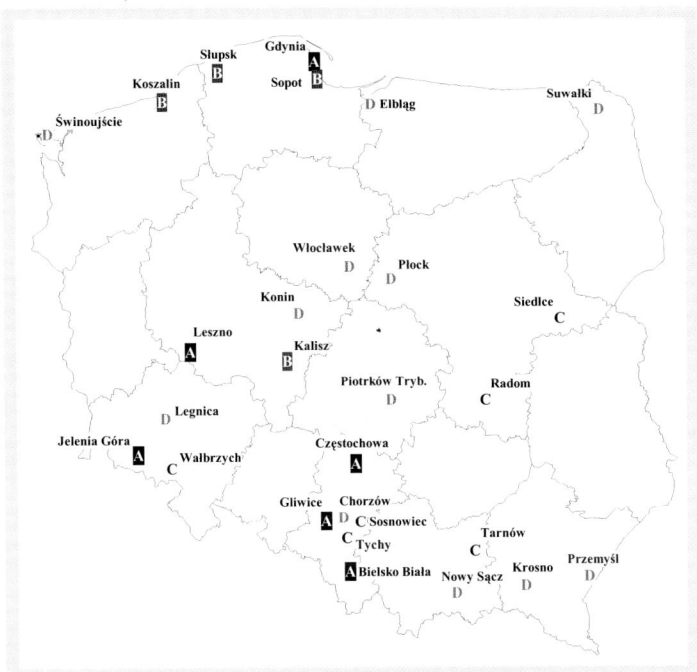

Source: P. Swianiewicz, W. Dziemianowicz, *op. cit.*

Map 6. Investment attractiveness of gmina towns.
Synthetic index of class A and B

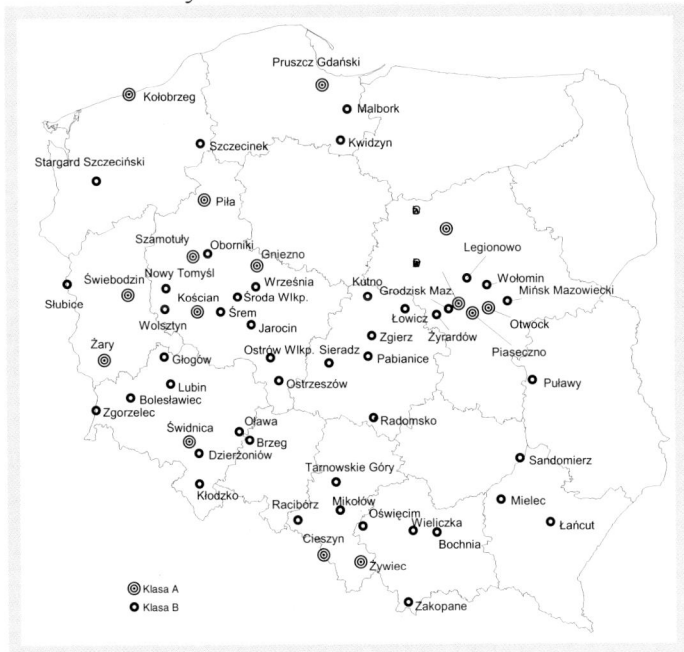

Source: P. Swianiewicz, W. Dziemianowicz, *op. cit.*

Map 7. Investment attractiveness of small towns – class A

Source: P. Swianiewicz, W. Dziemianowicz, *op. cit.*

The most attractive voivodeship town is Warsaw. Despite higher costs of conducting economic activity, Warsaw towers over remaining cities as regards the majority of the conditions and, in particular, as regards communication accessibility, market absorptivity, the quality of the labour market and the effectiveness of economic transformation.

A characteristic feature of three municipal gminas in the voivodeship, namely Radom, Siedlce and Płock, is average, or slightly above average investment attractiveness.

In turn, as many as nine gmina towns in the voivodeship under examination display extremely high or high investment attractiveness. These are mainly towns situated near Warsaw, the most attractive being Otwock, Piaseczno, Pruszków and Ciechanów.

The impact of localisation in relation to Warsaw is visible also in map 7, which marks the most attractive small towns. All twelve cities included into Class A of attractiveness are situated in the vicinity of Warsaw.

Wojciech Dziemianowicz

DEVELOPMENT OPPORTUNITIES IN MAZOVIA

As in the case of every other region, opportunities for the development of Mazovia are of a triple nature: inner-regional, inter-regional and international. The same features are characteristic for challenges.

INNER-REGIONAL OPPORTUNITIES FOR MAZOVIA

As a rule, a distinction is made between two categories of inner-regional factors (opportunities) for the development of a given region: "hard" and "soft". The former is composed of the production potential of the region, its branch structure and spatial distribution, the technological level of the economy, the technical infrastructure outfitting, etc. The "hard" factors may also include local purchasing power (dimension of the market), i.e. the level of the incomes and expenditure of the population and institutions in this region. The "soft" factors entail predominantly the so-called enterprising spirit of the local population (particularly the ability to create and absorb innovations), the faculty of social mobilisation (concentrated around tasks pertaining to the development of the region or its closest environs), the level of the skills possessed by the population, the effectiveness of regional institutions of authority and administration, etc.

In the case of Mazovia, Warsaw is the prime factor of development, combining both "hard" and "soft" aspects. This is the reason why the situation in Mazovia is exceptional – no other region has a capital with such a large economic and intellectual potential and performing such a prominent domestic and international role. At the same time, no other region reveals such considerable differentiation in the level of economic development (cf. table 6).

Warsaw has at its disposal development assets stemming from the fulfilment of the function of the capital of Poland. Such status offers indubitable marketing benefits – frequently, Warsaw is the only Polish town whose name is known abroad. Hence its superiority over other cities and regions as regards attracting foreign capital.

The rank of Warsaw is associated also with the localisation of the domestic decision-making centre – a network of political and administrative institutions, access to which provides specific "external profits" to economic subjects. Such institutions signify employers of thousands of well-educated and well-paid civil servants and state experts, who create the general intellectual potential and purchasing force of both the town and the region.

Warsaw is also the main communication centre of international and domestic rank (with the Okęcie airport playing a special role in the communication system of the country). Thanks to this function, Warsaw comprises the most important link between Poland and other countries, a feature which constitutes one of the causes of the attractiveness of the town for foreign capital, and especially the localisation of the management functions of international firms.

89

The capital of Poland is the key intellectual centre of the country. It concentrates the majority of Polish scientific-research institutions and leading schools of higher learning (together with a dense network of recently established private schools), the greatest number of research and academic workers, and a personnel with higher education, fluent in foreign languages and versed in computer technology.

Furthermore, the Polish capital is the largest domestic sales market, whose dimension depends both on the large population of the Warsaw agglomeration (concentrated in a relatively small area), high average incomes (the highest in the country) and expenditure of institutions – domestic and foreign. This phenomenon is confirmed by the fact that the Gross National Product per capita in the former voivodeship of Warsaw is about 100% higher than the domestic average.

The last, albeit not the least important asset is the spirit of entrepreneurship which distinguishes the capital from the rest of the country. This particular trait, perceivable already during the period of "real socialism", "exploded" at the time of the introduction of the market economy. It is certainly connected with the level of education, international contacts, prosperity, and the absorptivity of the local sales market. Yet another prominent factor is the *genius loci* of Warsaw, much more difficult to explain in rational terms.

The attractiveness of the Polish capital is a specific *perpetuum mobile* – a truly self-propelling factor. In the case of business ventures, it denotes the attraction of foreign and domestic capital, and facilitates the development of local business, thus increasing the economic-intellectual potential and the sales market. We are dealing with a globally known phenomenon of the concentration of the economy in the chief city of a given country.

The growing potential of Warsaw generates also certain negative side effects, predominantly transportation difficulties within the city, rapidly increasing prices of housing, and escalating rent. The latter tendency is the reason why despite a high level of wages and low unemployment Warsaw has not witnessed a considerable influx of a permanent population (although this flow is certainly larger than the officially registered one, since after the abolition of compulsory registration, which especially affected persons seeking employment in the capital, the majority of arrivals do not register themselves as residents). On the other hand, the number of commuters as well as seasonal workers and those employed for shorter periods of time discloses an ascending tendency, after a certain decline at the beginning of the 1990s.

An important economic asset of Mazovia consists of the fuel industry – Petrochemia Płocka (part of Polski Koncern Naftowy – PKN) – the supplier of about 60% of all fuel produced in Poland. The rapid growth of demand connected with the development of motorisation creates considerable opportunities for this branch of the industry and the PKN firm, as well as indirectly for the city of Płock and the region, despite increasing foreign competition. The prominence of this asset is limited slightly by the small regional multiplier effects of the fuel industry (i.e. its isolation from the economic fibre of the region).

The remaining areas of the region do not have at their disposal such obvious assets – both as regards "soft" and "hard" factors. Nonetheless, at the local level, even in the case of an unexploited pattern of "hard" factors, there can arise conditions conducive for economic development and for raising the civilisational level of particular localities or gminas.

The most important inner-regional opportunity for Mazovia is the diffusion of development impulses from Warsaw. Such diffusion may take place thanks to access to the Warsaw labour market, the commodity market (especially foodstuffs), tourist-recreation services (weekend leisure, the sale of land for vacation homes), and real estate markets (the sale of land for residential and economic construction as well as for communal infrastructure servicing the Warsaw agglomeration). The availability of the above mentioned markets is the reason for the flow of incomes from Warsaw to its closer and more distant regions. Equally important is the way in which those incomes are used – whether they will be invested on the spot in profitable activity, or spent in Warsaw or outside the region.

Another type of diffusion of potential development impulses is access to services offered by Warsaw, predominantly those of an intellectual and communication nature.

In this situation, the chief trends of undertakings intent on benefiting from inner-regional opportunities for the development of Mazovia include:
- favouring the economic development of Warsaw,
- facilitating the diffusion of development impulses from Warsaw to its surrounding,
- minimalising conflicts between Warsaw and the rest of the region.

The simultaneous realisation of all those activities from the perspective of a short period of time could be, to a certain degree, contradictory, and require a selection of priorities and the sequence of undertakings. Nonetheless, in a long-term perspective, those trends comprise a harmonious entity.

Efforts intent on the development of Warsaw economy are based on the premise that Warsaw is not only the capital of Mazovia, but also a town competing on the international arena for the best possible place within the global urban system. This competition involves predominantly money, and becomes apparent in the rivalry for international capital investments (especially seats of boards or the management of branches), international institutions, and events. The hitherto status of Warsaw in this competition is rather weak, and does not correspond to the potential and aspirations of the capital of a state with a population of 40 000 000.

An improvement of the competitiveness of Warsaw, and thus of the effectiveness of the local economy, could be achieved thanks to undertakings pursued both within the "hard" and "soft" sphere.

Basic significance within the "hard" sphere is ascribed to municipal transportation. Efforts already made or planned within this domain aim at:
- the expansion of rapid public transportation (the underground, rail transport);

- the construction of new routes and bridges integrating town space, particularly the Siekierki route and the Świętokrzyski Bridge (the latter will be open in the year 2000);
- the elimination of transit traffic from the City by means of ring roads;
- an increase in road capacity by improving the quality of the surface, constructing subterranean passages for pedestrians, solving parking problems in the City, etc.

Traffic jams in Warsaw, especially in worse weather conditions, pose a serious problem

An equally prominent significance for the international competitiveness of Warsaw is attached to its transportation links with its main partners, both in Poland (prime Polish agglomerations) and abroad. From this point of view, fundamental meaning belongs to:
- the realization of a programme concerning the construction of highways and rapid traffic routes;
- the modernisation of the railway system (an increase in speed and comfort);
- catching up with global progress in the realm of tele-informatics.

The coming years will probably bring decisions concerning the construction of a new airport in the vicinity of Warsaw or the expansion of the existing Okęcie terminal.

Other fields of communal economy requiring urgent reform are: waste management (sewage treatment plans, the removal, storage, destruction and utilisation of permanent refuse) and water supply (particularly the improvement of the quality of the water supplied by the Warsaw mains).

The so-called soft sphere ascribes basic significance to:
- an improvement in the pace and efficacy of the self-government and state administration as regards spatial planning and real estate management, which shall

The new passenger terminal at the Warsaw-Okęcie airport might soon prove to be too cramped

reduce construction cycles and the costs of building both economic objects and residential housing;

■ an improvement of <u>security</u>, particularly the battle against the veritable plague of car thefts;

■ an improvement in the effectiveness of <u>town administration</u>, achieved by a suitable reform (simplification and the introduction of order) of the prevalent system.

The aforementioned endeavours, intent on bettering the effectiveness of Warsaw economy and the efficiency of the functioning of the Warsaw municipal body, should provide benefits for an overwhelming part of the capital's population.

The economic well-being of Warsaw is the necessary, albeit not the ultimate condition for the economic welfare for Mazovia. The ability to profit from the possession of such an economic and intellectual centre as the one located in the capital of the country demands an increase in the diffusion of development impulses from Warsaw to its environs and an improved capability for absorbing those impulses by the environment. This task calls for:

93

- the expansion of <u>transportation links</u> between Warsaw and its surrounding area *via* the construction of highways, particularly exit routes from Warsaw to the largest towns in the region and the A-2 highway within the Warsaw area, the development of permanent bus connections, and an improvement in the effectiveness and security of the commuter railway system;
- a better <u>level of education,</u> enabling the population of the region to compete for a more favourable position on the Warsaw labour market than is the case today, to be capable of investing money, earned in Warsaw or elsewhere, in ventures located in the closest region as well as to be able to profit from the knowledge provided by contacts with or *via* Warsaw (I have in mind primarily the dissemination of the secondary school system and education involving foreign languages and computer know-how);
- the retention or improvement of the <u>quality of agricultural production,</u> so that the locally produced food – the basic regional product on the Warsaw market – could compete with other regions and foreign commodities. (Such a change in the competitiveness of Mazovian foodstuff will, naturally, create conducive conditions for sales on other markets, both abroad and at home, although success on the Warsaw market will continue to be of basic significance);
- the retention or improvement of the state of the <u>natural environment and landscape merits,</u> especially in regions attractive from the viewpoint of recreation (the Zegrzyński Reservoir, Kampinoska Forest, the valleys of the Vistula, the Bug, the Narew, the Pilica, etc.)
- the improvement of the <u>infrastructure outfitting</u> of terrains in the nearest vicinity of Warsaw in order to attract residential and economic construction (storehouses, trade centres, etc.), serving the Warsaw agglomeration.

It follows from the above reflections that the relations between the centre of the region and its surrounding could consist of mutual benefits and a diffusion of impulses from the centre to the region. On the other hand, existing projects do not foresee a direct transfer of measures from the capital to the rest of the region.

Inter-regional Opportunities for Mazovia

The inter-regional opportunities of any region are embedded in the relations between that region and its counterparts. Such relations may be the outcome of an impact exerted by objective forces or the result of intentional ascertainments by the interested regions or decisions made by central authorities.

The regions adjoining the voivodeship of Mazovia do not offer an essential opportunity. Voivodeships to the north-east and the south are the least prosperous in Poland; they experience the same problems and possess a similar economic and social structure as the peripheries of Mazovia. Furthermore, they do not contain strong centres that could act as the potential source of stimulus. A slightly different situation prevails along the western frontier of Mazovia – the borderland with the Łódź voivodeship. Here, a true opportunity is created by the establishment of a *duopolis* – a bipolar Warsaw–Łódź configuration. The latter, whose foundation and creation would be provided by rapid transport, reducing the time spent for travelling to half a hour, could offer the benefits of synergy, yielded by a merge of two local markets (Warsaw and Łódź). Its outcome would entail the growing investment attractiveness of both cities for domestic and international capital. The merge of the Łódź and Warsaw markets, especially the housing and labour markets, would generate multi-directional changes. An integration of the housing market, whose current characteristic feature are prices much higher in Warsaw than in Łódź, would signify falling prices in the capital, render the life of the inhabitants of Warsaw much easier, and make the capital much more accessible for immigration; this phenomenon would, in turn, prove to be highly profitable for the remaining population of Mazovia. On the other hand, integration of the labour markets might lead to a labour force influx from Łódź, a town affected by high unemployment; this trend would be beneficial for the Warsaw entrepreneurs, albeit slightly less so for the local employees, especially those with lower qualifications.

All told, it appears that in the case of both cities profits dominate over the sum of disadvantages. Such argumentation lay at the base of an agreement made in September 1998, and concerning co-operation between the presidents of the two towns. Its realisation creates an opportunity both for Warsaw and, indirectly, for the rest of the region.

The less prosperous parts of Mazovia could benefit from a regional state policy aiming at the prevention of growing differences between the level of development and the wealth of particular parts of the country. Imminent integration between Poland and the European Union produces an increase in the significance of regional policies, and creates consecutive opportunities for Mazovia.

International Opportunities for Mazovia

International opportunities and ensuing threats to the region result from the impact exerted by international factors upon its economy.

The most important factors, both today and in the foreseeable future, include:
- the integration of Poland and the European Union,
- Polish membership in NATO,
- the evolving globalisation of world economy.

Integration with the European Union yields two types of effects for the future development of Mazovia – direct and indirect.

Direct effects comprise the possibility of benefiting from auxiliary funds. During the present-day pre-access phase this denotes predominantly the availability of PHARE funds as well as the ISPA and SAPARD funds, to be set into motion in the year 2000; their purpose is to assist the development of the infrastructure (chiefly transportation) and the protection of the natural environment as well as the re-structuring of agriculture and the development of rural areas. After the formal acceptance of Poland into the European Union Polish regions will be able to enjoy funds intended for regional development, with the prime target being farming.

The scale of available measures is considerable, and could become an essential factor in the growth of the region.

The possibilities of utilising those measures depend upon numerous factors. An important place is occupied by the ability to formulate attractive projects to be financed by those funds; in turn, this faculty relies on the qualifications of persons devising the projects, familiarity with the rules and procedures applied in the Union, etc. For those reasons, by profiting from the intellectual potential of Warsaw, Mazovia has large chances for essential participation in auxiliary measures.

Presumably, the indirect impact would be greater than its direct counterpart. In this domain, special importance would be attached to the agricultural policy pursued by the Union and the conditions concerning agriculture and the international flow of the labour force according to which Poland will become a member of the Union. The eventual access of Polish farmers to measures intended for Union agriculture and farming regions is probably the greatest international chance for all Polish regions, including Mazovia.

Polish membership in NATO requires a thorough modernisation of the Polish army. This demand creates a certain opportunity for the Polish armament industry, at present in a state of crisis and located predominantly in Radom (Mazowieckie Voivodeship).

A characteristic feature of the contemporary world is economic globalisation, consisting predominantly of the liberalisation of financial markets. Its outcome is an increasingly rapid capital flow as well as growing competition between assorted countries, regions and towns interested in attracting such capital. In Poland, globalisation affects Warsaw – a city which is, to a relatively fullest degree, part of international capital circulation. Globalisation denotes both an opportunity and a threat: in order to profit from the former and avoid the latter Warsaw must improve its competitiveness.

Upon the threshold of the new millennium Mazovia faces assorted opportunities and hazards. The above conducted survey of assets and liabilities unambiguously indicates the domination of the former.

Roman Szul

Poviats of Mazowieckie Voivodeship

Counties (poviats, Polish: powiaty) are a new administrative unit whose significance will grow in time.

We present a brief characteristic of the poviats with the reservation that part of it is the outcome of a simple aggregation of data pertaining to communes (gminas) situated within their range. Nonetheless, even such a survey illustrates important differentiation within the voivodeship and the assets of particular poviats.

Select data on poviats in the voivodeship of Mazovia, 1998.

Poviat	area in sq. km.	total population	inner migration balance	unemployment rate in June 1999	no. of telephone subscribers per 1000 inhabitants	total no. of sewage treatment plants	economic subjects acc. to REGON	poviat revenues in thous. zlotys
Białobrzegi	639	34 555	-118	12,9	115,2	1	2 269	31 272
Ciechanów	1063	94 425	74	14,3	204,5	5	6 384	92 791
Garwolin	1284	108 801	-245	10,8	118,7	10	5 873	103 441
Gostynin	615	49 680	-31	16,7	176,7	7	2 771	46 063
Grodzisk Maz.	367	70 738	602	6,8	191,1	4	7 273	78 642
Grójec	1383	109 612	17	6,1	144,0	13	6 507	103 031
Kozienice	917	67 471	-140	13,0	155,5	8	2 936	64 603
Legionowo	393	85 935	374	9,3	271,1	6	8 644	114 698
Lipsko	748	41 814	-213	14,6	91,5	4	1 518	34 728
Łosice	772	35 666	-132	9,5	199,7	4	1 698	32 046
Maków Maz.	1065	50 491	-236	14,3	154,9	6	2 668	45 890
Mińsk Maz.	1187	149 093	819	6,7	220,6	17	11 229	144 972
Mława	1171	76 801	-71	17,8	143,6	4	4 144	66 269
Nowy Dwór Maz.	688	74 336	-93	15,3	204,7	9	4 824	79 408
Ostrołęka	2099	85 194	-269	15,1	68,7	10	2 730	79 130
Ostrowia Maz.	1225	79 842	-236	11,2	121,9	7	4 628	72 768
Otwock	615	110 947	288	9,0	226,3	2	10 248	139 284
Piaseczno	507	103 062	1944	4,0	318,5	14	11 579	174 017
Płock	1799	107 817	-220	14,2	88,9	23	4 312	101 012
Płońsk	1384	92 009	-299	14,2	162,1	7	4 679	81 288
Pruszków	246	133 147	1006	5,6	321,4	9	15 497	160 888
Przasnysz	1218	56 502	-299	15,7	113,7	3	3 436	51 586
Przysucha	801	47 870	-257	17,1	91,3	3	1 983	41 113
Pułtusk	829	51 898	-88	15,1	152,9	2	3 115	48 542
Radom	1530	143 062	198	17,6	112,3	9	6 765	130 314
Siedlce	1603	82 353	-147	11,5	128,7	5	3 287	71 460
Sierpc	853	57 310	-270	16,2	144,5	13	2 491	53 477
Sochaczew	731	84 896	-66	10,2	200,6	7	5 542	75 867
Sokołów Podlaski	1131	61 883	-125	8,8	165,0	7	2 924	54 632
Szydłowiec	488	46 095	-92	25,5	106,8	2	1 971	40 438
Warsaw	494	1 605 087	1445	1,6	483,4	11	226 232	3 960 157
Western Warsaw	533	84 727	1106	3,2	324,4	12	9 350	117 375
Węgrów	1219	71 933	-263	11,5	116,7	4	3 725	63 220
Wołomin	955	178 807	1163	9,9	207,4	13	15 931	191 030
Wyszków	876	71 562	-49	13,8	109,3	5	4 495	67 931
Zwoleń	571	39 520	-188	14,3	123,5	4	1 542	31 947
Żuromin	805	43 074	-231	15,6	95,2	3	2 077	37 157
Żyrardów	533	76 266	188	10,6	212,5	3	5 374	79 626
Ostrołęka	29	55 015	258	*	295,3	6	5 007	52 672
Płock	88	129 786	115	*	302,2	13	10 624	212 109
Radom	112	232 653	-452	*	298,1	2	23 412	276 661
Siedlce	32	75 342	180	*	304,4	2	6 883	71 076

* no data available

Source: *Bank Danych Lokalnych GUS 1998* (Local Data Bank, Main Statistical Office 1998), With the exception of data concerning the unemployment level in mid-1999. Such data are given jointly for towns with poviat status and poviats.

POVIAT OF BIAŁOBRZEGI

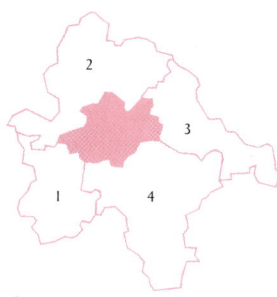

The poviat of Białobrzegi, situated in the southern part of the voivodeship, borders directly with the poviat of Radom, the third largest as regards the size of the population. A favourable position along the Warsaw–Radom–Kielce–Krakow–Zakopane highway, which comprises an important communication route towards the north-south, offers a chance for intensifying the economic development of the poviat. The area of the poviat of Białobrzegi totals 639 sq. km. A population of 35 000 denotes a rather moderate population density (55 persons per sq. km.). The poviat is composed of the following gminas: Białobrzegi (urban-rural), Promna, Radzanów, Stara Błotnica, Stromiec and Wyśmierzyce (urban-rural). This agricultural-industrial poviat is considered less affluent from the viewpoint of revenues and expenditure. According to the Centre for Development Research (CBR), its development potential is rather low. The number of economic subjects active in the poviat (2 269) is lower than the voivodeship average. The most important include the Italian firm of Allione Central Europe – food processing, Zbyszko – a producer of soft drinks, juices and concentrated beverages as well as traditional units such as Bank Spółdzielczy and insurance companies (PZU, TKA and Warta). The number of stationary telephone subscribers per 1 000 inhabitants is more than 115 – an annual increase of 9,2%.

Poviat of Białobrzegi borders with the following poviats:
1. Przysucha,
2. Grójec,
3. Kozienice,
4. Radom

POVIAT OF CIECHANÓW

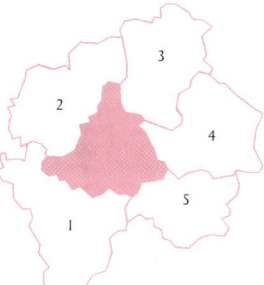

This agricultural-industrial poviat, with the capital in Ciechanów, is situated on the river Łydynia in the northern part of the voivodeship. Its characteristic features include a well-developed network of road and railway connections with nearby Warsaw and the Baltic coastline. The area of the poviat totals 1063 sq. km., of which 61% is occupied by arable land. The poviat is composed of the following gminas: Ciechanów (urban, rural), Glinojeck (urban-rural), Gołymin--Ośrodek, Grudusk, Ojrzeń, Opinogóra Górna, Regimin, and Sońsk. A population of 94 000 denotes a density of 89 persons per sq. km. The inner migration balance is positive (74 persons). The poviat is considered one of the medium prosperous in the voivodeship, and its development potential is evaluated as average. In 1998, there were 6 384 registered subjects, the largest ones being a poultry farm "Cedro", the Glinojeck sugar plant, whose strategic investor is the British "Sugar Firm" with an input of more than 35 mln. USD, Browary Warszawskie SA (brewery), H. Bauer Publishers, Fanar SA – a tool producer, Gryf – a publishing and printing enterprise and the Ciechanów dairy cooperative. Financial operations in the poviat are serviced by such banks as BGŻ, GE Capital, Kredyt Bank, NBP, PKO BP and Bank Zachodni. There are five telecommunication centres, and the number of subscribers per 1 000 inhabitants is 205 (an

Poviat of Ciechanów borders with the following poviats:
1. Płońsk,
2. Mława,
3. Przasnysz,
4. Maków Mazowiecki,
5. Pułtusk

increase of about 7,1% as compared to 1997). An essential role is played by such business organizations as the Mazovian Economic Chamber, the Ciechanów Society for the Support of Entrepreneurship, the Regional Development Agency and the Society for Economic Initiative.

POVIAT OF GARWOLIN

The poviat of Garwolin (the capital in Garwolin) lies on the river Wilga in the south-eastern part of the voivodeship. Its location – 60 km. from Warsaw, next to Route 17, which leads to Lublin and further on towards the frontier with Ukraine, together with Warsaw–Lublin train connections, favour economic activity. The area of the poviat totals 1 284 sq. km. (the seventh largest in the voivodeship), of which a considerable part is composed of woods. A population of 109 000 gives the poviat eighth place in the voivodeship. The poviat consists of the following gminas: Borowie, Garwolin (urban, rural), Górzno, Łaskarzew (urban, rural), Maciejowice, Miastków Kościelny, Parysów, Piława (urban-rural), Sobolew, Trojanów, Wilga, and Żelechów (urban-rural). CBR estimates the potential development of the poviat, considered as non-affluent, as rather low. Nevertheless, in 1998, there were 5 873 economic subjects, which is a relatively favourable result. The largest firms include Glass Factory Czechy SA, Cora Garwolin (garments), PKO BP, Bank Depozytowo-Kredytowy, Bank Spółdzielczy, Interdruk (printers), and the regional dairy cooperative. Furthermore, a Centre for the Training and Improvement of Cadres and a Complex of Farming Schools are situated in Miętno. Mention should be made of a noteworthy increase (more than 41%) of stationary telephone subscribers, from 70 per 1 000 inhabitants in 1997 to 119 a year later.

Poviat of Garwolin borders with the following poviats:
1. Kozienice,
2. Grójec,
3. Otwock,
4. Mińsk Mazowiecki,
5. Siedlce

POVIAT OF GOSTYNIN

The capital of this industrial-agricultural poviat, situated in the western part of the voivodeship, is Gostynin. Composed of the gminas of Gostynin (urban, rural), Pacyna, Sanniki, and Szczawin Kościelny, it has an area of 615 sq. km., mainly arable land. The population of the poviat totals 49 700, and population density is 81 persons per sq. km. The poviat is regarded as unaffluent, but its strong asset lies in attractive tourist facilities on the beautiful Lucińskie and Bialskie lakes to the north of Gostynin. In 1998, there were 2 771 registered economic subjects – a relatively small number. The largest firm in the poviat is ELGO from Gostynin, a leading Polish producer of lighting equipment. Other significant firms include Exdrob SA – a poultry hatching enterprise, and Dubinex – a meat processing plant. Concern for the protection of the natural environment is expressed by the presence of seven sewage treatment plants. The poviat has typical financial institutions such as Powszechny Bank

Poviat of Gostynin borders with the following poviats:
1. Płock,
2. Sochaczew

Gospodarczy SA, PKO BP, and PZU Życie (insurance). Telecommunication services are rendered by three centres and the index of subscribers per 1 000 inhabitants is 177 (an increase of 11% in relation to 1997).

POVIAT OF GRODZISK MAZOWIECKI

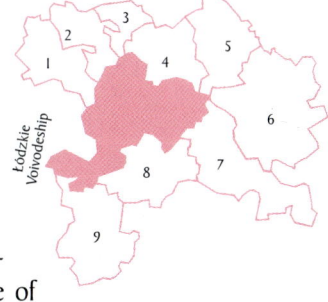

An industrial poviat in the centre of the voivodeship, 30 km. to the south-west from Warsaw, along the Łódź–Warsaw highway. Convenient connections with Poznań, Katowice and Krakow render the poviat particularly attractive for investment. The capital is Grodzisk Mazowiecki, one of the most vital towns in the voivodeship. Apart from Grodzisk, the poviat is composed of the following gminas: Baranów, Jaktorów, Milanówek (urban), Podkowa Leśna (urban) and Żabia Wola. The area of the poviat totals 367 sq. km., and a population of 70 700 results in a rather high population density of 192 persons per sq. km. (the fourth in the voivodeship). The poviat is one of the most prosperous in Mazovia, with a development potential assessed by CBR as high. In 1998, there were 7 273 registered firms, well above the average. The largest enterprises include: Polfa Grodzisk Mazowiecki (pharmaceutics), PepsiCo (a soft drinks bottling plant), and Danfoss (producer of central heating valves). The relatively high number of telephones continues to grow (4,9% in 1998). The poviat has four functioning sewage treatment plants. The number of apartments completed by 1997 was 365 – higher than the voivodeship average. The positive inner migration balance (602 persons) is yet another confirmation of the considerable attraction of the poviat.

Poviat of Grodzisk Mazowiecki borders with the following poviats:
1. Żyrardów,
2. Sochaczew,
3. Western Warsaw
4. Pruszków,
5. Grójec

POVIAT OF GRÓJEC

This industrial-agricultural poviat (the capital in Grójec) is widely known at home and abroad for its orchards. In the future, its favourable localisation (the central-southern part of the voivodeship) along the Warsaw–Radom–Kielce–Krakow route will stimulate the economy to an even greater extent, especially as regards the food industry and trade. The poviat is composed of the following gminas: Belsk Duży, Błądów, Chynów, Goszczyn, Grójec (urban-rural), Jasieniec, Mogielnica (urban-rural), Nowe Miasto on the Pilica, Pniewy, Tarczyn and Warka (urban-rural). The area of the poviat totals 1 383 sq. km, of which 42% is arable land. From the viewpoint of population density (79 persons per sq. km.) the poviat of Grójec does not distinguish itself in the region. CBR assesses the development potential of the poviat as average. The country itself is regarded as of average prosperity too. In 1998, there were 6 507 enterprises (an increase of 6,7%), which constitutes a relatively good result. The largest enterprises in the poviat are firms in the food branch: the PepsiCo bottling plant in Pniewy, the

Poviaty of Grójec borders with the following poviats:
1. Żyrardów,
2. Grodzisk Mazowiecki,
3. Pruszków,
4. Piaseczno,
5. Otwock,
6. Garwolin,
7. Kozienice,
8. Białobrzegi,
9. Przysucha

101

Warka brewery in Warka, Tarczyn – a producer of fruit juices and beverages in Tarczyn, and the Italian firm of Ferrero in Belsk Duży – a renowned confectionery producer. The index of stationary telephone subscribers – 144 per 1 000 inhabitants – denotes an increase of 10,3% as compared to 1997. Considerable progress has been noted in the domain of the protection of the natural environment – there are 13 sewage treatment plants. The above-the-average tourist merits of the poviat are enhanced by the river Pilica and a picturesque landscape, especially in the spring when apple trees blossom on thousands of hectares of orchards. The poviat has at its disposal a sufficient number of hotels – nine objects with 430 beds.

POVIAT OF KOZIENICE

Poviat of Kozienice borders with the following poviats:
1. Zwoleń,
2. Radom,
3. Białobrzegi,
4. Grójec,
5. Garwolin

The industrial poviat of Kozienice (the capital in Kozienice), situated in the southern part of the voivodeship, is composed of the following gminas: Garbatka-Letnisko, Głowaczów, Gniewoszów, Grabów on the Pilica, Kozienice (urban-rural), Magnuszew and Sieciechów. The woodland area of the poviat totals 917 sq. km. – Kozienicka Forest is one of the most attractive tourist offerings of the region. The population of the poviat totals about 68 000, i.e. the population density is 74 persons per sq. km. The poviat is regarded as a rather wealthy region but CBR assesses its development potential as exploited to a considerable degree. In 1998, there were 2 936 registered firms (an increase of 6% as compared to 1997). Owing to the presence of a great power plant this index does not characterise the economy of the country accurately. At the same time, the Kozienice plant, with the power of 2 750 MW, is the largest employer in the poviat (2 800 workers). Other prominent firms include Zakład Kondensatorów Ceramicznych (ceramic condensers), Prefabet-Kozienice SA (prefabricated concrete, Energomontaż-Północ Kozienice (power engineering), and Energoaparatura. The local firms are serviced business surroundings units. The index of stationary telephone subscribers per 1 000 inhabitants is 156 (an increase of 11,4% as compared to 1997) – the effect of the activity of eight telecommunication service enterprises. Furthermore, the poviat has at it disposal eight sewage treatment plants. A sufficient lodging and hotel network is composed of five objects with 818 beds.

POVIAT OF LEGIONOWO

The industrial poviat of Legionowo (the capital in Legionowo) is extremely attractively situated in the fork of the Vistula and the Narew; moreover, it serves as a dormitory for Warsaw. The poviat is known for the largest Audio-Tele Centre in Poland (Legion Polska) and for military and police academies. Just as widely renowned is the Zegrzyński Reservoir – the main tourist offering of the region. Its localisation (the proximity of Warsaw) and tourist-recreation assets are well-exploited. The poviat is composed of the following gminas: Jabłonna, Legionowo (urban), Nieporęt, Serock (urban-rural) and Wieliszew. The area of the wooded poviat totals 393 sq. km. A population of 86 000 signifies a density of 218 persons per sq. km. (fourth place in the voivodeship, without municipal poviats). After the poviats of Warsaw and Piaseczno, the poviat of Legionowo is the wealthiest in Mazovia. In 1998, it had 8 644 registered firms, which constitutes a very high index considering the rather small area of the poviat and the size of its population. Legionowo itself is the site of Leaf Poland, a well-known chewing gum producer, MFC – a clothes producer, and MABEG (waste recycling). The poviat has a well-developed stationary telephone network, with 271 subscribers per 1 000 inhabitants (ninth place in the voivodeship and an increase of 20,2% as compared to 1997). The subscribers are serviced by eight telecommunication centres. There are six functioning sewage treatment plants. Ten hotels offer 2 391 beds. The positive inner migration balance is 374.

Poviat of Legionowo borders with the following poviats:
1. Warsaw,
2. Western Warsaw,
3. Nowy Dwór Mazowiecki,
4. Pułtusk,
5. Wyszków,
6. Wołomin

POVIAT OF LIPSKO

An agricultural poviat (the capital in Lipsko) on the river Krępianka, along the south-eastern edge of the voivodeship; its eastern boundary is the Vistula. Localisation along the Warsaw–Radom–Sandomierz route, at the point of contact of three voivodeships, could become the poviat's strong asset. The poviat is composed of the following gminas: Chotcza, Ciepielów, Lipsko (urban-rural), Rzeczniów, Sienno, and Solec on the Vistula. As much as 67% of the total area of 748 sq. km. is arable land. The population totals 42 000 (56 persons per sq. km). The poviat in question is one of the poorest in the voivodeship and its development potential, assessed by CBR, is rather low. In 1998 there were 1 518 registered enterprises (an increase of 8,6%). The most important institutions in the poviat include HORTEX, a fruit and regetable processing firm with a long tradition, Ruch SA (press distribution), Pomer – services for agriculture, PZU (insurance), PKO BP and Bank Spółdzielczy. The rather small number of stationary telephone subscribers (91,5 per 1 000 inhabitants) is rising dynamically – by 15,7% as compared to 1997. The poviat has at its disposal four sewage treatment plants.

Świętokrzyskie Voivodeship

Lubelskie Voivodeship

Poviat of Lipsko borders with the following poviats:
1. Radom,
2. Zwoleń

POVIAT OF ŁOSICE

Poviat of Łosice
borders with the
following poviats:
1. Siedlce

This traditionally agricultural poviat, with the capital in Łosice, is the most easterly part of the voivodeship, situated in the Siedlce Rising. Its plains are crossed by the river Toczna – a left-bank tributary of the Bug. The poviat lies along the Białystok–Lublin route, near an international connection with Belarus (frontier crossing in Terespol). It is also a convenient point of departure for tourists setting off for the nearby beautiful terrains on the Bug. The poviat is composed of the following gminas: Huszlew, Łosice (urban-rural), Olszanka, Platerów, Sarnaki and Stara Kornica. The area of the poviat totals 772 sq. km. with a population of 36 000, which signifies a population density of 46 persons per sq. km. Despite the fact that the poviat is one of the less affluent, CBR assesses its development chances as average. In 1998, there were 1 689 registered enterprises (an increase of 10,7% as compared to the previous year). The prime enterprises, active for years, are the "MITEX" dairy works and "POLFER" in Woźniki, WFSS "PERUN", GS "SCh" (farmers' cooperatives), and CHZ "ROLIMPEX" (foreign trade) Biała Podlaska. The stationary telephone subscribers index per 1 000 inhabitants is 200 (an increase of 8,5%), exceeding considerably many wealthier poviats. A well-developed hotel and lodgings network offers a total of 2 434 beds. There are four sewage treatment plants; the latest – opened in Łosice – is one of the most modern facilities of this sort in Poland.

POVIAT OF MAKÓW MAZOWIECKI

Poviat of Maków
Mazowiecki
borders with the
following poviats:
1. Pułtusk,
2. Ciechanów,
3. Przasnysz,
4. Ostrołęka,
5. Wyszków

An agricultural-industrial poviat (the capital in Maków Mazowiecki) in the northern part of the voivodeship on the rivers Orzyc and Narew. The poviat is composed of the following gminas: Czerwonka, Karniewo, Krasnosielc, Maków Mazowiecki (urban-rural), Młynarze, Płoniawy-Bramura, Różan (urban-rural), Rzewnie, Sypniewo and Szelków. The area totals 1 065 sq. km, of which 51,5% is arable land. With a population of about 51 000 persons it is rather thinly populated (48 persons per sq. m.). The poviat is crossed by two domestic routes, of which the one from Warsaw to the Mazury region has heavy traffic, especially during the summer season. CBR assesses the economic development of this rather unaffluent poviat as rather low. In 1998, there were 2 668 registered firms (an increase of 12,2%), the prime being Cukrownia Krasiwiec SA (sugar plant) and Zakład Przemysłu Drzewnego (wood industry). The stationary telephone subscribes index of 155 per 1 000 inhabitants demonstrates a considerable rise as compared to 1997 (24,5%). The poviat has typical institutions providing services for agriculture; banking services are rendered primarily by cooperatives. There are six sewage treatment plants.

POVIAT OF MIŃSK MAZOWIECKI

This industrial-agricultural poviat, whose capital is Mińsk Mazowiecki, is situated in the central part of the voivodeship. Its terrain is crossed by a very important communication route leading
towards Terespol. The poviat is composed of the following gminas:
Cegłów, Dębe Wielkie, Dobre, Halinów, Jakubów, Kałuszyn,
Latowicz, Mińsk Mazowiecki (urban, rural), Mrozy, Siennica, Stanisławów, Sulejówek (urban) and Wesoła (urban). This is one of the
largest poviats in Mazovia (1 187 sq. km.) with a population of 149 000
(i.e. the population density is 125 persons per sq. km – seventh place in the
voivodeship). Although the poviat of Mińsk is regarded as rather unaffluent, the
proximity of Warsaw exerts a positive impact on an assessment of its development
potential. It seems worth mentioning a considerable differentiation of the poviat,
which is composed of traditionally agricultural gminas, such as Latowicz, and residential gminas, such as Sulejówek or Wesoła (dormitories of Warsaw). In 1998,
there were 11 229 registered enterprises (seventh place in the voivodeship and an
increase of 8,6%% as compared to 1997). The most important firms functioning in
the poviat include Colgate Palmolive in Halinów, part of an international concern,
a meat plant in Stanisławów, the Catzy cosmetic factory in Wesoła, Fabryka Wyrobów
Metalowych (metal articles), Fabryka Urządzeń Dźwigowych (crane equipment),
Mazowieckie Mosty (bridge construction), Budopol (building industry), and Sawiren
– Mińskie Zakłady Obuwia (shoes). The index of stationary telephone subscribers
per 1 000 inhabitants is rather high (221). The poviat has at its disposal as many as
17 sewage treatment plants and ten hotels and lodgings. A positive inner migration
balance of 891 indicates considerable development dynamic. In the near future, the
poviat will gain a strong asset in the form of the A2 highway, linking Western and
Eastern Europe. This venture should attract investors and exert a favourable impact
on the economic development of the region.

Poviat of Mińsk
Mazowiecki
borders with the
following poviats:
1. Garwolin,
2. Otwock,
3. Warsaw,
4. Wołomin,
5. Węgrów,
6. Siedlce

POVIAT OF MŁAWA

A predominantly industrial poviat (the capital in Mława) in the northern part of the voivodeship, crossed by a convenient communication
connection between Gdańsk and Warsaw. The poviat is composed of
the following gminas: Dzierzgowo, Lipowiec Kościelny, Mława (urban), Lubań, Radzanów, Strzegowo, Stupsk, Szreńsk, Szydłowo,
Wieczfnia Kościelna and Wiśniewo. The area totals 1 171 sq. km., while
a population of 77 000 gives a density of 66 persons per sq. km. The
economic potential of this rather unaffluent poviat is assessed by CBR as low.
In 1998, there were 41 244 registered firms (an increase of 8,1% in relation to
1997), i.e. not very many for a poviat of this size. Mława is known throughout
Poland for the Curtis television factory, a leading domestic producer. Other significant

Poviat of Mława
borders with the
following poviats:
1. Przasnysz,
2. Ciechanów,
3. Płońsk,
4. Żuromin

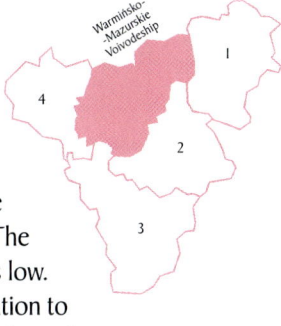

firms include: Zakłady Wytwórcze Urządzeń Wodociągowych (water-main equipment), Dźwigpol SA (cranes), Insbud SA (construction installations), Eksbut – a shoe producer, Zakład Opakowań i Produkcji Mechanicznej (packaging and mechanicsô and Aqua – Zakład Wody Mineralizowanej (mineral water). The rather low index of stationary telephone subscribers – 144 per 1 000 inhabitants – is growing rapidly (12,7% as compared to 1997). The poviat boasts of a Municipal Science, Culture and Sports Centre in Mława – a true focal point of local recreation and social life.

POVIAT OF NOWY DWÓR MAZOWIECKI

Poviat of Nowy
Dwór Mazowiecki
borders with the
following poviats:
1. Western Warsaw,
2. Sochaczew,
3. Płońsk,
4. Pułtusk,
5. Legionowo

This industrial poviat (the capital in Nowy Dwór Mazowiecki) is situated in the central part of the voivodeship, in the immediate vicinity of Warsaw. The poviat is composed of the following gminas: Czosnów, Leoncin, Nasielsk (urban-rural), Nowy Dwór Mazowiecki (urban), Pomiechówek and Zakroczym (urban-rural). The area of the poviat totals 688 sq. km; a population of 74 000 signifies a density of 108 persons per sq. km. (eleventh place in the voivodeship). CBR assesses the development potential of the poviat – one of the more prosperous in the voivodeship – as average. In 1998, there were 4 824 registered firms, including such world-known enterprises as the German firm of Benckiser – producer of cleansers, and the French Elf, which deals with the distribution of liquid fuel. Other important firms are Instal, Elopak – a producer of packaging, and Hansen Poland – the food industry. The index of stationary telephone subscribers per 1 000 inhabitants is 205 (an increase of as much as 16,1% as compared to 1997). There are nine sewage treatment plants and nine hotels and lodgings. The poviat is highly attractive from the viewpoint of weekend tourism due to terrains on the river Wkra, woods in the region of Pomiechówek, the Vistula, and the proximity of Kampinoska Forest.

POVIAT OF OSTROŁĘKA

Poviat of Ostrołęka
borders with the
following poviats:
1. Ostrowia
Mazowiecka,
2. Wyszków,
3. Maków
Mazowiecki,
4. Przasnysz

An industrial-agricultural poviat, with the capital in Ostrołęka, situated in the north-eastern part of the voivodeship. There is a convenient communication connection – Warsaw is 120 km. away. Moreover, a similar distance separates the poviat from the large towns of Białystok and Olsztyn. The poviat lies in an ecologically pure region, known as the "green lungs of Poland". It is composed of the following gminas: Baranowo, Czarnia, Czerwin, Goworowo, Kadzidło, Lelis, Łyse, Myszyniec (urban-rural), Olszewo-Borki, Rzekuń and Troszyn. The area of the poviat – 2 099 sq. km. – is one of the largest in the voivodeship; its considerable part is composed of woods, some of which are remnants of old forests. A population of more than 85 000 means a density of 41 persons per sq. km. The prime asset of the poviat lies in its location along the main route from Warsaw to the Mazury region. Although the poviat is rather prosperous, CBR assessed its development potential as low. In 1998, there were 2 730 enterprises. The economy of the poviat cannot be separated easily from that of the municipal poviat of Ostrołęka. The activity of such globally known firms as Intercell (paper), SIAS (fruit components), Ytong (building material) or the "Ostrołęka" power plant is of fundamental significance for both these administrative units. At the moment, the poviat still lags behind as regards the number of stationary telephone subscribers – only 69 per 1 000 inhabitants. There are ten functioning sewage treatment plants. The inner migration balance is 269 – one of the highest in the voivodeship, testifying to the considerable attractiveness of the poviat.

POVIAT OF OSTROWIA MAZOWIECKA

This industrial-agricultural poviat (the capital in Ostrowia Mazowiecka), situated in the eastern part of the voivodeship, is composed of the following gminas: Andrzejewo, Boguty-Pianki, Brok (urban-rural), Małkinia Górna, Nur, Ostrów Mazowiecka (urban, rural), Stary Lubotyń, Szulborze Wielkie, Węsewo and Zaręby Kościelne. The area of the poviat totals 1225 sq. km., with a population of 80 000 (a population density of 65 persons per sq. km.). A considerable area is composed of the compact woodland complex of Biała Forest. The poviat is regarded as unaffluent, but CBR assesses its development potential as average. The local woods and the river Bug, exceptionally picturesque in the regions of Brok, comprise the foremost tourist assets of the poviat, which has at its disposal convenient facilities for tourism and recreation (by no means only for weekends). In this domain, the leading role is played by the gmina of Brok. In 1998, there were 4 628 registered enterprises (an increase of 10,8%). The rising number of firms indicates a large economic activity of the region. The best known economic subject is the dairy in Ostrowia Mazowiecka, which competes with other enterprises in this branch (including foreign firms in Mazovia). Other firms are: Forte SA (furniture), Alpha Opakowania z Tworzyw Sztucznych (synthetic packaging) and Schneider Polska sp. z o. o. Technika Samochodowa (automobile technology). The index of the number of stationary telephone subscribers per 1 000 inhabitants is 122 (an increase of 7%). Moreover, the poviat has at its disposal seven sewage treatment plants.

Poviat of Ostrowia Mazowiecka borders with the following poviats:
1. Sokołów Podlaski,
2. Węgrów,
3. Wyszków,
4. Ostrołęka

POVIAT OF OTWOCK

This poviat, located in the immediate vicinity of Warsaw and with the capital in Otwock, is part of the Warsaw agglomeration. It is composed of the following gminas: Celestynów, Józefów (urban), Karczew (urban-rural), Kołbiel, Osieck, Otwock (urban), Sobienie Jeziory and Wiązowna. The poviat fulfils residential, sanatorium and recreational functions for Warsaw. Its predominantly woody area, totalling 1615 sq. km., is inhabited by 111 000 persons, which signifies a popu-

Zakłady Mięsne Sochocin (meat plant). Numerous smaller firms represent primarily the agricultural-food branch. The poviat has a well developed communication and telecommunication infrastructure. The index of the number of stationary telephone subscribers per 1 000 inhabitants is 162 (an increase of 15,7%). Furthermore, the poviat is situated along the Warsaw–Gdańsk route, which in Płońsk joins the important domestic route to Toruń and then to the West.

POVIAT OF PRUSZKÓW

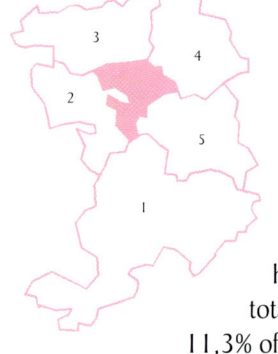

Poviat of Pruszków borders with the following poviats:
1. Grójec,
2. Grodzisk Mazowiecki,
3. Western Warsaw,
4. Warsaw,
5. Piaseczno

This industrial poviat (the capital in Pruszków) in the central part of the voivodeship is composed of the following gminas: Brwinów (urban-rural), Michałowice, Nadarzyn, Piastów (urban), Pruszków (urban) and Raszyn. The immediate proximity of Warsaw influences the development of the poviat, resulting in a positive inner migration balance (1 006 persons – fifth place in the voivodeship) and good effects of residential housing construction (673 flats completed in 1997). The area of the poviat totals 246 sq. km., of which 50,5% is composed of arable land and only 11,3% of woods. A population of 133 000 signifies a density of 539 persons per sq. km. (second place in the voivodeship). CBR assesses the development potential of this prosperous poviat as high. In 1998, there were 15 497 registered enterprises (fifth place in the voivodeship), of which as many as 400 are with foreign capital participation. More significant firms include: Daewoo, specialising in the annually growing production of television sets, Munksjo Packaging – cardboard packaging, and Lek – pharmaceutics. The gmina of Raszyn is a terrain of particularly intense investment due to the region of Janki, which concentrates routes leading towards Katowice, Wrocław and Krakow and is the site of numerous trade centres: IKEA, Metro and Casino. The poviat is known for an excellent telecommunication infrastructure (the index of the number of stationary telephone subscribers per 1 000 inhabitants is 321) and financial services. Moreover, it has at its disposal nine sewage treatment plants. Pruszków is celebrated for the HOOP PEKAES Pruszków basketball team, a leading team in Poland.

Poviat of Przasnysz borders with the following poviats:
1. Ostrołęka,
2. Maków Mazowiecki,
3. Ciechanów,
4. Mława

POVIAT OF PRZASNYSZ

Warmińsko-Mazurskie Voivodeship

The agricultural-industrial poviat with the capital in Przasnysz lies on the river Węgierka in the northern part of the voivodeship. Crossed by the rivers Orzyc and Ulatówka, it is composed of the following gminas: Chorzele (urban-rural), Czernice Borowe, Jednorożec, Krasne, Krzynowłoga Mała, and Przasnysz (urban, rural). The area of the poviat totals 1 218 sq. km. and is dominated by woods. A population of 57 000 signifies a density of 46 per sq. km. The development potential is assessed by CBR as average, although the poviat is regarded as unaffluent. In 1998, there were 3 436 enterprises, of which 3319 were natural persons conducting economic activity. The best known firms in the poviat are ABB – a producer of electrical power engineering parts, and KROSS – a well-known bicycle producer. The index of the number of stationary telephone subscribers per 1 000 inhabitants is 114 (an increase of 5,2%). Moreover, the poviat has at its disposal three sewage treatment plants.

POVIAT OF PRZYSUCHA

Situated in the southern part of the voivodeship, this agricultural-industrial poviat has the capital in Przysucha. The poviat is composed of the following gminas: Borkowice, Gielniów, Klwów, Odrzywół, Potworów, Przysucha (urban-rural), Rusinów and Wieniawa. The area of the poviat, crossed by the river Radomka, totals 801 sq. km. is composed mainly of woods. The population totals 48 000, with a density of 60 persons per sq. km. CBR assessed the potential of this unaffluent poviat as low. In 1998, there were 1 983 firms, and an increase of 12,1% as compared to the previous year testifies to the rising entrepreneurship of the local population. The most important economic subjects active in the poviat include: HORTEX – fruit and vegetable processing, RUPP Ceramika – ceramic roof tiles, ZPC Przysucha – ceramic plates, and FWM Przysucha – foundry products. The index of the number of stationary telephone subscribers per 1 000 inhabitants is 98. There are three functioning sewage treatment plants.

Poviat of Przysucha borders with the following poviats:
1. Grójec,
2. Białobrzegi,
3. Radom,
4. Szydłowiec

POVIAT OF PUŁTUSK

The capital of this agricultural-industrial poviat is Pułtusk – one of the oldest and most beautiful towns of Mazovia. The poviat, which lies on the river Narew in the north-central part of the voivodeship, is composed of the following gminas: Gzy, Obryte, Pokrzywnica, Pułtusk (urban-rural), Świercze, Winnica and Zatory. The area of the poviat totals 829 sq. km., of which 53,9% is composed of arable land. A population of 52 000 signifies a population density of 63 persons per sq. km. The poviat is regarded as medium prosperous, and its development potential is assessed by CBR experts as average. In 1998, there were 3 115 registered enterprises (an increase of 9,7%), the most active being Polam-Pułtusk (lighting) and Wytwórnia Prefabrykatów Betonowych (prefabricated concrete products). The index of the number of stationary telephone subscribers per 1 000 inhabitants is 153 (an increase of 7,8%). The poviat has at its disposal two sewage treatment plants. A significant asset of the poviat of Pułtusk is the dynamic private Higher School in the Humanities, attended by more than 10 000 students not only from Mazovia, but also from the neighbouring voivodeships. As a result, Pułtusk is becoming an important academic centre.

Poviat of Pułtusk borders with the following poviats:
1. Legionowo,
2. Nowy Dwór Mazowiecki,
3. Płońsk,
4. Ciechanów,
5. Maków Mazowiecki,
6. Wyszków

111

POVIAT OF RADOM

Poviat of Radom borders with the following poviats:
1. Radom (municipal county),
2. Szydłowiec
3. Przysucha,
4. Białobrzegi,
5. Kozienice,
6. Zwoleń,
7. Lipsko

This industrial poviat (the capital in Radom) in the southern part of the voivodeship along the Warsaw–Krakow route, is composed of the following gminas: Gózd, Iłża (urban-rural), Jastrzębia, Jedlińsk, Jedlnia-Letnisko, Kowala, Pionki (urban, rural), Przytyk, Skaryszew (urban-rural), Wierzbica, Wolanów and Zakrzew. The poviat is known in Poland for leather tanning and a shoe and clothes production. Two local airports are situated in Małęczyn and Dąbrówka Podłężna. The area of the poviat totals 1 530 sq. km. (one of the largest in the voivodeship), and the population – 143 000 (a population density of 93 persons per sq. km.). The poviat is regarded as unaffluent, and its development potential is assessed by CBR as rather low. In 1998, there were 6 765 registered enterprises, which constitutes an average index in the voivodeship. The best known firms are Cementownia Wierzbica (cement), Berta – Huta Szkła Gospodarczego (glassware) in Jedlińsk, Tussitura Bresciana (clothing) in Pionki, and Steffen Pionki. The number of stationary telephone subscribers per 1 000 inhabitants is 112. The poviat has nine functioning sewage treatment plants.

POVIAT OF SIEDLCE

Poviat of Siedlce borders with the following poviats:
1. Siedlce (minicipal poviat)
2. Garwolin,
3. Mińsk Mazowiecki,
4. Węgrów,
5. Sokołów Podlaski,
6. Łosice

An agricultural poviat, with the capital in Siedlce, in the eastern part of the voivodeship, along the route leading to the Belarussian frontier. The poviat is composed of the following gminas: Domanice, Korczew, Kotuń, Mokobody, Mordy, Paprotnia, Przesmyki, Siedlce, Skórzec, Suchożebry, Wiśniew, Wodynie and Zbuczyn Poduchowny. The area totals 1 603 sq. km. (third in the voivodeship), of which 53,6% is arable land, and 17,6% – woods. A population of 82 000 signifies a density of 51 persons per sq. km. The development potential of this unaffluent poviat is low. In 1998, there were 3 287 registered enterprises, of which 3 165 were self-employed, involved in economic activity. The economy of the poviat is not easily distinguishable from that of the municipal poviat of Siedlce where the majority of the inhabitants of nearby gminas are employed. The most active subjects outside Siedlce include: Silbet – Zakłady Produkcji Materiałów Budowlanych (building material) in Skórzec and Prefabet (prefabricated concrete products) in Suchożebry. The index of the number of stationary telephone subscribers per 1 000 inhabitants is 129. The poviat has at its disposal five sewage treatment plants.

112

POVIAT OF SIERPC

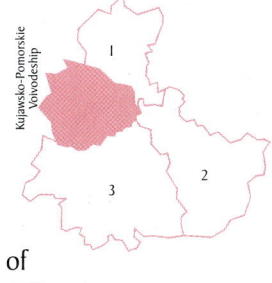

The capital of this agricultural poviat in the north-western part of the voivodeship is Sierpc. The poviat is composed of the following gminas: Gozdowo, Mochowo, Rościszewo, Sierpc (urban, rural), Szczutowo and Zawidz. The area of the poviat, crossed by the rivers Sierpnica and Skrwa, totals 853 sq. km, of which as much as 61,9% is composed of arable land; Szczutowskie Lake lies to the north-west of Sierpc. Together with the famous Skansen (Museum of the Mazovian Village) those are the prime tourist attractions of the poviat. A population of 57 000 denotes a density of 67 persons per sq. km. The poviat is regarded as unaffluent, and has a rather low development potential. In 1998, there were only 2 491 registered firms, but their number grew dynamically as compared to 1997 (an increase of about 14,3%). The best known enterprises are Cargill – animal fodder, Okręgowa Spółdzielnia Mleczarska (dairy cooperative), Zakłady Piwowarskie (brewery) in Sierpc, and Drukarnia Sp. z o. o. (printers). Economic subjects are serviced by, i.a. Bank Spółdzielczy, Bank Pekao SA, PKO BP, and PZU Życie. The telephone subscribers index is rather favourable – 145 per 1 000 inhabitants. The poviat has 13 functioning sewage treatment plants.

Poviat of Sierpc borders with the following poviats:
1. Żuromin,
2. Płońsk,
3. Płock

POVIAT OF SOCHACZEW

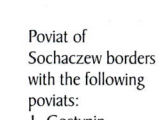

An industrial poviat, with the capital in Sochaczew, situated on the Bzura in the central-western part of the voivodeship. The poviat is composed of the following gminas: Brochów, Iłów, Młodzieszyn, Nowa Sucha, Rybno, Teresin and Sochaczew (urban, rural). The poviat and town of Sochaczew are crossed by one of the busiest routes from Warsaw to Poznań, and then *via* Swieck towards Western Europe. The area of the poviat totals 731 sq. km, of which 58,9% is arable land, one of the best in Mazovia. A population of 85 000 denotes a rather high density of 116 persons per sq. km. According to the strict criteria applied by CBR, the development potential of this moderately prosperous poviat is average. There is an airport in the locality of Dębówka. The most attractive tourist offering of the poviat is Żelazowa Wola – the birthplace of Frederic Chopin. In 1998, there were 5 542 registered enterprises, whose number grows dynamically (an increase of 13,9% as compared to 1997). The largest and best known enterprise is Master Food, an American firm employing more than 1 000 workers, and an investor of 150 mln USD in Sochaczew. Another important firm is Bakoma in Szymanów, a leading Polish yogurt producer. The stationary telephone index is high – 201 subscribers per 1 000 inhabitants (an increase of as much as 27% as compared to 1997).

Poviat of Sochaczew borders with the following poviats:
1. Gostynin,
2. Płock,
3. Płońsk,
4. Nowy Dwór Mazowiecki,
5. Western Warsaw,
6. Grodzisk Mazowiecki,
7. Żyrardów

113

POVIAT OF SOKÓŁOW PODLASKI

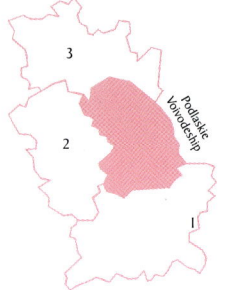

Poviat of Sokołów
Podlaski borders
with the following
poviats:
1. Siedlce,
2. Węgrów,
3. Ostrowia
Mazowiecka

This industrial-agricultural poviat (the capital in Sokołów Podlaski) lies in the eastern part of the voivodeship. It is composed of the following gminas: Bielany, Ceranów, Jabłonna Lacka, Kosów Lacki, Repki, Sabnie, Sokołów Podlaski (urban, rural) and Sterdyń. The area of the poviat totals 1 131 sq. km., and the population – 62 000, which gives a density of 55 persons per sq. km. In 1998, there were 2 924 registered enterprises (an increase of 7,5%), of which 2 785 were self-employed persons conducting economic activity. The poviat is regarded as rather unaffluent, and CBR specialists consider its development potential as low. The best known local enterprise is Zakłady Mięsne – a leading producer of cured meat. Other significant firms are Okręgowa Spółdzielna Mleczarska (dairy cooperative) in Sokołów Podlaski and Kosów Lacki, Cukrownia Sokołów (sugar plant) and ZDZ. The index of the number of stationary telephone subscribers per 1 000 inhabitants is 165. There are seven functioning sewage treatment plants.

POVIAT OF SZYDŁOWIEC

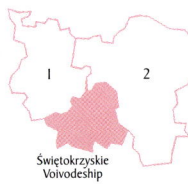

Poviat of
Szydłowiec borders
with the following
poviats:
1. Przysucha,
2. Radom

An industrial poviat, with the capital in Szydłowiec, situated in the southern part of the voivodeship. The poviat is composed of the following gminas: Chlewiska, Jastrząb, Mirów, Orońsko and Szydłowiec (urban-rural). The area totals 488 sq. km. (one the smallest in the voivodeship) and is woody. A population of 46 000 denotes a density of 94 persons per sq. km. This rather unaffluent poviat has a low development potential. In 1998, there were 1 971 registered economic subjects (an increase of 12,3%), of which 1 893 were firms run by individual entrepreneurs. The most important active institutions include: Szydłowieckie Kopalnie Kamienia Budowlanego (building stone mine), Zakłady Elektroniki Przemysłowej PROFEL (industrial electronic engineering), Spółdzielnia Inwalidów ELEKTRON (invalids' cooperative) and Huta Szkła GRACJA (glassworks). The index of the number of stationary telephone subscribers in the poviat per 1 000 inhabitants is 107 (an increase of 7,4%). There are two functioning sewage treatment plants.

Poviat of Warsaw
borders with the
following poviats:
1. Piaseczno,
2. Pruszków,
3. Western Warsaw,
4. Legionowo,
5. Wołomin,
6. Mińsk
Mazowiecki,
7. Otwock

POVIAT OF WARSAW

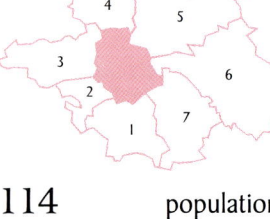

As fitting for the capital of Poland, this poviat, whose authorities are situated in Warsaw, is the largest in the voivodeship from the viewpoint of economic indices. The poviat is composed of the following gminas: Warsaw-Bemowo, Warsaw-Białołęka, Warsaw-Bielany, Warsaw-Centrum, Warsaw-Rembertów, Warsaw-Targówek, Warsaw-Ursus, Warsaw-Ursynów, Warsaw-Wawer, Warsaw-Wilanów and Warsaw-Włochy. The poviat, with an area of 494 sq. km, has a population of 1,6 mln, i.e. there are 3 239 persons per sq. km. (first place in the voivodeship). Warsaw is the most prosperous poviat not only in Mazovia, but in the country, and the revenues of its gminas exceed those of the poviat of Piaseczno (second place) by as much as 28 times! In 1998, there were 226 323 registered enterprises (first place in the voivodeship, and an increase of 9%), of which 10 554 were firms with the participation of foreign capital. This number signifies one-third of all firms in the whole country. It is impossible to propose a characteristic of the poviat of Warsaw as a distinct administrative-economic unit, since it overlaps with the town itself which, due to its status as the capital of Poland, comprises the centre of political, economic and cultural life. In order to demonstrate the attractiveness of Warsaw for foreign investors it is worth mentioning that the State Agency for Foreign Investments estimates the value of such investments as more than 10 billion USD (since 1990), contributing to the flourishing growth of Warsaw.

POVIAT OF WESTERN WARSAW

This industrial poviat, with its main seat in Warsaw, encompasses several gminas in the immediate vicinity of Warsaw. Participation in the Warsaw agglomeration is the greatest asset of the poviat, influencing the development of its gminas and creating enormous opportunities for the local population as regards education and the labour market. The poviat is composed of the following gminas: Błonie (urban-rural), Izabelin, Kampinos, Leszno, Łomianki (urban-rural), Ożarów Mazowiecki (urban-rural) and Stare Babice. A considerable part of the area, which totals 533 sq. km., is composed of the surroundings of Kampinoska Forest, the greatest tourist attraction of the poviat. A population of 85 000 gives a density of 159 persons per sq. km. The poviat is one of the wealthiest, and its development potential is assessed by CBR as high. In 1998, there were 9 350 registered enterprises (an increase of 10,2% as compared to 1997), of which 197 are subjects with the participation of foreign capital. Foreign investors in the poviat include Delphi Automotive Systems (automobile components), Nutrexpa (cocoa), Lindab (metal parts for industry and construction), Weber Maschinentechnik (electrical power engineering equipment), and Renault (spare parts distribution). The index of the number of stationary telephone subscribes per 1 000 inhabitants is 324 – second place in the voivodeship (an increase of 11,1% as compared to 1997). The positive inner migration balance of 1 110 persons also testifies to the attractiveness of the poviat.

Poviat of Western Warsaw borders with the following poviats:
1. Grodzisk Mazowiecki,
2. Sochaczew,
3. Nowy Dwór Mazowiecki,
4. Legionowo,
5. Warsaw
6. Pruszków

115

POVIAT OF WĘGRÓW

Poviat of Węgrów
borders with the
following poviats:
1. Mińsk
Mazowiecki,
2. Wołomin,
3. Wyszków,
4. Ostrów
Mazowiecka,
5. Sokołów
Podlaski,
6. Siedlce

An agricultural-industrial poviat (the capital in Węgrów), situated in the eastern part of the voivodeship. Its northern boundary is delineated by the river Bug, joined by the Liwiec, which flows across almost the very centre of the poviat. The poviat, whose area totals 1 219 sq. km., is composed of the following gminas: Grębków, Korytnica, Liw, Łochów, Miedzna, Sadowne, Stoczek, Węgrów (urban) and Wierzbno. The Miedzyńskie and Łochowskie woods, together with Liw Castle, the oldest in this part of Mazovia, and several historical monuments in Węgrów itself are regarded as the main tourist assets of the poviat. The local tourist and recreation merits are insufficiently popularised. A population of 72 000 means that this is a rather thinly populated region (59 persons per sq. km.). The development potential of this unaffluent poviat is assessed by CBR experts as low. In 1998, there were 3 725 registered enterprises (an increase of 11,9%). The leading firm is Okręgowa Spółdzielnia Mleczarska (dairy cooperative – part of the Nutricia firm), a producer of, i.a. baby food. The index of the number of stationary telephone subscribers per 1 000 inhabitants is 117 (an increase of as much as 17,1%). The poviat has at its disposal four sewage treatment plants.

POVIAT OF WOŁOMIN

Poviat of Wołomin
borders with the
following poviats:
1. Warsaw,
2. Legionowo,
3. Wyszków,
4. Węgrów,
5. Mińsk
Mazowiecki

This industrial poviat, with the capital in Wołomin, is a direct neighbour of Warsaw. The poviat is composed of the following gminas: Dąbrówka, Jadów, Klembów, Kobyłka (urban), Marki (urban), Poświętne, Radzymin (urban-rural), Strachówka, Tłuszcz (urban-rural), Wołomin (urban-rural), Ząbki (urban) and Zielonka (urban). The poviat is rather diversified, since some of the gminas are rural (e.g. Strachówka) and some are residential (e. g. the Warsaw dormitories of Zielonka or Ząbki). The area of the poviat totals 955 sq. km, of which 37,8% is arable land, and 25,4% – woods. A population of 179 000 signifies a density of 187 persons per sq. km. The development potential of this relatively prosperous poviat is assessed by CBR as average. In 1998, there were 15 933 enterprises (an increase of 9,4%), of which 102 are subjects with the participation of foreign capital. The best known are CocaCola, with a bottling plant in Radzymin, Italian Fashion (clothes), and Fantasy Foods. The poviat has a relatively good telecommunication infrastructure – 207 subscribers per 1 000 inhabitants, and a well-developed sewage treatment plant network (13).

POVIAT OF WYSZKÓW

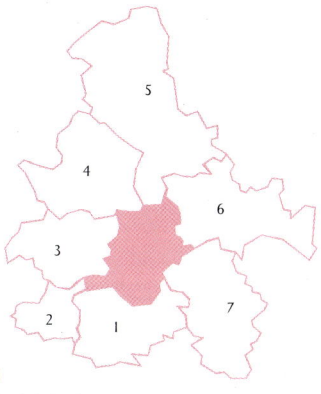

An industrial poviat (the capital in Wyszków), to the north-east of Warsaw. The poviat is crossed by the river Bug, and encircled by the Lochowskie Woods to the east and Biała Forest to the north – both enhancing its tourist offerings. The poviat, composed of the following gminas: Brańszczyk, Długosiodło, Rząśnik, Somianka, Wyszków (urban-rural) and Zabrodzie, lies along the busy route from Warsaw to Białystok and further to the Belarussian frontier crossing in Kuźnica Białostocka. The area of the poviat totals 876 sq. km., of which 37,6% is arable land, and 32,9% – woods. A population of 72 000 denotes a density of 82 persons per sq. km. The development potential of this rather unaffluent poviat is assessed by CBR as average. In 1998, there were 4 495 registered firms (an increase of 7,5% as compared to 1998). The most active firms in the poviat include: Fama-Wyszkowska Fabryka Mebli (furniture), Huta Szkła (glass-works), Daewoo-FSO Motor, Warszawskie Przedsiębiorstwo Budowlane (construction), and Browary Wyszków (brewery). The index of stationary telephone subscribers per 1 000 inhabitants is 109. There are five functioning sewage treatment plants.

Poviat of Wyszków borders with the following poviats:
1. Wołomin,
2. Legionowo,
3. Pułtusk,
4. Maków Mazowiecki,
5. Ostrołęka,
6. Ostrów,
7. Węgrów

POVIAT OF ZWOLEŃ

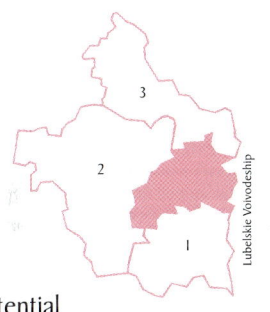

This agricultural poviat, with the capital in Zwoleń, is situated in the south-eastern part of the voivodeship. The poviat is composed of the following gminas: Kazanów, Policzna, Przyłęk, Tczów and Zwoleń (urban-rural). The area of the poviat totals 571 sq. km., of which as much as 70,1% is arable land. A population of 40 000 means a relatively low density of 69 persons per sq. km. The poviat is crossed by two small rivers: the Iłżanka and the Zwoleńka. CBR assesses the development potential of this unaffluent poviat as low. In 1998, there were 1 542 registered enterprises. One of the best known firms is Bobrowskie Kopalnie Granitu (granite mine), whose strategic investor is the American Enterprise Investors fund. Other subjects are: Rawska Odlewnia Żeliwna (iron foundary), Zakłady Mechaniczne Łucznik-Zwoleń (mechanics) and Przedsiębiorstwo Robót Drogowych (road works). The index of the number of stationary telephone subscribers per 1 000 inhabitants is 124. The poviat has at its disposal four sewage treatment plants.

Poviat of Zwoleń borders with the following poviats:
1. Lipsko,
2. Radom,
3. Kozienice

Lubelskie Voivodeship

117

POVIAT OF ŻUROMIN

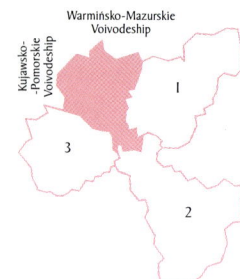

Poviat of Żuromin
borders with the
following poviats:
1. Mława,
2. Płońsk,
3. Sierpc

An agricultural-industrial poviat (the capital in Żuromin), situated in the north-western part of the voivodeship, and composed of the following gminas: Bieżuń (urban-rural), Kuczbork-Osada, Lubowidz, Lutocin, Siemiątkowo Koziebrodzkie and Żuromin (urban-rural). A population of 43 000 in an area of 805 sq. km. gives a population density of 54 persons per sq. km. The poviat is regarded as rather unaffluent, and CBR specialists assess its potential as low. In 1998, there were 2 077 registered enterprises (an increase of 11,3% as compared to 1997). The best known firms in the poviat are Zakłady Produkcji Towarów i Komponentów Samochodowych (car parts) and EMF (German), both in Żuromin, as well as Seatech Corporation in Bieżuń (spare car parts). The rather low index of the number of stationary telephone subscribers per 1 000 inhabitants (95) grows dynamically, and increased by as much as 21,1% as compared to 1997. There are six sewage treatment plants.

POVIAT OF ŻYRARDÓW

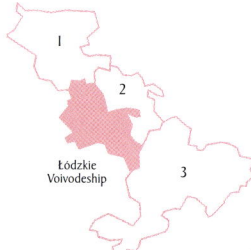

Łódzkie
Voivodeship

Poviat of Żyrardów
borders with the
following poviats:
1. Sochaczew,
2. Grodzisk
Mazowiecki,
3. Grójec

This industrial poviat, with a capital in Żyrardów, lies in the central-western part of the voivodeship. The poviat is composed of the following gminas: Mszczonów (urban), Puszcza Mariańska, Radziejowice, Wiskitki and Żyrardów (urban). The area of the poviat totals 533 sq. km,; a population of 76 000 signifies a density of 143 persons per sq. km. The poviat is not regarded as prosperous, but CBR assesses its development potential as average. In 1998, there were 5 374 registered enterprises (an increase of 11,3%), the largest being Thomson Polkolor, a French producer of television sets, employing 700 workers. Other significant firms include: FM Polska (transport and storage services), Rautauuruki (metal products), Knauf, which is building a construction material factory, Żyratex SA – Zakłady Technicznych Wyrobów Włókienniczych (technical textiles), Poldres – Zakłady Przemysłu Odzieżowego (garments), and Polfa (pharmaceutics). The index of the number of stationary telephone subscribers per 1 000 inhabitants is 213 (an increase of as much as 23,9%). The poviat has at its disposal three sewage treatment plants.

OSTROŁĘKA

Ostrołęka is a town with an imposing history – in the past, it was one of the most important urban centres in Mazovia. The town, with the status of a poviat, lies on the river Narew in the north-eastern part of the voivodeship, and occupies an area of 29 sq. km., of which 20,6% is arable land. Ostrołęka is a member of the Union of Polish Towns, and cooperates with the twin towns of Alytus

(Lithuania) and Meppen (Germany). A population of 55 000 gives a density of 1 897 persons per sq. km. In 1998, there were 5 007 registered enterprises. The economic structure is dominated by the following industries: wood and paper (Intercell), construction material (Ytong), and food (Zakład Przetwórstwa Mięsnego, SIAS Polska). Another attention-worthy factor is the high degree of the self-organisation of the local enterprises, as evidenced by the BCC Lodge, the Regional Business Club, the Ostrołęka Movement for the Support of Entrepreneurship, the Regional Initiatives House and the Trade and Services Association. In addition, Ostrołęka is the site of Agencja Rozwoju Regionalnego SA (regional development), Agencja Rozwoju Mazowsza Północno-Wschodniego (development of north-eastern Mazovia), and representatives of ten banks. The index of the number of stationary telephone subscribers per 1 000 inhabitants is 295.

The municipal poviat of Ostrołęka borders with the poviat of Ostrołęka

PŁOCK

A town with the status of a poviat (88 sq. km), situated on the Vistula in the north-western part of the voivodeship. A ranking of picturesque Polish towns would certainly place Płock at the very summit. The local assets are easily discernible upon entry into the town centre from Radziwie, along the bridge on the Vistula. Płock – the original capital of Mazovia – is a dynamically developing and second most important economic-industrial centre of the voivodeship after Warsaw. The population of the poviat totals 130 000, and the population density is 147 persons per sq. km. In 1998, there were 10 628 registered enterprises. The most significant branches of the industry are petrochemical, food, clothing, machinery and construction. The largest and best known firm, not only on a local scale but also throughout Poland, is Polski Koncern Naftowy – a supplier of liquid fuel for the domestic market, employing about 7 000 workers in Płock alone. After a fusion with CPN, the revenues of Polski Koncern Naftowy (about 20 billion złotys) place it first among all economic subjects active in Poland. Polish farmers are familiar with the Bizon combine harvester, produced in Płocka Fabryka Maszyn Żniwnych. Another local firm is Levi-Strauss, the world known producer of jeans wear. An Incubator of Innovations and Undertakings was created for the purpose of assisting small and medium enterprises; its target is the creation of places of work by exploiting the intellectual and technological potential of the local scientific and research-development centres. Furthermore, Płock has a Business Support Centre, and local entrepreneurs are associated in the Płock branch of the Business Centre Club and the Płock Capital Club. Finally, Płock is an academic centre with several thousand students in four schools of higher education. It is also a town of numerous outstanding historical monuments.

The municipal poviat of Płock borders with the poviat of Płock

RADOM

The municipal poviat of Radom borders with the poviat Radom

This town, with the status of a poviat, lies in the southern part of the voivodeship. Situated on important communication roules, both road and railroad, it has an area of 112 sq. km. and a population of 233 000, rendering it the second largest town in the voivodeship of Mazovia. In 1998, there were 23 412 registered enterprises, of which 111 were firms with the participation of foreign capital. The most vigorous firm in the town is Seita (the French purchaser of Zakłady Przemysłu Tytoniowego – tabacco), employing about 1 400 workers. Up to now, Seita has assigned 120 mln. US dollars for direct investments. Radom is the centre of numerous enterprises of the machine and armament industry, which at present face certain difficulties, but which have at their disposal numerous opportunities for further development, basically thanks to a highly skilled work force. Radom is an important academic centre with the following schools of higher education: the Radom Polytechnic, a seminary, the Private Higher School for the Protection of the Natural Environment, and the Higher School of Finances and Banking. The city of Radom in an important cultural centre, i.a. it hosts the Jan Kochanowski Theatre. The Voivodeship Police Station also enhances the status of the city.

SIEDLCE

The municipal poviat of Siedlce borders with the poviat of Siedlce

A town with the status of a poviat (32 sq. km.), situated on the E-30 Route in the central-eastern part of the voivodeship. Localisation along important communication – train and highway – routes, at a distance of about 90 kilometres from Warsaw and the Belorussian frontier, offers a chance for strengthening the role of the town as the regional, cultural and educational centre of this part of the voivodeship. The planned construction of the Świecko–Terespol highway, which is to cross the southern fragment of the town, will constitute a successive impulse for its development. The modernisation of a section of the railway E-20 route, to be completed in 2000, will considerably facilitate contact with Warsaw: the Siedlce –Warsaw journey will take less than a hour (instead of two hours). The population of the town totals 74 000. In 1998, there were 6 883 registered enterprises. Quite possibly, one of the best known commodities made in Siedlce is the "Chopin" luxury vodka, produced by Polmos SA. Other leading firms include: Real SA, Mostostal Siedlce (bridge construction), Drosed – Siedleckie Zakłady Drobiarskie (poultry), KWANGJIN – ZPP Poland and Siedlecka Fabryka Mebli (furniture). Siedlce is an important educational centre for the eastern part of the voivodeship of Mazovia. An essential role is played by the Podlasie Academy, which provides an opportunity for higher education for pedagogues and future representatives of modern agriculture. Two sewage treatment plants operate there. The Higher School of Finances and Management was opened this year. The town signed friendship and cooperation agreements with the gmina of Dasing (Germany), the town of Pescantina (Italy), and the self-government region of Vilnius (Lithuania). Furthermore, it maintains contacts with Denmark, Ukraine and Russia.

Jacek Żurowski

CULTURE

■

One of the most prolific artistic conceptions propagated by Mazovia was the utilisation of folk culture in music, literature and the plastic arts as well as the elevation of the qualities of this category of culture to a national level. The fullest and most perfect expression of this idea was achieved in the music of Frederic Chopin, the works of Stanisław Moniuszko and the Kurpie songs by Karol Szymanowski. Inspiration sought in folk culture appeared in yet anther form in *Promethidion* by Cyprian Kamil Norwid, which accentuates not so much artistic merits as the ethical and aesthetic order of folk culture. In times less distant to us, folk art inspired graphic works by Władysław Skoczylas and Tadeusz Kulisiewicz, stagings by Kazimierz Dejmek, stage design by Andrzej Stopka and Adam Kilian and the prose of Kazimierz Nowak and Wiesław Myśliwski.

HERITAGE

The cultural heritage of lands comprising Mazowieckie voivodeship constitutes the most vital and richest component of the cultural tradition of contemporary Poland. This holds true predominantly for Warsaw whose function as the capital coincides with the period of an intense shaping of the Polish nation. Nevertheless, it should be kept in mind that this was also the time of the emergence of the Warsaw cultural environment which absorbed the most ambitious and talented individuals from the entire country; their greatest source proved to be Mazovia. Both Mazovia and Podlasie comprised regions which, in numerous aspects, remained backward – overpopulated, with an economy ruined during the seventeenth and eighteenth century, and with almost one-quarter of the inhabitants representing the petty, poor, but valiant gentry.

The Mazovian legacy is much more extensive than those motifs which became part of the great cultural tradition. Many components were irretrievably damaged and scattered, or their traces became obliterated. Even the culture bequeathed by the population of Warsaw is known only superficially and selectively, not to mention its material devastation incurred during the Warsaw Uprising. Let us not forget the variegated legacy of other Mazovian centres, predominantly Płock, which during the reign of Władysław Herman and Bolesław the Wrymouth played the role of the capital, or the cultural accomplishments of Czersk, Sochaczew, Pułtusk, Ciechanów, Grójec and all those towns which were never part of historical Mazovia, but which today find themselves within the administrative boundaries of Mazowieckie voivodeship (e.g. Radom and Szydłowiec).

The history of many of those urban centres goes back to the distant past, and the political and economic impact exerted by some of them exceeded the influence of Warsaw. The seventeenth and eighteenth century saw a decline caused by many wars. Mazovia was by no means a land which enjoyed peace. Generation after generation fell in battle. The gravest population losses took place during the second world war. The extermination policy implemented by the Nazi occupant led to the annihilation of almost the entire Jewish community which perished in ghettos and death camps. The Warsaw population ceased to exit as a community, and the toll of the Warsaw Uprising of 1944 reached almost a quarter million of the residents of the Polish capital; the survivors were resettled and dispersed, and the town itself was reduced to rubble. It is not surprising, therefore, that Mazovia found it so difficult to preserve tradition and continue cultural processes.

Regardless of which Mazovian town or locality we examine closer, we discover in their history admirable cultural achievements, testimony of former grandeur, and the names of people who were born, brought up, and worked there – men who made great contributions to the development of the arts and science and to

From the Mazovian pantheon

Jan Kochanowski

Fryderyk Chopin

Hugo Kołłątaj

Władysław Reymont

Henryk Sienkiewicz

Zygmunt Krasiński

Oskar Kolberg

Bolesław Prus

Maria Curie-Skłodowska

123

shaping national self-awareness. Without Jan Kochanowski, Piotr Skarga, Julian Ursyn Niemcewicz, Hugo Kołłątaj, Joachim Lelewel, Frederic Chopin, Cyprian Kamil Norwid, Oskar Kolberg, Henryk Sienkiewicz, Bolesław Prus, Aleksander Świętochowski, Stanisław Brzozowski, Władysław Reymont, Bolesław Leśmian, Wacław Berent, Leopold Staff, Julian Tuwim, Władysław Broniewski, Janusz Korczak, Krzysztof Kamil Baczyński, Maria Dąbrowska, Konstanty Ildefons Gałczyński, Antoni Słonimski, Jarosław Iwaszkiewicz, Maksymilian and Aleksander Gierymski, Jacek Malczewski, Stanisław and Stanisław Ignacy Witkiewicz, Karol Szymanowski and Witold Lutosławski, to mention only some of the outstanding examples, the spiritual structure of the Polish nation would have been different, and Polish culture poorer. Alongside their accomplishments, which constitute not only a legacy, but also tradition, i.e. the live contents of the thoughts and images cherished by generations of modern Poles, there exists a myriad of the names of less celebrated men of letters and artists who prepared wider groups of society for the reception of supreme creative achievements generating the cultural development of society. Such men include Władysław of Gielniowo, author of the oldest Easter hymn in Polish, and an entire legion of poets from the era of national uprisings, from Gustaw Ehrenberg to Krystyna Krahelska – a poetess born in Belorussia who studied, wrote, and fought in Warsaw.

Without delving into the distant history of present-day Mazovia and Podlasie – the age of Celtic and German peoples – we shall concentrate our attention on the more recent past, keeping in mind that the culture of those lands, and primarily the towns, was moulded by two large communities: German and Jewish. Up to the second world war, the Jewish minority formed a significant part of the residents of the towns and townlets of Mazovia, Podlasie and the Kielce region; hundreds of thousands of Jews lived in Warsaw alone. The two ethnic groups remained in a certain isolation, determined by, i.a. religious and cultural differences. The population of German descent was more open to contacts with others, and in the second or third generation succumbed easier to Polonisation, as witnessed by the numerous biographies of Polish patriots of German origin. The permeation of mutual impacts between Poles and Jews followed a slower course, hampered by greater obstacles, particularly in the plebeian strata. Nevertheless, despite the retention of cultural distinctness, we encounter numerous examples of conciliation between attachment to a national group and involvement in the struggle for the independence of Poland. Widely known examples include Berek Joselowicz, merchant and colonel of the Polish army during the Kościuszko Insurrection and the Duchy of Warsaw, Beer Meisels, a Warsaw rabbi active in preparations for the November and January uprisings or the truly heroic and saintly figure of Janusz Korczak.

The cultural life of the Polish, Jewish, and German communities possessed distinct features; nonetheless, mutual cultural influence and a suffusion of impacts, rendered indelible also in language, continued to take place. Unfortunately, the impression made by the cultures of particular ethnic minorities within the network of the society of a single state and its tradition, and, even more so, the shaping of features decisive for a certain cultural community, well above all differences, did not become the theme of more thorough studies; worse, living forms of such relations have already become part of the irretrievable past. An overwhelming fragment of the material legacy and written sources has been destroyed. This process was not incurred by time itself, a fact which could be regarded as the outcome of natural neglect, but due to the intentional activity of the Swedes, Prussians, Russians and Germans who occupied Mazovia. The plight of the castles of the Mazovian dukes and of the Royal Castle in Warsaw, bombed in 1939 and methodically reduced to ruins by the Germans already in the wake of the Uprising of 1944, as well as the devastation of the magnificent collections of the Załuski Library, the National Library, and the Municipal Archive of Warsaw are an example of particularly painful losses and unprecedented crimes perpetrated against cultural legacy.

Time proved to be ruthless also for the resources of material heritage. Almost all traces of the Mennonites who came to Mazovia from the Netherlands and Friesland have been obliterated, leaving behind mere remnants of dams, houses and cemeteries. Such vestiges have to be sought by resorting to methods resembling those applied by archeologists searching for prehistorical evidence of the past. Relics of the material culture of the Jewish community are scarce – the Jews themselves are no longer, only a few lived through the Holocaust, and a fraction of the survivors stayed in Poland. The limited material testimony of Jewish culture includes the beautiful Sezession orphanage of the Jewish Kahal in Stara Praga district of Warsaw, the tsadik palace and the prayer-house in Góra Kalwaria, and the original and charming villas in Świder, Konstancin and Otwock.

An equally small number of buildings survived in Warsaw itself; let us remember that the majority of the houses in the Old Town, along the Royal Tract, and in the New Town are actually restored historical monuments. The process of restoration was based on thorough studies, and, to a great measure, on old building material and technologies – nonetheless, it was the recreation of something with whose loss the local population did not want to come to terms. The outcome of this unprecedented undertaking was the reconstruction of the barbarously destroyed town. In its course, it became apparent that not everything could be rebuilt and restored in its former shape.

Polish society perceived the attractiveness of the culture of Mazovia in supplying ideas which integrated assorted social forces, and which at a given historical moment were of prime importance for the further existence of the nation. Let us now take a closer look at prominent notions associated directly with artistic creativity.

The importance of the aforementioned conception of the restitution of material and institutional resources, connected with the names of, i.a. Stanisław Lorentz, Jan Zachwatowicz and Piotr Biegański, reached far beyond the protection of historical monu-

The "Mazowsze" Song and Dance Ensemble made great contributions to the popularisation of Mazovian foklore

ments and artistic culture. At the same time, it defined a specific attitude towards the reinstatement of those resources and institutional forms which had been intentionally destroyed by the occupant, and whose existence was to signify a return to the normal life of a nation and its functioning within the family of European nations.

One of the most prolific artistic conceptions propagated by Mazovia was the utilisation of folk culture in music, literature and the plastic arts as well as the elevation of the qualities of this category of culture to a national level. The fullest and most perfect expression of this idea was achieved in the music of Frederic Chopin, the works of Stanisław Moniuszko and the Kurpie songs by Karol Szymanowski. Inspiration sought in folk culture appeared in yet anther form in *Promethidion* by Cyprian Kamil Norwid, which accentuates not so much artistic merits as the ethical and aesthetic order of folk culture. In times less distant to us, folk art in-

Sierpc, Skansen-
-Museum of the
Mazovian Village

spired graphic works by Władysław Skoczylas and Tadeusz Kulisiewicz, stagings by Kazimierz Dejmek, stage design by Andrzej Stopka and Adam Kilian and the prose of Kazimierz Nowak and Wiesław Myśliwski. The idea of resorting to folk

126

creativity conceived as a reservoir of national culture found its best examples in Mazovia where it is based on the most profound interpretations of its meanings. This pertains both to high-level artistic accomplishments and to diverse forms of popular art as exemplified by the "Mazowsze" Song and Dance Ensemble created by Tadeusz Sygietyński and Mira Zimińska. The earliest and fullest expression of reference to sources of urban, plebeian folklore also took place in Mazovia and, in particular, in Warsaw.

At this point, it seems worth indicating a certain general feature of a comprehension of culture which probably distinguishes Mazovia from other regions of the country and defines a specific ethos. The population of the capital and the environs of Płock, Siedlce, Węgrów and Żyrardów attaches high rank to artistic culture, primarily literature, but also to science, technology and social work. This attitude is testified by tokens of memory which take into consideration equal proportions of assorted domains of culture and which are expressed in the names of streets, buildings, cultural institutions, statues, commemorative plaques, showrooms, and various publications. The names of Maria Curie-Skłodowska, Tytus Chałubiński, Ludwik Krzywicki, Tadeusz Kotarbiński, Stefan Bryła and Janusz Groszkowski are well embedded in our memory.

At the same time, it should be noted that ideas endowed with a wide resonance are accompanied by an acknowledgement of the right to pursue independent art and to focus exclusively on one's own artistic workshop and aesthetic values free from all ethical obligations (Zenon Przesmycki-Miriam, Karol Szymanowski and Wacław Berent). In a similar vein, models of involvement in combat contrast with attention concentrated on intimacy or privacy – as in the works of Miron Białoszewski and, predominantly, his *Pamiętnik z powstania warszawskiego* (Diary from the Warsaw Uprising).

Naturally, it is impossible to outline, even approximately, the role played by creativity originating in the capital of Mazovia in the shaping of the cultural consciousness of successive generations of Poles. In order to render its characteristic more complete, special attention should be paid to the diversity of ideological proposals and a *sui generis* "surplus" of creative accomplishments. The latter is essentially the indispensable property of a leading cultural centre (the capital) if it is to guarantee the cultivation of all important domains, forms and manners of comprehending culture.

CONTEMPORANEITY

A distinctive trait of the culture of contemporary Warsaw and Mazovia is the aforementioned "surplus". It is the outcome of the enormous resources represented by the creative milieus of Mazowieckie voivodeship, the immense potential of environs interested in participation in culture and a well-developed infrastructure serving culture.

127

Warsaw is a focal point for numerous professional groups dealing with the arts, the protection of the cultural legacy, scientific research within the widely comprehended humanities, and education (the arts and the humanities). It is the largest environment of this kind in the country, and the place of residence for almost half of all Polish creators representing assorted disciplines of art – men of letters, theatrical actors, conductors, soloists-instrumentalists, composers and film directors. The same holds true for architects, painters, graphic artists, sculptors, stage designers, conservators of paintings, sculptures, books and incunabula, as well as photographers. In each of the above mentioned fields we encounter the names of outstanding and renowned creators. Suffice to mention several out of a total of almost 5 000 artists, a thousand men of letters, a hundred composers of so-called serious music, cultivated by philharmonics and the theatre, and almost a thousand architects – all told, tens of thousands of representatives of the milieu associated with Warsaw and the present-day Mazowieckie voivodeship. Our choice is just as subjective as is our highly selective memory and the variegated values regarded as prominent. The list includes celebrated artists together with the slightly forgotten, those barely inaugurating their career, and those who find themselves in the midst of their *Sturm und Drang* phase. Each name deserves a distinct and by no means brief justification, since the accomplishments of every single person are different and highly individual and it is difficult to capture the richness of talents and attitudes in each domain. This feature, decisive for the force of the inspirational tension prevailing in the artistic milieu of Warsaw, co-creates conditions conducive for creativity.

Mention is due to the following representatives of literature living in the capital: Halina Auderska, Julia Hartwig, Lesław Bartelski, Julian Wiktor Gomulicki, Józef Hen, Marian Grześczak, Ryszard Kapuściński, Tadeusz Konwicki, Piotr Kuncewicz, Janusz Krasiński, Zygmunt Kubiak, Wiesław Myśliwski, Jarosław Marek Rymkiewicz, Eustachy Rylski, Andrzej Szczypiorski and Wojciech Żukrowski.

The leading artists are: Magdalena Abakanowicz, Teresa Pągowska, Erna Rosenstein, Magdalena Więcek, Stefan Gierowski, Józef Szajna, Henryk Tomaszewski, Jacek Sienicki, Rajmund Ziemski, and the equally brilliant Franciszek Starowieyski, Waldemar Świerzy, Gustaw Zemła, Xymena Zaniewska, Zofia de Ines, Andrzej Kreutz-Majewski and Krystian Jarmuszkiewicz, Wojciech Szańkowski, Ryszard Kowalski, Edward Dwurnik, Eugeniusz Dobkowski, Jerzy Kalima, Zofia Kulik, Andrzej Fogt, Marian Czapla, Jarosław Modzelewski, Marek Sobczyk, Andrzej Strumiłło, Aleksander Kozyrski, Jacek Ziemiński, and Daniel Wnuk. Among the youngest painters let me mention Małgorzata Szołtysik and Kuba Grydniewski.

The composers residing in Warsaw include: Witold Rudziński, Włodzimierz Kotoński, Henryk Czyż, Zbigniew Rudziński, Zygmunt Krauze, Marian Borkowski, and the youngest Paweł Mykietyn.

128

Attention is due to the following film directors – Jerzy Kawalerowicz, Andrzej Wajda, Jerzy Hoffman, Krzysztof Zanussi, Janusz Kondratiuk, Marek Piwowski, Juliusz Machulski.

The large group of Warsaw-based architects is represented by Roman Dziekoński (a rare example of three successive generations working the same field), Marek Budzyński (author of the new seat of the Supreme Court in Warsaw), the visionary architect Jacek Damięcki, Czesław Bielecki and Oskar Hansen, author of futuristic projects and the most accomplished contributor to shaping the awareness of Warsaw architects and town planners.

Just as varied is the milieu of the humanities, aesthetes, historians and theoreticians of art, scholars dealing with Polish studies, historians of philosophy, philosophers and historians of culture.

The artistic environment attaches foremost significance to the work conducted by scientific institutes dealing with contemporary culture, the philosophy of art and aesthetics, and cultural transformations within society. Such institutes include noteworthy centres in the Polish Academy of Sciences, such as the Institute of Literary Studies and the Institute of Art, which concentrates its attention on the arts, the theatre, music, and the cinema. A distinct position is occupied by the Institute of Culture, supervised by the Ministry of Culture and studying transformations of contemporary culture, the philosophy of art, and the cultural policy of the state and territorial self-governments. The Institute of Polish Culture at Warsaw University examines the evolution of social consciousness and new forms of artistic communication as well as alternative culture. Assorted departments of the National Library investigate readership and problems associated with publications; they also set up bibliographies. The Podlaska Academy in Siedlce deals with

Radziejowice. Larch manor house from eighteenth century

contemporary culture and focuses its attention on regionalism and changes of local environments. Warsaw is also the place of residence and work of numerous art, music, film and theatre critics.

Much could be written about the creative milieu of Warsaw, its eminent representatives and achievements. In our attempted outline of culture in Mazowieckie voivodeship it seems worth accentuating three essential features of the creative environment of the capital: its complimentariness, diversity, and innovativeness, and to emphasise the increasingly discernible tendency towards development and migration among people associated with the arts.

Complimentariness denotes a representation, within a single centre, of all those domains and specialisations characteristic for contemporary artistic culture, which make it possible to undertake every artistic venture under the condition of sufficient financial means.

The diversity of the creative environment of Warsaw is tantamount to the occurrence of numerous types of artistic-aesthetic awareness and equally multiple trends. This feature permits the cultivation of popular art as well as art intended for "high" circulation, which demands equally "high" competence from its audience. Thanks to this trait, the creative milieu of a given town or region may effectively satisfy the needs or tastes of assorted recipients. Indubitably, the artistic environment of Warsaw, enriched by the potential of artists from other, lesser or greater cultural centres of the voivodeship, in particular Radom, Płock, Siedlce, Ostrołęka and Ciechanów, has full chances for this type of effective activity, for meeting the diverse requirements of the community of the region and for exerting extensive impact upon other parts of contemporary Poland.

The creative environment of the capital, conceived as a collective category, discloses yet another feature decisive for its dynamics, namely the ability for innovation. Naturally, innovation is always a proposal made by a creative individual, although, in certain circumstances, this concept may be referred to a group, i.e. whenever we wish to draw attention to an approval of new ideas or attempts. Such a reception stems from positive anticipation and an orientation towards novelties.

Tendencies distinctly present in the voivodeship include the emergence of new cultural centres. The matter at stake concerns not only former voivodeship seats, such as Płock, Radom and Siedlce, where the past quarter of a century witnessed significant cultural investments, but also lesser urban centres, either distant from the cultural centre of Poland or constituting its satellites. A rule prevailing in the recent years is the construction of new creative environments thanks to secondary schools, polytechnics and branches of higher schools based in Warsaw. Such investments require pedagogues representing assorted fields, always with skills suitable for the humanities, and at times, with practical artistic training. Another discernible tendency is the settling down of professional artists in centres outside Warsaw. Decisions to move to smaller towns and, at times, villages are the outcome of diverse factors, i.a. lower living costs, the construction of a home and a studio, or a desire to free oneself from city hub-bub which hinders concentration; other reasons include an easier maintenance of contacts with the centre and its institutions as well as the economic and social animation of Mazovia. Finally, this trend is also favoured by a tendency towards situating certain institutions, which serve particular functions, out-side Warsaw. In the past, this approach was expressed by the conversion of the manor house in Obory , designed by Tylman of Gameren, into a creative work centre intended for men of letters; a similar role is played by the palace in Radziejowice, adapted for international courses addressed to young com-posers. Suburban Konstancin is the site of the Creative Work House and a Home of Artists – Vet-erans of the Polish Stage, Karolin near Otrębusy is the seat of the "Mazowsze" Song and Dance Ensemble, and Łucznica has a Centre of Cultural Animation. A unique Polish Sculpture Centre has been organised in Orońsko near Radom.

In smaller urban centres, creative environments are devised by teachers, prima-rily of history, Polish, and music as well as amateur theatre instructors and artists. All constitute probably the most active category of representatives of the arts, engaged in seeking favourable conditions for opening workshops as well as bene-fiting from available material and cheaper technical assistance. Teachers are also the prime animators of numerous Mazovian cultural associations of lovers of the region, which endeavour to cultivate local tradition and, frequently, to restore interrupted traditions of the past.

THE PUBLIC

An essential factor in the cultural dynamics of Warsaw and the entire voivode-ship is the great potential represented by active recipients of culture. Naturally, this potential is found predominantly in Warsaw, a town of numerous higher edu-cation institutions and secondary schools, the place of residence of employees of state and self-government administration as well as civil servants, the seat of as-sorted central institutions and enterprises, and a centre visited daily by thousands of clients and tourists.

The most active section of this public is, naturally, academic youth and students of assorted-level schools. Foreign visitors attending spectacles staged by Warsaw theatres are struck by the predominating presence of young people among the audience, in contrast to the West where participation in theatrical events has succumbed to a certain ritualisation cultivated by the wealthier and more stable social strata, even if only due to high costs.

In Warsaw, with its 53 schools of higher learning and more than 160 000 students, the asset of people intensively interested in public cultural life is of enormous significance for shaping the cultural style of the entire population of the city, the voivodeship and, ultimately, the country. Other centres of the voivodeship of Mazovia, such as Radom, Płock, Ostrołęka, Siedlce, Grodzisk Mazowiecki,

Pułtusk, Sochaczew and Żyrardów have their own student environments, which total about 45 000 persons. The entire population of the present-day region, and particularly its young generation, upon the initiative of schools, visit the attractive artistic institutions of Warsaw, and thus constitute the cultural public of the capital. A second, rather numerous, category of recipients of culture, disclosing "heightened activity", is made up of senior citizens.

■

Cultural Infrastructure

Typical features of the cultural infrastructure of the voivodeship are its great variety and disproportions. This most extensive configuration has at its disposal almost all types of institutions and facilities characteristic for the contemporary culture of civilisationally advanced states. Warsaw, in particular, plays the role of an all-sidedly developed centre of artistic institutions – the largest and, in numerous realms, dominating in relation to other domestic centres. With the exception of Warsaw, Płock and Radom, cultural centres in the voivodeship fulfil chiefly local functions. Now for a rough survey of the most important artistic institutions in Warsaw and the voivodeship.

Theatres

A special role among all the dramatic theatres is played by the National Theatre not only owing to its rank in the past, contemporary form, and status of the national stage – as expressed in direct supervision of the Ministry of Culture and National Legacy – but, predominantly, due to the fact that its ensemble is composed of outstanding Polish actors; artistic management is entrusted to Jerzy Grzegorzewski, the eminent director and stage designer. The theatre, situated in a building reconstructed after a fire, which broke out in 1987, has at its disposal two stages, of which the larger uses modern technical equipment and a fire-alarm system. The theatre presents leading examples of Polish and world drama, interpreted by the most outstanding Polish directors: Kazimierz Dejmek, Adam Hanuszkiewicz, Kazimierz Kutz, Maciej Prus, Henryk Tomaszewski, Janusz Wiśniewski and, obviously, Janusz Grzegorzewski. Future collaborators will include such directors as Jan Englert and Mikołaj Grabowski. The current repertoire is composed of plays by Gombrowicz, Różewicz, Wyspiański, Strindberg, Kleist and Shakespeare. The National Theatre boasts of such celebrated actors as: Teresa Budzisz-Krzyżanowska, Anna Chodakowska, Dorota Segda, Jan Englert, Mariusz Benoit, Krzysztof Kolberger, Olgierd Łukaszewicz, Jerzy Łapiński, Jerzy Trela and Zbigniew Zamachowski.

The Polski Theatre, specialising in Polish drama, is a stage of rich tradition and with excellent Polish actors, such as Nina Andrycz, Grażyna Barszczewska, Magdalena Zawadzka, Bogdan Baer, Damian Damięcki, Ignacy Gogolewski and Wiesław

Gołas. Until recently, the head of the Polski Theatre was Andrzej Łapicki – celebrated actor, unrivalled director and a nonpareil performer in comedies by Aleksander Fredro. Today, the artistic manager is Jarosław Kilian, a representative of the younger generation. Public opinion eagerly awaits further proposals, and attaches great hope to the style in which the new manager will continue the tradition of this second most prestigious stage in Warsaw.

Twenty stationary theatres, with a steady repertoire, include at least five other noteworthy stages, whose distinct artistic profile was shaped in the course of a longer period of time, and whose specificity is delineated by an outstanding creative personality and a permanent ensemble. Such theatres include the Ateneum, for many years headed by Janusz Warmiński and, today, by Gustaw Holoubek, with such excellent actors as Anna Seniuk, Ewa Wiśniewska, Michał Bajor, Piotr Fronczewski, Jan Matyjaszkiewicz, Janusz Michałowski, Bartosz Opania and Leonard Pietraszak. Both stages present the classical Polish dramatic repertoire, with a certain predilection towards a psychological interpretation of the plays; the small Scena 61 features contemporary European drama, enacted by a limited group of actors, and recitals of songs performed by members of the theatre.

From many years now, the Współczesny Theatre, headed by Maciej Englert, continues the artistic line conceived by Erwin Axer, outstanding director and long-term head of the theatre. This stage specialises in contemporary dramatic literature, accentuating the relations between the *personae dramatis* and psychological analysis. Furthermore, it has at its disposal a select group of fine actors, and is concerned with the presence of talented artists capable of creating comic roles; today, such a position is held by Krzysztof Kowalewski.

Another distinguished group of actors is to be found in the Powszechny Theatre, whose repertoire is based on contemporary European dramas and popular plays. Ewa Dałkowska, Mirosława Dubrawska, Krystyna Janda, Joanna Żółkowska, Janusz Gajos Władysław Kowalski and Piotr Machalica guarantee success for each play in which they appear. A particularly admirable career is pursued by Janusz Gajos, who did not succumb to the stereotype of a popular hero of a television series, but due to his theatrical roles enjoys the highly regarded rank of a dramatic actor.

The Nowy Theatre is headed by Adam Hanuszkiewicz, excellent actor and highly controversial director. Similarly as the National Theatre, which Hanuszkiewicz managed in the past, the Nowy Theatre stages classics of Polish dramas interpreted and adapted for the purpose of stirring the interest of the young audience, and embarks upon a discourse about contemporaneity seen through the prism of texts by nineteenth-century Polish Romanticists (e.g. *Balladyna* by Słowacki) and naturalists (e.g. *Moralność pani Dulskiej* [The Morality of Mrs. Dulska] by Zapolska). The staging conceptions proposed by Adam Hanuszkiewicz are questioned by certain theatrical critics, but highly approved by the young theatregoers, even

133

more so considering that the Nowy Theatre has an equally youthful group of well-trained actors.

A similar path towards winning the young audience is followed by Zbigniew Jarzyna, artistic director of the Rozmaitości Theatre and an interpreter of plays by Stanisław Ignacy Witkiewicz (*Bzik tropikalny* [Tropical Craze]) or Aleksander Fredro.

The above mentioned Warsaw stages are supplemented by the theatres of Płock and Radom. The former has the Jerzy Szaniawski Theatre, named after a playwright who lived in Jadwisin (Mazovia) and whose works have become part of the canon of Polish twentieth-century drama. In Radom, the same rank is ascribed to the Jan Kochanowski Powszechny Theatre.

The Płock theatre proposes a greatly ambitious classical repertoire, contemporary plays, adaptations of European literature as well as titles intended for youth and children. Alongside *Dziady* (Forefathers' Eve) by Mickiewicz, *Faustus* by Goethe, and *Dulska* by Zapolska, directed by A. Hanuszkiewicz, other greatly popular titles include Hasek's *History of the Moderate Progress Party* and *The Snow Queen* by Andersen. The Kochanowski Theatre attracts large audiences by including into its programme lavish musicals, staged at great expense, and classical plays involving small groups of actors.

While focusing our attention on stationary theatres with permanent groups of actors, we should keep in mind the fact that the very conception of the theatre evolves towards a much more flexible structure. The attractiveness of the dramatic art is determined to an increasing degree by groups formed by directors and by actors not tied to a repertoire theatre who prepare a certain spectacle and, as in the past, present it independently in various towns. Moreover, the number of theatrical ensembles founded by students or even secondary school pupils is rising. At times, thanks to their admirable efforts, they attain impressive artistic results. Such theatres present their spectacles in various parts of Warsaw during the summer season. The Festival of Garden Theatres, held in the capital in July, is a review of youth theatres which has won the approval of large audiences.

Music

A strong aspect of the cultural life of Warsaw are concerts, musical theatres, and performances given by assorted musical ensembles. In this domain, cultural life takes place at various levels and differs as regards artistic contents, the style of the music and types of reception.

Supreme status is enjoyed by the National Philharmonic and the Wielki Theatre – National Opera. Connoisseurs of old opera praise the Warsaw Chamber Opera. Popular music, both in its nineteenth-century Parisian-Venetian version and as American musicals, is part of the repertoire of the Roma-Musical Theatre.

The National Philharmonic is headed by the excellent conductor by Kazimierz Kord, an outstanding interpreter of great oratorio-orchestra forms; the second artistic individuality is Jerzy Maksymiuk, a frequent conductor of symphonies. Apart from a permanent series of Friday and Saturday symphonic concerts, the Philharmonic presents (usually on Tuesdays) extremely attractive chamber concerts and performances given by celebrated Polish soloists or, more frequently, world renowned artists.

Żelazowa Wola. Birthplace of Frederic Chopin

Warsaw boasts of many orchestras, chamber ensembles, and excellent choirs, to mention only "Symphonia Varsovia", whose honorary conductor was Yehudi Menuchin, and the Wilanowski Quartet. The Polish capital also has numerous concert halls with excellent acoustics, a feature characteristic for certain Warsaw historical objects and churches, which often become the site of orchestral, choral and organ concerts. An active organiser is the National Concert Bureau which has great experience in this field and expertise in combining a programme with the given architectonic object or plein-air conditions. Other localities in the voivodeship also propose attractive concerts, such as those organised in Żelazowa Wola near Sochaczew – the birthplace-museum of Frederic Chopin and surrounding park.

Assorted towns in the voivodeship of Mazovia also harbour the ambition of possessing permanent symphonic orchestras or chamber ensembles. Such is the role performed by the Płock Symphonic Orchestra, which holds concerts for the local music-lovers and educational events for young listeners – part of a well-conceived music curriculum. The high level of the work carried out by this orchestra is testified by joint performances with such outstanding soloists as Barbara

135

Hesse-Bukowska, Stefania Woytowicz, Konstanty Andrzej Kulka and Janusz Olej-
niczak.

Radom has a chamber orchestra of its own – the Capella Radomiensis.

Mention is due to the representative stage of the capital – the National Opera, which has at its disposal a vast theatrical building, one of the largest European stages equipped with superb technical facilities, and a smaller chamber
hall. The building itself contains all that is indispensable for a large group of
musicians-instrumentalists, singers, dancers and technicians, together with the
showrooms of the Theatre Museum. The National Opera is directed by Jacek
Kaspszyk, a well-known conductor who in the course of the past two years has
already elevated musical performance to a superior level thanks to, i.a. a first-rate

National Opera,
performance of
"Halka"
by Stanisław
Moniuszko, group
scene from Act I

group of soloists, including such acclaimed names as Ewa Podleś, Hanna Lisowska,
Andrzej Hiolski, Bogdan Paprocki, Bogusław Morka and Wiesław Ochman. Not
all the singers have a permanent contract with the Opera which relies on the cooperation of renowned European soloists, engaged for particular spectacles; at
the same time, attempts are made to promote young Polish opera singers. In the
nearest future, Jacek Kaspszyk will once again stage *The Valkyrie* by Wagner, an
opera prepared some ten years ago by the late Robert Satanowski, the eminent
art director of the Wielki Theatre. In the current repertoire opera lovers emphasise stagings of *Der Rosenkavalier* by R. Strauss, *Don Giovanni* by Mozart,
Halka by S. Moniuszko, and a ballet interpretation of the *Third Symphony* by
Michał Górecki, with choreography by Krzysztof Pastor, a representative of the
young generation who already enjoys world-wide acclaim. The Warsaw stage at-

taches considerable attention to the presentation of ballets, and features its own realisations as well as those proposed by excellent European ensembles, i.a. Russian and Italian.

The European uniqueness of the Warsaw Chamber Orchestra, directed by Stefan Sutkowski, is due to the fact that it is probably the only ensemble whose repertoire embraces all the operas by Mozart, including those written by the young composer, as well as numerous Baroque operas by Monteverdi and Hasse. Previous realisations became the basis of the Mozart Opera Festival, organised usually in June and July, and the Baroque Opera Festival held in the autumn. Singers of the Chamber Opera perform in a small theatre on a miniature stage – but it is this quality which enables the audience to concentrate its attention on the excellent music.

Every September, the Polish capital becomes the site of the "Warsaw Autumn" Music Festival, which comprises a review of contemporary works by composers from Poland and the world, as well as compositions which initiated twentieth-century modern music. The programme is extensive, and the concerts are held in assorted concert halls and theatres as well as in the Witold Lutosławski television hall, known for its excellent acoustics. The festival is celebrated for creating an atmosphere of a true meeting of lovers of modern music, and an opportunity for becoming acquainted with musicians from different parts of the world. Moreover, it is usually accompanied by discussions concerning contemporary music and art exhibits.

Naturally – highest rank is ascribed to the International Frederic Chopin Piano Competition, held every five years, an event which facilitated the artistic debut of many young virtuosos.

MUSEUMS

One of the essential attractions of Warsaw and numerous other towns in the voivodeship are 92 museums, of which 37 are situated in the capital. They include typical art museums, amassing and presenting artworks, theatrical memorabilia, documents of literary life and musical instruments. Others are museums-residences, biographical museums of writers, sculptors and scientists as well as natural history and history of technology museums; those frequently encountered in smaller localities gather objects and sources concerning local issues.

The National Museum in Warsaw has the largest collection of art and a large staff composed of scientists, historians of art, and conservators. Established in 1862 as the Museum of Fine Arts, in 1916 it became known as the National Museum, originally situated in Podwale Street. The construction of the buildings designed by Tadeusz Tołwiński specially for museum purposes was inaugurated in 1926, and completed in 1938. During the second world war part of the collection was plundered by the German occupant; a considerable fragment of the loot was returned after the war. Today, the most valuable

137

exhibits are monuments of ancient art, Polish and European painting and the crafts. The fundamental part of the monuments of ancient art originates from excavations conducted by Prof. Kazimierz Michałowski during the 1930s, 1950s and 1960s in Egypt, the Crimea, Syria, Sudan (the famous frescoes from Faras) and Cyprus.

The National Museum features an extensive collection of North European, Italian, French, Russian and Old Russian paintings and sculptures; particularly outstanding canvases include examples of the Old Dutch masters and paintings from the eighteenth-century Low Countries (J. Momper, J. Breughel). Valuable Italian works by Pinturicchio and Gentile Bellini are supplemented by a set of Venetian paintings from the eighteenth century. Apart from a large collection of seventeenth – nineteenth-century icons, special attention among Old Russian and Russian canvases is due to the so-called pieredvizhniki (Kramskoy and Makovsky), the seascape painter Ayvazovsky, and the nineteenth-century artists Levitan, Niestierov and Sierov.

A superb collection is composed of mediaeval altar paintings from Pomerania, Toruń and Lower Silesia. Unfortunately, due to the lack of sufficient space, only a fragment of the extensive collections of the decorative arts, engravings, drawings, coins and medals is on display. The best-known and relatively best-featured is a popular set of paintings depicting the development of Polish art from the sixteenth century to contemporary times. Part of the rich collection, totalling 10 000 paintings and sculptures, is on loan in other museums, while another part remains in storage. Nevertheless, a permanent exposition of Polish paintings features the most brilliant works by Polish artists, headed by Bacciarelli, Grassi, Orłowski, Wojnarowski, Brodowski, Michałowski, Suchodolski, Brandt,

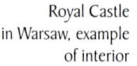

Royal Castle in Warsaw, example of interior

138

Rodakowski, Matejko, Maksymilian and Aleksander Gierymski, Pankiewicz, Podkowiński, Jacek Malczewski, Wojtkiewicz and painters closer to our times – i.a. Pronaszko, Witkacy, Chwistek and Cybis. Only a personal acquaintanceship with this collection makes it possible to become aware of the trends in the progress of Polish art. Let us note that an excellent supplement of the image of the historical evolution of Polish art, presented in Warsaw, is to be found in the museums of Płock, specialising in the Secession, and the regional museum of Radom, with its valuable and well-selected collection of contemporary Polish paintings, especially the avantgarde.

The National Museum is connected with the Museum in Royal Łazienki, located in the most beautiful park in the capital, and with the Museum in Wilanów, a palace-garden complex encompassing the seventeenth-century suburban residence of King Jan III Sobieski. The lavish outfitting of the palace is enhanced by a charming portrait gallery of Polish monarchs, magnates, outstanding men, artists and townspeople, which provides a basis for reflection on the development of artistic consciousness in Poland and brings the viewer closer to the personalities of many known historical figures.

One of the new pavilions in Wilanów contains a Poster Museum, opened in 1968, which collects and displays world and Polish exhibits. Together with the International Poster Biennial, the museum has made Warsaw one of the most important centres of the propagation of this field of art.

While we are on the subject of museums, it is simply impossible to omit the Royal Castle, whose interior houses a large collection of paintings by, i.a. Rembrandt, Bacciarelli and Canaletto, as well as old furniture. Greatly popular periodically held exhibitions, often feature true gems of European art.

SCULPTURE, CONTEMPORARY PAINTING

Exhibition of works by Salvador Dali in the X. Dunikowski Museum

Polish modern sculpture is the theme of the Xawery Dunikowski Museum in Warsaw and the Contemporary Sculpture Centre in Orońsko. The museum, situated in the Królikarnia park and Classicistic palace designed by Merlini (and modelled on the Palladian Villa Rotunda), bears the name of the most eminent Polish twentieth-century sculptor, author of numerous sculptures and monumental premises, such as the one commemorating the Silesian Uprisings, featured on St. Anne Hill. The museum displays a collection of sculptures by Dunikowski, and accumulates works by other Polish artists. It also holds cyclic exhibitions of contemporary Polish and European painters and sculptors.

A more extensive programme is pursued by the Sculpture Centre in Orońsko near Radom. Situated in the estate of Józef Brandt, the nineteenth-century painter of battle scenes, the Centre occupies a manor house, former manorial outbuildings and a newly erected exhibition object, all situated in a magnificent park. Apart from collecting works by Polish and European sculptors, the museum has well-equipped studios, gathers documentation on creativity, organises plein air shows and symposia, and publishes a periodical and studies dealing with sculpture. In recent years, the Centre suffered from a lack of funds necessary for continuing its endeavours. Hopefully, those are temporary difficulties, especially considering that the Centre is a well-devised cultural institution, not merely on a domestic scale. Investments in Orońsko could produce profitable artistic effects and multiply capital.

Contemporary art, primarily painting and akin genres, is the theme of two institutions in Warsaw: the state-owned "Zachęta" Gallery and the Contemporary Art Centre in Ujazdowski Castle; the latter is known as "Zuj", a witty and abbreviated name devised by young artists. The activity pursued by "Zachęta" has a long history, marred with tragic events (the gallery was the scene of the assassination of Gabriel Narutowicz, the first President of the Republic of Poland, killed by a fanatic nationalist). "Zachęta" fulfils the function of an official state exhibition centre – hence its important role in an exchange programme with galleries abroad; nonetheless, it remains free of all official and academic qualities, thanks to the character of the cultural policy of the state, open to variegated artistic phenomena and focused on interesting events in European art.

The Contemporary Art Centre, situated in the reconstructed, originally eighteenth-century Ujazdowski Castle, concentrates its attention on the latest, experimental and, frequently, controversial art. It conducts lively cooperation with numerous artists and creative groups in Eastern and Western Europe. A distinguishing feature of the Centre are presentations of the visual arts within the context of other forms of contemporary art: the theatre, music, poetry and dance. Moreover, the Centre documents contemporary art and issues its own publications. Apparently, as in the case of the Orońsko-based Sculpture Centre, suitably financed and programmed "Zuj" could become one of the significant art centres of Europe, and a place for confrontations between European artists from the East and the West, the North and the South.

Numerous galleries propagating art and showrooms selling old and new art emerged after 1989, especially in Warsaw, which also has a number of auction houses. More than twenty galleries in the Polish capital hold periodical exhibitions of contemporary art and specialise in the sale of featured works; there are also over 50 salons.

Galleries and art showrooms are to be found in all the larger towns in the voivodeship. A rapid growth of exhibition rooms and centres designed for the exchange of works of art testifies, primarily, to a large supply of contemporary art. In a situation characterised by a certain insufficiency of old objects d'art, attempts at enlivening the turnover in contemporary art, based on predictions of an increased prestigious "consumption" of art, appear to be especially apt. The problem, however, consists in the absence of traditions of an art market in Poland. A stimulation of the exchange calls for extensive financial input, and, predominantly, for the application of experience and knowledge at the disposal of the well-developed Western art market institutions. The progressing development of an exchange of works of contemporary art, large supply, the convenient localisation of Warsaw at the crossing of numerous art routes, contacts and, finally, the existing resources of art institutions in the capital – all those factors indicate conducive chances for the development of the art market.

Private collections. A new and valuable phenomenon in the last decades is the emergence of new museums, memorial chambers and private collections documenting the life of creators associated with local environments or presenting private art collections. Such institutions include the museum of Polish Folk Art in Otrębusy near Warsaw, created by the ethnographer Prof. Marian Prokopek (encompassing also the celebrated collection created by the late Ludwig Zimmerer, a German journalist), the Museum of Small Towns in Bieżuń, conceived by Stefan Gołębiowski, a local teacher, a gallery in the historical manor house in Patrykozy, displaying contemporary Polish paintings collected by Wojciech Siemion, actor and the "Sculpture Garden" in Mogielnica, established by the outstanding sculptor, the late Franciszek Starynkiewicz. Together with existing state museums, private collections are evidence that the population of the voivodeship acknowledges the importance of the protection of historical monuments and testimonies of the past as well as the need to render indelible select persons connected with the region through birth, upbringing, work, and contributions made in their capacity as social activists.

141

Libraries comprise those cultural institutions which are often insufficiently appreciated and reduced to the function of book storehouses. In reality, they constitute a foundation for a system of popularising culture and an extremely significant element in the educational infrastructure of society. Certain libraries also comprise a direct component of science. With the exception of Warsaw, the network of Mazovian libraries remains underdeveloped. The largest institution, also on a domestic scale, is the National Library, with 6,5 million volumes as well as specialised workshops and institutes at its disposal. The second largest library, albeit entrusted with entirely different tasks, is the Municipal Public Library in Warsaw, encompassing seven district libraries and 187 branches across Warsaw.

In 1999, the immense collection of the Library of Warsaw University was transferred to a new seat. All told, there are 1 112 libraries in the voivodeship, with the total of about 16 million volumes.

The index of the number of books per 1 000 inhabitants in the voivodeship is, however, rather unfavourable: 3 180 volumes signifies one of the last places in the ranking of voivodeships. In recent years, the development of higher education brought about a veritable siege of all available libraries and scientific reading rooms.

CULTURAL "INDUSTRIES"

This name, which to a certain degree veers from the intuition of everyday language, embraces such institutions as publishing houses, the press, radio and television centres, film production, musical recording enterprises, and assorted organisations specialising in the distribution of "cultural property". Warsaw is relatively well-equipped with this type of infrastructure. The term "relatively well" entails a comparison with other cultural centres in Poland, which is not to say that after a decade of so-called transformations Warsaw achieved a state enabling fully balanced cooperation with other centres of the cultural industries in the world.

Publishing houses. Changed economic and legal rules prevailing in the cultural industries generated a dynamic development of publishing. In Warsaw, there are at present some 600 publishing houses (although about 3 000 are registered, most do not conduct systematic activity). More than ten publishing houses were created upon the basis of former state firms, but the majority are entirely new. These well-developing, and vigorous firms compensate a certain insufficiency of capital by apt orientation as regards readers' expectations, familiarity with the potential of the authors, and profiling an editorial programme concurrent with the competence of the editors and collaborating authors. An obstacle hampering the assumption of the final shape by the publishing industry is the constantly unsatisfactory distribution of books. Retail book warehouses, albeit numerous, posses small capital. Similarly, bookstores are forced to tackle high rents, the seasonal nature of demand, and the competition of media other than books. There are about 700 bookstores throughout Mazovia, but only a few offer more than 5 000 titles.

The development of new mass media and an increased supply of mass culture products were followed by a rapid growth of stores selling newspapers and popular publications as well as musical recordings and video cassette equipment. The expanding network of shops selling musical recordings and video cassettes is accompanied by a large increase in the number of video receivers, portable players and all types of electronic equipment.

Cinemas. On the other hand, the network of cinemas is gradually diminishing. According to the data supplied by the Main Statistics Office, at the end of 1997 there were 71 permanent cinemas in the voivodeship, with 4,6 seats per 1 000 inhabitants. Those data situate the voivodeship in one of the last places among the new voivodeships, well below the national average, which is 55,2 seats per 1 000 inhabitants. The lowest indices occur in the counties of Piaseczno, Otwock, and Szydłowiec – 1,8 statistical seat per 1 000 inhabitants. There are no permanent cinemas in as many as 14 counties (including the county of Białobrzegi, Lipsko, Ostrołęka, Nowy Dwór Mazowiecki, Przasnysz, Sierpc and Zwoleń). At the same time, the residents of Mazovia go to

A multiplex in the Ursynów district of Warsaw. Other such objects are being built

the cinema much more frequently than in the past. In 1998, the index of the public per 1000 inhabitants totalled 864, while in the voivodeship of Pomerania, the second ranking, it amounted to only 690. In recent years – a period which witnessed a transference of interest from films seen in the cinema to those available on cassettes – concern for encouraging the audience to return to the cinema resulted in modernisation. The first effects involved the introduction of modern equipment, raising the standard of interiors, and opening so-called multiplex cinemas which have at their disposal numerous showing rooms as well as excellent apparatus and equipment.

Concert and show halls, mass-scale events. The voivodeship distinctly lacks fully safe and large-capacity concert and show objects, outfitted with satisfactory technical equipment and intended for mass-scale events. For this purpose, use is made of on-the-spot adapted sports and recreation objects or provisionally converted unused buildings (by way of example, in Głowaczów, disco-polo concerts, greatly

143

popular in the east-southern part of the voivodeship, are held in a former farming machinery and artificial fertilisers storehouse).

Successful examples of truly mass-scale events, such as the Holiday Assistance Orchestra Concerts, organised by Jerzy Owsiak, the "Wreaths" – an event held in Płock, "Earth Days" in Agrykola, or the Bregovic-Kayah concert in Warsaw, testify to the possibilities of developing this form of participation in culture, and might encourage to embark upon profitable investments. The network and technical state of public institutions engaged in cultural initiation and education, the amateur pursuit of the arts, and assorted forms of serving local groups, which disclose diverse interests and attract various age categories, remain highly unsatisfactory.

The worst situation predominates in rural communes. Local self-governments have limited financial means for the programme activity of clubs and local culture centres. Enterprises have resigned from maintaining their own cultural institutions. In larger towns, often only residential co-operatives continue financing cultural clubs. Fortunately, select schools and parishes remain interested in cultural endeavours, but, as a rule, they concentrate their attention almost exclusively on school children.

Diverse benefits are ensured by cyclical events, organised in many localities of the voivodeship, and either featuring the cultural and economic accomplishments of local communities, or providing occasions for stimulating interest in music, dance and the theatre. The discovery of a sufficiently attractive formula of a "cultural event" whose programme could capture the attention of the media and encourage tourists and lovers of the given region to attend, which could combine artistic, social or economic targets, and, finally, which would enable an independent conducting of assorted ventures, forms an essential condition for overcoming the inertia of local communities, for winning organisational experiences, and for accomplishing the active integration of a certain group of people. Events of this sort include Mława Days, Ostrołęka Days, Płock History Days, Sochaczew Days, the "Wreaths" in Płock, the "Kwiecień-Plecień" Song, Dance and Theatre Festival in Sierpc, National Children's and Youth Circus Workshops in Ciechanów, the "Kasztelania" International Folklore Festival in Sierpc, the National Meeting of Folk Dance Ensembles in Płock, the "Kupalnocka" International Folklore Festival in Płońsk, Kolberg Days in Przysucha, the birthplace of Oskar Kolberg (June), the Jazz Evergreens Festival in Siedlce (April), the National Scouting Song Festival in Siedlce (May) and the "Szantynocki" Shanty Night Concert in Węgrów.

The above mentioned events cannot equal renowned artistic competitions held in Warsaw, such as the international Chopin competitions, the "Warsaw Autumn" Music Festival or the International Poster Biennial. Events held in suburban cultural centres possess direct local significance, sometimes of a wider environmental or domestic range; nevertheless, their direct dimension does not correspond fully to their rank.

Folk Culture

The current situation of folk culture, i.e. unprofessional art which refers to the creativity of the old Mazovian village, deserves to be discussed separately. Ethnographic museums, departments of folk art in historical museums, and Skansen museums contribute to the protection of traces of folk culture of the past, which characterised the lifestyle of local peasants during the eighteenth and nineteenth century. Specialised museums include the State Ethnographic Museum in Warsaw (whose extremely valuable and rich collections of folk art and Judaica were burnt down as a result of German bombings carried out during the first wartime days in 1939), the Museum of the Radom Village, together with a Skansen, and the Museum of Folk Musical Instruments in Szydłowiec. Ethnographic departments are to be found in the Regional Museum in Kozienice, the Regional Museum in Ostrołęka, the Mazovian Museum in Płock, the Regional Museum in Pułtusk, the Regional Museum in Siedlce, the Museum of the Mazovian Village and the Skansen in Sierpc, the Municipal Museum in Wyszków and the Regional Museum in Żyrardów.

Despite the fact that the generation of folk artists acquainted with the uninterrupted tradition of old customs, modes of regulating the life and work of farmers, and production technologies is no longer, and despite the increasingly waning features of the "old way of life", the knowledge and practical-technical skills of the former countryside are cultivated, even if only "for display". Mazovia constitutes a special region in Poland which, regardless of the levelling impact of the urbanisation and industrialisation of the village, has retained astonishingly numerous traces of old culture. The folk culture of this voivodeship is composed of five distinct groups in which we may come across traces of the past either in architecture, the utilisation of old production techniques and manners of cultivating art, or local customs and linguistic peculiarities. Those groups constitute the Kurpie from Biała Forest and Zielona Forest, the Płock sub-region, the Warsaw suburban region, Podlasie and former Kozienicka Forest.

Unhampered reference to folk art, which involves a mixture of the impacts of assorted cultures, is disclosed in the cultural life of numerous communities, and assumes diverse forms. The economic breakdown of many rural regions and the absence of perspectives for employment inclined part of the village population to turn to the crafts, whenever there is a chance for a permanent demand for such products. Respect for the rules of old styles and the type of produced objects is turning into a secondary matter. Naturally, ethnographers and historians of art assessing those products could voice many reservations towards what today is known as folk art. Today, we deal with folkloristic creativity undertaken in a world so radically different from that of the old Mazovian village that it would have been strange and "unauthentic" if it were to disclose great similarities to nineteenth-century folk culture.

Regardless of all the reservations made by the supporters of "authentic" folk creativity, the Mazovian voivodeship has a large potential of folklorists; some of those highly talented people are already widely known, while others await discovery and acclaim. Many have gained such renown in their local environment, including Jan Rybczyński and Józef Rzepka, sculptors from Przysucha, Alojzy Przerwa, a folk painter from Policzna, and numerous other poets, painters, blacksmiths and basket weavers whose products are universally admired.

*   *   *

A consequence of the self-government reform will be certainly a growing autonomy of regions delineated in the new administrative division of the country. The second factor to exert an impact on social and cultural life will be the unification accomplished by strong cultural industries. The increasingly vital development potential of the entire society of the region will become a condition for retaining resources of the cultural infrastructure and the cultivation of traditional motifs that serve the solution of important existential problems. This process will demand the expansion of local institutions without which it is impossible to accomplish the initiation and adaptation of aesthetic values. Another requirement will be the reconstruction of a programme of the variegated and extensive activity of the cultural structure of the capital of Mazovia, as well as the establishment of new bonds between the population and artistic institutions of Warsaw, on the one hand, and the society of the whole new region, on the other hand.

Krzysztof Kostyrko

THE TOURIST PANORAMA
OF MAZOWIECKIE VOIVODESHIP

Mazowieckie voivodeship is undoubtedly one of the great surprises in the Polish lowlands – a land of enormous attraction that continues to grow in the course of a suitable development of tourist facilities. With the exception of Warsaw, the entire area still awaits discovery. This is a territory intended for true connoisseurs, where every turn of the road discloses locations and objects worthy of interest.

WARSAW

Warsaw is situated on the banks of the Vistula, in the very centre of Mazovia. It is the capital of the historical region of Mazovia, the voivodeship and the state as well as the site of the seats of the supreme authorities of the Republic; in addition, it fulfils the function of the prime centre of political life, the largest Polish academic and cultural centre, a significant industrial centre and the largest town in the country. Visits are by no means associated merely with business, as witnessed by tides of tourists arriving from all over the world.

TOWARDS THE OLD TOWN

Upon arrival, all visitors make their way towards Castle Square, situated at the foot of the Column of Zygmunt III, topped by the figure of the king who four hundred years ago granted Warsaw the rank of the state capital. The originally Gothic (fourteenth-century) and subsequently expanded Royal Castle was carefully rebuilt after total devastation incurred during the second world war. The royal chambers, open to visitors, display valuable historical souvenirs and works of art. Only a few steps away lies the Old Town. Not surprisingly, this extremely charming part of town is the most frequented. Reduced to ruins during the Uprising of 1944, it was conscientiously rebuilt and remains encircled by defensive walls dating from the fourteenth century. The Old Town Market Square is surrounded by narrow, initially Gothic burgher houses, redesigned in the Baroque style during the seventeenth and eight-

Views of Zamkowy Square. In the foreground: the Royal Castle destroyed during World War II and reconstructed in the 1970s.

eenth century. Several of these objects have been turned into the Historical Museum of Warsaw, worthy of special attention. Nearby there towers the Gothic cathedral of St. John whose crypts contain tombs of the dukes of Mazovia, state Presidents and distinguished men of letters. One of the highlights of the tour is a stroll along the narrow lanes of the Old Town, followed by a rest in one of the innumerable cafes, taverns and restaurants. A horse-carriage trip will take us to the nearby New Town Market Square whose prime accent is the white silhouette of the Baroque church and convent of the Sisters of the Blessed Sacrament.

AROUND SASKI GARDEN

A fascinating westward walk from Castle Square ends in Saski Garden – an oasis of peace and quiet in the midst of the City. This district boasts of numerous magnificent monuments typical for the era of Classicism. A number of palaces and a Capuchin church whose Royal Chapel is the resting place of the heart of King Jan III and the ashes of King August II are located along Miodowa Street. Krasiński Street features a true masterpiece of the Baroque: the Palace of the Republic, designed by Tylman of Gameren, and framed by the modern architecture of the Palace of Justice. Senatorska Street and adjoining squares provide an opportunity for admiring monumental works by the celebrated Antonio Corazzi: the imposing façade of the Wielki Theatre in Teatralny Square and a complex of buildings of the former Ministry of Finances, today the seat of the authorities of the capital, in Bankowy Square.

Old Town Market Square – a tourist favourite

149

The Royal Tract leads from Zamkowy Square towards the royal residence in Wilanów. The Tract itself encompasses a sequence of streets, starting with Krakowskie Przedmieście, regarded as the most beautiful in Warsaw and including some twenty palaces from the seventeenth and eighteenth century, once the property of famous Polish families. Today, many of these buildings serve other purposes; one of the objects is the residence of the President of the Republic of Poland and others are used by Warsaw University. The most important churches in this area are St. Anne's, the church of the Visitant nuns, and the Holy Cross, keeper of an urn with the heart of Frederic Chopin; one of the nearby palaces (today: the Academy of Fine Arts) was the place of residence of the young composer and his parents (the Chopin salon is open to visitors). A prolongation of Krakowskie Przedmieście is the Nowy Świat Street with a number of Classicistic houses from the end of the eighteenth century and the nineteenth century. Both streets are full of elegant restaurants and cafes, shops, antique and art shops and numerous bookstores, such as the "MPiK", the Bolesław Prus bookstore and the "Resursa" – Warsaw is truly a town of book lovers.

The Radziwiłł Palace (seventeenth century), redesigned upon numerous ocassions. Today – the seat of the President of the Republic of Poland

Along Ujazdowskie Avenue

The representative Ujazdowskie Avenue, where the nineteenth-century aristocracy and wealthy merchants raised their palaces, villas and houses, stretches beyond Trzech Krzyży Square. The Avenue and its environs are a concentration of embassies, government buildings and the Sejm (Parliament). This is also a district of parks: the elegant Ujazdowski Park, the charming albeit small Botanical Gardens of Warsaw University, and the magnificent Royal Łazienki, indubitably one of

the most splendid palace-garden complexes in Europe, designed for King Stanisław August Poniatowski during the eighteenth century. This unique landscape park contains several buildings, including the Palace on the Isle, the summer residence of the last Polish monarch, a veritable Classicistic gem and today a museum of interiors. Nearby lies the stylised Theatre on the Isle. Strolling across the park we come across two statutes: of King Jan III Sobieski, the famous victor of the siege of Vienna (1683), and Frederic Chopin; during the summer season, concerts featuring the works of this brilliant composer are held at the foot of the latter monument every Sunday at noon.

THE RESIDENCE OF KING SOBIESKI

Wilanów is situated at the southern end of Warsaw. This country residence of King Jan III Sobieski, from the end of the seventeenth century, is composed of a Baroque palace surrounded by a superb park – an excellent example of this type of architecture both in Poland and Europe. The palace is flanked by other historical buildings: a poster museum and tastefully designed restaurants and cafes. The most important object is the museum of interiors arranged in the palace and displaying lavish royal apartments as well as an extensive gallery of Polish portraits ranging from the fifteenth to the nineteenth century – an extraordinary history lesson. The same benefits are to be enjoyed by a closer examination of the historical statues in Warsaw.

151

Wilanów – one of the most valuable Baroque complexes in Poland. During the seventeenth century – a residence of Jan III Sobieski

ON THE TRAIL OF WARSAW STATUES

This excursion comprises a true journey into the innermost recesses of history. A vivid impression is made by the statues of Adam Mickiewicz, Prince Józef Poniatowski, Cardinal Stefan Wyszyński and Mikołaj Kopernik, standing in Krakowskie Przedmieście Street. No sightseer can ignore the column in Obozowa Street in the more distant Wola district, marking the site of the election field where the Polish gentry gathered to choose the monarch. An equally strong impact is made by monuments commemorating the Warsaw Uprising of 1944 and its participants (near the Sejm and in Krasińskich Square). Just as imposing are monuments honouring the memory of Poles who perished in battle or were murdered in the East (Muranowska Street) and the monument of the Heroes of the Ghetto and the Umschlagplatz (Stawki Street), from which the Nazis deported thousands of Warsaw Jews to death camps. The cemeteries in Powązki (Catholic, Protestant and Jewish) comprise a pantheon of two centuries of the fame and glory of Warsaw. Here, old trees shade the graves of numerous famous Poles, and the tombs frequently possess enormous artistic merits.

TRACING ASSORTED VARIANTS OF HISTORICISM

Warsaw is a town of numerous residential houses and edifices erected in the spirit of the eclectic style and the national variety of historicism, especially in the City: in Ujazdowskie Avenue, Jerozolimskie Avenue, Mokotowska, Nowowiejska and Lwowska streets and adjoining ones; the objects in question include the church in Zbawiciela Square and the nearby main building of the Warsaw University of Technology. Excellent examples of socialist historicism are the Palace of Culture and Science and Konstytucji Square.

THE NATURE RESERVATIONS OF WARSAW

The residents of the capital are immensely proud of municipal woodlands recognised as nature reservations: the Bielański Wood, with centuries-old oaks, situated in the northern part of the town, the Sobieski Wood in the east, and the Kabacki Wood in the south, whose environs encompass the locality of Powsin – a favourite resort – and the sprawling Botanical Garden of the Polish Academy of Sciences. The locality of Natolin features the largest and oldest oak in Mazovia, bearing the name of Mieszko I. No other European capital borders with a protected nature area as large as the Kampinoski National Park.

The Mermaid – symbol of Warsaw. One of scarce monuments referring to the legend

Monoment commemorating the Warsaw Uprising of 1944; in the background: the Palace of Justice

Żelazowa Wola and Its Closest Environs

Żelazowa Wola, one of the most frequently visited spots in Poland, lies along the edges of the Kampinoski National Park. From the beginning of the nineteenth century, this former landed estate of Żelazów, situated on the river Utrata, belonged to the impoverished family of Count Skarbek, whose children were taught by the French tutor Mikołaj Chopin. Here, he met his future wife, Tekla Justyna Krzyżanowska, and here their son, Frederic (Fryderyk) Chopin was born on 22 February 1810, spent his childhood and holidays – the last visit took place in 1830. The Skarbek manor has not survived, but in 1931 a manorial outbuilding in which Frederic was born was designed to resemble Polish manors of the period; now, situated in the park, it is a museum attracting numerous tourists and lovers of music by the brilliant composer, whose birthplace is always adorned with fresh flowers. Concerts of Chopin's works are given in Żelazowa Wola during the summer season.

To the West of Żelazowa Wola

At a small distance from Żelazowa Wola we come across Brochów, whose red-brick Renaissance basilica originated from a Gothic church, redesigned by Jan Baptysta of Venice in 1551–1561. Three lofty towers with embrasure windows grant the building a defensive character. Here, the parents of Frederic Chopin were married in 1806 and Frederic himself was baptised on 23 April 1810.

The nearby small industrial town of Sochaczew may not be one of the most attractive local centres, but this important castle-town on a ford across the Bzura features several interesting objects, including the picturesque ruins of a fifteenth-century

Church in Brochów
(sixteenth century)

154

castle. The Classicistic town hall from 1828 contains the Museum of the Region of Sochaczew and the Battlefield on the Bzura whose collections include an exhibit of uniforms and complete soldiers' outfit from the time of the September 1939 campaign. The local Narrow-gauge Railway Museum is the largest European collection of narrow-gauge rolling stock, admired by hobbyists and specialists alike.

A Visit to a National Park

The name of the village of Kampinos (on the highway to Warsaw), to the west of Żelazowa Wola, was given to the nearby forest and then to the Kampinoski National Park; established in 1959 for the purpose of protecting the unique natural landscape and historical merits of this fragment of the Vistula antecedent valley, together with a complex of well-preserved inland dunes, peat-bogs and the remnants of Kampinoska Forest, it bears enormous significance both for science and tourism. The astonishing plant and animal world is composed of elks, red deer, beavers, the lynx, cranes and eagles. The façade of the wooden church in the village of Kampinos, built of fine-knot local pine in 1783, is an example of the impact exerted by brick Baroque and Classicistic architecture upon wooden constructions. The didactic-museum centre of the Kampinoski National Park, situated in adjoining Granica, features a historical-natural exhibit, a small Skansen museum, and a nature trail: this copious offer includes nature films and guided tours. The centre, located in the very midst of the Forest, provides parking facilities, a children's recreation area, and a woodland buffet.

The Sanctuary in Niepokalanów

Niepokalanów is but a short trip away from Kampinos. The Marian sanctuary, of extreme importance for Polish Catholics, is now devoted to St. Maksymilian Kolbe, the founder of the monastery, who in 1941 suffered a martyr's death in the Auschwitz concentration camp. The old wooden church contains a showroom commemorating the life and martyrdom of Father Kolbe. The brick church, with assorted modernistic features, was completed in 1954. Nearby lies Paprotnia, whose historical inn and smithy (eighteenth-nineteenth century) are supposedly the place where Mrs. Walewska reminded Napoleon of his promises as regards Poland. Today, the smithy has been converted into "Kuźnia Napoleońska", a fine period restaurant.

PŁOCK AND ITS ENVIRONS

The characteristic features of Płock, the most important town in Mazovia next to Warsaw, are ancient history, splendid historical monuments and outstanding location on the high escarpment of the Vistula, with a unique promenade. Populated for several thousand years, from 1047 Płock held the rank of the capital of a bishopric, and during the reigns of Władysław I Herman and Bolesław III the Wrymouth (1079–1138) it was the capital of the Polish state. The town boasts of almost 150 monuments of architecture, thousands of magnificent works of art, three museums and a theatre. Tourist trails start in the city, too. Sightseeing in the oldest part of Płock, around the Old Market Square, which already in the Middle Ages acted as the centre of municipal life – a role it played up to the nineteenth century – is particularly captivating.

THE CATHEDRAL ON TUMSKI HILL

Sacral and lay monuments on Tumski Hill are evidence of a thousand year long tradition of this extraordinary site. The cathedral, regarded as one of the most valuable monuments of Polish history and art, features the tombs of the rulers of Poland and the dukes of Mazovia as well as numerous works of art, including sepulchral objects. At the beginning of the twentieth century, the building, with Romanesque, Gothic, Renaissance and Classicistic motifs, was redesigned by Stefan Szyller in the spirit of the then fashionable historicism. The porch features the famous bronze Płock Portal – a two-wing door with bas-relief plates depicting Biblical scenes. Commissioned by Bishop Alexander of Mallone for the cathedral in Płock, and made in the twelfth century in Magdeburg, the portal never reached its original destination: today, Płock has a precise copy of the original which embellishes the Russian town of Novgorod.

Płock – the first
capital of Mazovia

156

Gothic Castle Towers and Splendid Museums

The Mazovian ducal castle, known as the royal or the Benedictine abbey, was erected in the fourteenth century by Kazimierz the Great; during the following centuries, it was redesigned upon numerous occasions. The preserved fragments of Gothic defensive walls are the tallest in the country (17 metres high). The Szlachecka (Noble) Tower, originating from the mid-fourteenth century, is a remnant of the brick Gothic castle of Kazimierz the Great. From the end of the fifteenth century, the Gothic Zegarowa (Clock) Tower, topped with a Baroque helmet, served as a cathedral bell tower, well above the traces of a palatium built of stone blocks, where Bolesław the Wrymouth was born in 1085. Today, the Castle interiors display the exceptional collection of the Mazovian Museum. A second, diocesan museum is located in a building specially erected alongside the cathedral; its inner walls feature assorted stone fragments of the original cathedral.

The Sierpc Churches, Skansen and Beer

While in Płock it is simply mandatory to pay a visit to Sierpc and its three historical churches, the most valuable being the Late Gothic church of the Benedictine nuns from 1483, redesigned in subsequent centuries. This old sanctuary features the particularly venerated fifteenth-century Gothic statue of the Madonna, standing in the main altar and adorned with silver garments. Next to Sierpc we find a museum dealing with the Mazovian village, accompanied by a fascinating ethnographic park. The numerous displayed wooden objects include an eighteenth-century tavern from Sochocin, where we can taste the celebrated Sierpc beer, and then visit the museum either on foot or by carriage; the assistance of a professional guide is highly recommended.

The Spectacular Landscape of the Płock Region

The Brudzeński Landscape Park was created to the west of Płock, where the river Skrwa Prawa flows along the deep valley and forms a fiord-shaped lake at the mouth of the Vistula. The variegated local woods are composed of rich vegetation interspersed with carpets of early spring flowers. The edges of the Park are enhanced by a number of historical monuments, such as the small wooden church from 1711 in Brwino Górne, standing in the midst of centuries-old linden trees, the charming Late Romanesque church in Rokić (thirteenth century) and the Gothic-Renaissance brick church from 1611 in Siecień.

The Gostynińskie Lake District stretches along the southern edge of the region, partly within the boundaries of a landscape park; scattered lakes associated with the withdrawal of the iceberg during the last glaciation are accompanied by assorted geomorphological forms such as eskers, kames, and dunes. The park and its immediate surrounding contain as many as sixteen nature reservations, numerous historical trees, and an imposing number of species of the local flora and fauna. This is also a region of summer vacation villages and hotels – some of the lakes are renowned for attractive beaches and swimming facilities. The particularly appealing area of Łąck is famous for its beautiful woods and lakes as well as a palace built in 1873 in the style of a neo-Renaissance Italian villa for Robert Fuhrman, master of the hunt of Tsar Alexander II. The palace, which prior to 1939 was the residence of Edward Rydz-Śmigły, the Marshal of Poland, adjoins the buildings and stables of the State Stud-horse Farm, one of the best known Polish breeding stables open to visitors (by appointment only).

■

OPINOGÓRA – THE RESIDENCE OF ZYGMUNT KRASIŃSKI

Opinogóra, neo--Gothic castle, seat of the Museum of Romanticism

Opinogóra – the acknowledged birthplace of Polish Romanticism – is connected with the great poet Zygmunt Krasiński, who spent his childhood and part of his adult life here, and was buried in a crypt of the local Classicistic church from the mid-nineteenth century. A hillock situated in the centre of a pleasant park is crowned by a Romantic gem – a neo-Gothic castle from 1843, today adapted for the small and excellently arranged Museum of Romanticism. All traces of the hunting lodge of the Mazovian dukes, where Bolesław IV, Duke of Warsaw, Czersk, Zakroczym, Ciechanów and Łomża died in the mid-fifteenth century, have been obliterated; a sandstone cross erected in the Opinogóra park by General Wincenty Krasiński commemorates this historical figure. Another non-extant building is the palace itself, but visitors may admire the preserved neo-Gothic outbuilding.

Neighbouring Ciechanów was the castle-town of the legendary Ciechanów, whose statue stands at the foot of Farska Hill, an early mediaeval stronghold. Here, Zygmunt Krasiński situated the plot of the opening chapters of one of his earliest works – a novel about Władysław Herman. Above the hillock there towers a Gothic parish church, whose erection lasted from 1353–1356 to the sixteenth century; after 1920, it received its present-day form, designed by Stefan Szyller. The most valuable historical monuments in Ciechanów are the brick ruins of the castle of the Mazovian dukes, whose retained and partially reconstructed interiors now house a museum. The picturesque ruins were discovered during the era of Romanticism; from that time on, they became the goal of veritable pilgrimages and the inspiration of such poets and writers as the young Zygmunt Krasiński, Maria Konopnicka, Bolesław Prus and Henryk Sienkiewicz.

Touring in this fragment of Mazovia entails a visit to the village of Krasne, the family nest of the Krasińskis of the Ślepowron coat of arms and the Korwin cognomen. Representatives of this aristocratic Mazovian family include many famous Poles, holders of high offices. The outline of the local church dates back to the Late Gothic period; the Baroque elements were added probably in the first half of the seventeenth century. The present-day historicising form was granted after 1826. The interior of this family necropolis presents a collection of artistically important tombstones and epitaphs.

Puɫtusk

Puɫtusk is situated on the river Narew – a legend mentions the town of Tusk, whose remnants, after a calamitous flood, became known as "Póɫ Tuska" (half of Tusk). Written records go back to the thirteenth century: the settlement was granted town rights in 1257. At the beginning of the millennium, the dukes of Mazovia presented the bishops of Pɫock with the ownership rights to Puɫtusk and the adjoining forest along the eastern banks of the Narew. The town thrived under the bishops, who encircled it with defensive walls. From 1440, it became celebrated for its famous academy whose scholars included eminent Poles; as late as the seventeenth century, the greatest Polish families sent their sons "for instruction to Puɫtusk". Picturesque location, partially on an island between the armlets of the river, together with a fascinating past and monuments, place Puɫtusk among the most captivating small towns in Poland.

A Town on an Island

The Puɫtusk town square is regarded as the longest in Poland, and its four hundred metre-long axis is simultaneously the axis of an island. The rows of houses surrounding the Market Square originate from the second half of the nineteenth century and the beginning of the twentieth century. One of the edifices bears a plaque informing that Napoleon stayed here after the battle of Puɫtusk in 1806. The centre of the square is occupied by a Late Gothic town-hall tower from the sixteenth century, a symbol of the town and now a regional museum. Today, the former bishop's castle, high above the market square, is basically a modern object, raised by using elements of the old castle and completed in 1989; its interiors have been turned into the exclusive Polonia House, composed of a hotel, restaurants, clubs and conference and reception rooms. Visitors may enjoy the adjoining harbour, recreation and sport grounds, and a parking lot. Magdalenka, the

Puɫtusk, Late Gothic town-hall tower – symbol of the town

former Castle chapel, built in 1538, is situated at the foot of the hill. The oldest framework of the collegiate church, on the opposite side of the square, originated in the sixteenth century; after 1650, it was redesigned in the Renaissance spirit by the acclaimed Italian mason, Jan Baptysta of Venice. The church, preceded by a Classicistic bell tower from the 1795, whose erection involved the use of sixteenth-century walls, remains one the outstanding monuments of Mazovian architecture; a particularly striking impression is made by the interior – ceilings, altars and chapels as well as Gothic, Renaissance and Baroque tombstones and epitaphs. At the beginning of the nineteenth century, tsarist authorities pulled down the defensive town walls, and today the only surviving fragments are two bastilles.

LOCAL MONUMENTS OF NATURE AND ARCHITECTURE

The opposite bank of the river offers a view of Biała Forest. Three hiking trails leading towards the Forest along a comfortable footbridge across the Narew, start in front of the town hall in the market square. Just as recommendable is a day-trip along a pleasant woodland trail, marked with red signs, to the village of Obryte, whose attractions include the Kurpiowska Cottage. Serock, situated next to the Warsaw highway, has a square-shaped market on the eastern side of the main street, with an architecturally interesting contemporary town hall and a pleasant restaurant. The construction of the adjacent handsome Late Gothic church was commenced prior to 1525. Its picturesque surrounding is composed of tempting paths along the wooded and deep ravines of the steep bank of the Narew, which joins the Bug near Serock.

◼

THE KURPIE REGION

Ostrołęka,
Classicistic town
hall from first half
of nineteenth
century

This is one of the most attractive parts of Mazovia, with vestiges of Kurpie Forest and the last wild bee-keeping facilities in Poland, preserved up to our times in the "Czarnia" reservation. The region makes a distinct imprint on the ethnographic map of Poland. The local population (the Kurpie) is known for its dialect, customs, costumes and architecture, as well as folk art and culture, both ascribed an exceptional place in Polish folk tradition. A trip to Ostrołęka, Kadzidło, Myszyniec and the "Czarnia" reservation are simply a "must" in any sightseeing programme. Unfortunately, part of the Mazovian Kurpie region is situated within the boundaries of the neighbouring Podlaskie voivodeship (i.a. the localities of Łomża and Nowogród, with the famous Skansen founded by Dr. Chętnik).

IN OSTROŁĘKA

Ostrołęka is the gateway to the Kurpie region. Its strategic location was the reason for the numerous armed confrontations which took place in the area – the battle waged by the French army in 1807 is commemorated on the Parisian Arc de Triomphe as one of the most important of the Napoleonic era. On 26 May 1831, Ostrołęka became the site of a battle between tsarist troops and Polish insurgents, marked by a monument-mausoleum situated in the old Russian fort. The main square in the oldest part of the town displays a statue of General Józef Bem, another participant of hostilities at Ostrołęka and a national hero of Poland and Hungary. The houses encircling the square include the town hall, the former starosty office, a post office from the first half of the nineteenth century and a museum. The former Bernardine church and monastery are another prime monument, dating back to the second half of the seventeenth century; in the first half of the eighteenth century, this complex was preceded by a characteristic Calvary courtyard, surrounded by galleries adorned with picturesque turrets. The Late Baroque-Rococo polychromy embellishing the church interior was completed in the seventeenth century. The church, recently damaged by fire, is being restored to its former state.

In Kadzidło and Myszyniec

Kadzidło and the surrounding area are known for local folklore and the Kurpiowska Farmstead which features the interior of a local cottage and examples of regional folk art. A typical Kurpie wedding is staged every third Sunday in June. The polychromy and organs in the neo-Baroque church are the work of local artists: the feretories disclose partly folk features and the interior houses a collection of folk craft and art works. On the feast day of St. Blaise members of the congregation carry the wax vota, while the Eucharistic procession held on Corpus Christi is an occasion for viewing regional costumes. The holiday of St. Roch is celebrated by religious ceremonies which involve chasing cattle across burning fire – a trace of magical practices from the distant past, whose purpose was to overcome the plague.

The name of Myszyniec, acknowledged as the most prominent settlement and capital of the Kurpie region, is borne also by Myszyniecka Forest, earlier known as Zagajnica and, subsequently, as Zielona. From 1791 to 1869, Myszyniec enjoyed town rights and is still regarded by the Kurpie population as an urban centre. The red brick neo-Gothic parish church, erected in 1859, adjoins a bell tower-gate, probably from the second half of the seventeenth century; next to the entrance, the interior of the tower contains two walled-in stocks used for imprisoning felons. Local wooden roadside shrines feature folk sculptures. The settlement plays the role of a significant folk culture centre; on the last Sunday in August a meadow in Zawodzie becomes the site of a bee-honey harvest accompanied by a tasting festivity: honey served on horseradish leaves, assorted baked goods and liqueurs. The lavish St. Martin's fair held after 12 October is a widely-known local event.

■

Węgrów

This town – once the private property of the Kiszki, Radziwiłł and Krasiński families – is well worth visiting. Valuable Baroque monuments include two exceptional churches founded by Dobrogost Krasiński and built by Karol Ceroni, probably according to projects by the celebrated Tylman of Gameren; they are the parish church from 1703–1706 and the former Reformed Franciscan church from 1693–1706. Both are decorated with polychromy by Michelangelo Palloni, paintings and statues; in addition, the parish church displays the mysterious Twardowski Mirror, used by the famous sorcerer to show a likeness of the deceased Barbara Radziwiłł to bereaved King Zygmunt August. The main altar in the former Reformed Franciscan church was designed by Tylman of Gameren; the interior also contains a wooden crucifix from 1688–1690 and a Baroque tombstone of Jan Dobrogost Krasiński, one of the most remarkable monuments of its kind in Poland, situated above the portal in the sepulchral chapel of the founder of the church. The town-planning configuration of Węgrów is typical for Baroque urban

161

centres, especially those in Podlasie. The premise is based on the shape of the market square and the introduction into one of sides of the market of a church with a developed façade. The market square is also the site of the Gdański House, an excellent example of a Baroque town residence, today a library. A bell foundry

Węgrów, parish church (sixteenth century), redesigned at the beginning of seventeenth century

belonging to the Kruszewski family, where two bells for the Royal Castle in Warsaw were cast in 1973, is situated in the northern part of the town.

On the Liwiec

The former town of Liw, today a large village, lies on the western bank of the Liwiec. In 1041, when the river comprised a boundary with the Grand Duchy of Lithuania, a Mazovian defensive castle-town was built on the western bank. The only vestige of this distant past is the ruin of the ducal castle which was completed prior to 1423; the sole extant part is a massive gate tower. In 1792, the Gothic, so-called smaller house, was replaced by a Baroque building of the chancery of the starost. A museum now, it presents a collection of military objects, paintings depicting battle scenes, and Sarmatian portraits.

On the Węgrów side of the Liwiec we come to Stara Wieś. In the seventeenth and eighteenth century, it was the seat of the Węgrów landed estates owners – the magnate families: Radziwiłł, Krasiński, Swidziński, Ossoliński, Jezierski, Golicyn, and once again Krasiński and Radziwiłł (until 1945). In the middle of the nineteenth century, the early Baroque palace was redesigned in the Romantic Gothic style. Today, this charming object, destroyed during the second world war and carefully rebuilt for the National Bank of Poland, is open only to select visitors.

Siedlce

Almost every town has its symbol, monument or building. Siedlce, the capital of western Podlasie, for decades associated with Mazovia, has Jacek – a figure of Atlas carrying the globe, which tops the helmet of the town-hall tower, built in the Late Baroque-Classicistic style during the mid-eighteenth century. Although Siedlce enjoyed municipal status already in 1547, its retained and distinct outline dates back from the eighteenth century when it belonged to Aleksandra Ogińska, born Czartoryska, founder of the town hall and author of the addition of a lavish façade and the main altar in the church of St. Stanisław the Bishop. The Princess also commissioned the Ogiński chapel, built in the Classicistic style and designed by Zygmunt Vogel. The oldest object in the town is the Ogiński Palace, raised in 1698 at the request of Kazimierz Czartoryski; thoroughly expanded, it was granted a fashionable neo-Classicistic form by Ogińska. The palace has been the seat of administrative authorities at the gubernia, voivodeship or county level. Princess Ogińska was also the founder of the first Romantic sentimental garden in Poland whose only traces remain concealed in the town park.

Monuments of the Region

A monument to the west of the town commemorates the important battle waged in Iganie on 10 April 1831 by Polish insurgents; led by General Ignacy Prądzyński and assisted by an artillery commanded by General Józef Bem, the participants of

Siedlce, Late Baroque town hall (mid-eighteenth century)

163

the November Uprising defeated the twice as large tsarist forces. A historical complex with a Classicistic manor house and a church from the second half of the eighteenth century in the nearby village of Niwiska on the Liwiec recalls the resplendent past of this locality. The Classicistic church in Mokobody, on the Liwiec, was redesigned at the turn of the eighteenth century according to a project by Jakub Kubicki, and envisaged as a smaller version of the Church of Providence whose erection in Warsaw was declared by a parliamentary statue commemorating the Third May Constitution. Further to the north, a Late Baroque church in the village of Wyszków, on the same river, retained a uniform Classicistic interior dating from 1788. The same village is known for exquisite brick roadside shrines whose stone polychromy sculptures depict St. Florian and St. Jan Nepomucen.

A closer inspection of two local manors calls for leaving the main Warsaw highway. A side road in Broszków leads to the village of Chlewiska where in 1923 the widow of Władysław Reymont purchased the "Reymontówka" villa for part of the Nobel Prize in literature, awarded for the epic *Chłopi* (Peasants). Today, it is a creative work centre, open to guests and offering accommodation and meals. Slightly further along the side road we reach, *via* Chojeczno and Kopcie, the village of Sucha with its wooden manor house of the Cieszkowski family (first half of the eighteenth century, partially redesigned during the nineteenth century). The manor, now a museum with guided tours, is inhabited and has preserved the atmosphere of a typical rural residence on the borderland of Mazovia and Podlasie. Another worthy object is a small Skansen museum which includes a nineteenth-century cottage from the environs of Garwolin; here, Rev. Stanisław Brzóska, a hero of the January Uprising in Podlasie, found refuge.

■

KONSTANCIN JEZIORNA

This charming town offers ample opportunities for dining well, enjoying excellent coffee and strolling in the local park or along the tree-lined streets. Konstancin is a complex of historical villas and other buildings dating from the beginning of the twentieth century, all located in a woodland landscape. From the end of the nineteenth century, Konstancin developed as an exclusive summer resort and has retained this character up to this very day. The local villas comprise a veritable survey of the fashions and styles functioning in architecture at the beginning of the twentieth century. The resort includes also numerous sanatoria and hospitals, i.a. rheumatological, neurological, therapeutic and the world-famous Centre for Orthopaedic Rehabilitation (the so-called STOCER). Rich brine springs, with a temperature of about 30 degrees, are used in a graduation tower located in the pleasant resort park. Our walk around Konstancin may begin next to the local church and park or at the bus stop and parking lot near the tower. Well-marked trails, offering two-hour excursions, e.g. following the black signs of a route encircling the town, start at the church at the intersection of Piłsudskiego and Sienkiewicza Streets.

Just a few steps away lies Obory, beautifully situated in the Vistula valley and with as many as three nature reservations and a Baroque manor house from 1681–1688, built probably according to a project by Tylman of Gameren or an architect from his circle; in 1893, partially redesigned by Henryk Marconi. The manorial complex, which includes an outbuilding from the second half of the eighteenth century, is surrounded by a historical park. Since for years the manor has been used as a work centre for men of letters, its area remains closed to visitors.

The Chojnowski Landscape Park, bordering with Konstancin, features numerous old pines, ancient oaks, and an exceptional amassment of nature reservations and monuments. This convenient excursion terrain is the beginning of numerous marked tourist trails, i.a. from the train station and parking lot in Zalesie Górne. The whole region abounds with woodland parking spots and includes the outdoor recreation facilities in Zimne Doły. It is advisable to spend some time in nearby Piaseczno, with its historical pattern of streets around the market square in the old centre, deling back to the location of the town in 1429. The Late Gothic church from the sixteenth century blends elements of Renaissance, Baroque and contemporary design into a unique whole. The tower of the Classicistic town hall from 1824 bears the municipal coat of arms, and the dome displays a half-moon, which recalls the arrival to Piaseczno of an envoy of the Ottoman Empire who in 1777 was sent on a mission to the Polish monarch.

■

HISTORICAL MONUMENTS IN AND AROUND CZERSK

To the south of Konstancin the picturesque ruins of Czersk Castle overlook the Vistula valley. In the mid-thirteenth century this was the most important political and Church centre of Mazovia. At the end of the fourteenth century, the dukes of Mazovia replaced the wooden castle-town with a mighty brick castle, redesigned in the middle of the sixteenth century. From the following century, the castle became increasingly neglected, and by the mid-nineteenth century its ruins turned into an object of interest conceived as testimony of the past; today, it is one of the most frequently visited Mazovian monuments, with a spectacular scenic view of extensive orchards, stretching to Warka and Grójec. Czersk Castle was part of the widow's endowment of Queen Bona who was the first to introduce fruit cultivation.

To the north, the panorama from the Czersk towers includes Góra Kalwaria. Preserved remnants of the Calvary premises from 1666–1667 disclose a spatial composition based on the plan of a cross whose core consists of the present-day Kalwaryjska Street while the arms comprise Dominikańska Street and Pijarska Street. A chapel known as Pilate's House, built at the crossing of the axis, was converted to the extant church of the Elevation of the Holy Cross (1680, redesigned in 1791). On the opposite side of the square – the former market square – stands a Classicistic town hall with market halls from the first half of the nineteenth century on the right. The Baroque Bernardine church was erected in 1755–1759 according to the project by Jakub Fontana. In Marianki, beyond the compact development of the town, the interior of the small church of the Cenacle (1674), considerably redesigned in modern times, features the eighteenth-century sarcophagus of Rev. Stanisław Papczyński, chaplain and close friend of King Jan III Sobieski, and founder of the Marian order, the present-day user of the church.

In the past, Góra Kalwaria was one of the prime centres of the Chassidic Jews in Poland and from 1859 – the site of the manor built by Izaak Meir Rothenberg, the famous tsadik. Jews inhabited a quarter in the region of Pijarska Street which included the tsadik's residence and two synagogues. Today, both the manor house (10 Pijarska Street) and the former municipal synagogue (5 Pijarska Street) have been put to different uses. The Beit hamidrash, i.e. prayer house, remains under the supervision of the Chief Rabbi of the Republic of Poland. The Jewish cemetery, situated in Zakalwaria Street, is frequently visited by Jews from abroad, especially the United States, who make it the focal point of their tours.

Czersk. At the end of the fourteenth century the dukes of Mazovia erected a mighty castle

Within the Range of Podkowa Leśna

The garden-city of Podkowa Leśna, to the west of Warsaw, is composed of detached houses surrounded by old trees merging with the nearby woods. Founded in the 1920s, this locality was divided into several spheres, composed of streets named after birds, trees, flowers, animals or men of letters. The Warsaw line, opened in 1927, was the first electric train line in Poland. The town was and continues to be associated with numerous outstanding representatives of Polish science and culture, i.a. Anna and Jarosław Iwaszkiewicz, whose museum is situated in their home in Stawisko, where they lived in 1928–1980. Podkowa encompasses nature reservations – the Prof. Bolesław Hryniewiecki reserve, bordering with the town, is one of the oldest and most beautiful suburban woodland reservations of its kind, while the "Parów Sójek" deciduous wood occupies the very centre of the town. Up to 1945, the variegated and magnificent Nadarzyńskie Woods were the property of the landed estate in Młochów; today, they display all the features of a large and natural suburban woodland park, with plenty of Romantic nooks and trees more than 180 years-old. The entire region is ideal for walks along footpaths, woodland routes and attractive, well-marked tourist trails, open all year round.

Near Podkowa

The environs of Podkowa include a noteworthy motorisation museum in Otrębusy and Karolin, situated to the south of the Warsaw Commuter Train line in the midst of a wood – the seat of the world-famous "Mazowsze" State Song and Dance Ensemble, established by Tadeusz Sygietyński and after his death supervised for many years by his wife, Mira Zimińska-Sygietyńska.

The same Warsaw highway brings us to – at first glance – unimposing, albeit noteworthy town of Pruszków. A large number of factory buildings scattered throughout this considerable industrial centre dates back to the turn of the nineteenth century and possesses certain historical merits. The town centre is composed of an extensive former manorial park with numerous old trees; along its edges we find the museum of ancient Mazovian metallurgy – one of the most interesting objects on the trail. Opposite the hospital in Armii Krajowej Street, stands a house built in the Polish manorial style; it was to this villa that in March 1945 Soviet authorities invited the leaders of the underground Republic of Poland, later abducted by the NKVD to Moscow, where they were unlawfully imprisoned and sentenced during the so-called Trial of the Sixteen.

The neighbouring locality of Pęcice, situated amidst fields and meadows, includes the Classicistic palace of the Sapieha family (1809), surrounded by a historical park and bearing the inscription: "I am a Polish manor house that battles valiantly and guards faithfully". Today, this is the "Dom polski" boarding-house – offering respite over a cup of coffee or dinner, apartments adapted for longer stays and conference or reception rooms.

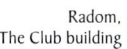

RADOM AND ITS ENVIRONS

THE LAND OF FAMOUS POLES ALONG THE SOUTHERN EDGES OF THE VOIVODESHIP

The preserved fragments of Kozienicka Forest, secluded in reservations, recall that this was the favourite site of royal hunts and the resting place of Polish rulers during their journeys to and from Wilno and Krakow. In 1467, one of such sojourns coincided with the birth of future King Zygmunt, later known as the Old, an event commemorated by a Latin inscription on a column from 1518, standing in the palace garden. In the twenty fourth year of the reign of this monarch, Jan Kochanowski was born in a manor house in the village of Sycyna, to the south of the Forest.

THE NATIVE LAND OF A GREAT POET

"Guest, sit down under my leaves and partake of leisure" – this verse from an epigram by Jan Kochanowski is familiar to every Pole. The greatest Polish poet of the Renaissance era was fond of passing time under a linden tree growing in front of his manor house in the village of Czarnolas near Zwoleń. Today, both the famous tree and the wooden edifice are gone. A brick manor from the second half of the nineteenth century has been converted into a biographical museum. A monument of Jan Kochanowski stands in Czarnolas and a second one was erected opposite the Sycyna residence, where the poet was born in 1530. Yet another monument is found in the former market square in the town of Zwoleń; all three bear the only surviving likeness of the poet, taken from a marble bust above an epitaph on the wall of the Kochanowski chapel (1610) in the sixteenth-century

Radom,
The Club building

168

parish church in Zwoleń. Master Jan was buried in the church crypt, but the turbulent course of history rendered the exact location of his ashes uncertain.

RADOM – AN INDUSTRIAL AND CULTURAL CENTRE

Radom is the capital of a large region in the Mazovian Lowland, sharing voivodeship boundaries with historical Mazovia. It is also associated with great names – that of Dr. Tytus Chałubiński (b. 1820), the famous discoverer of the Tatra Mts. and the outstanding Symbolist Jacek Malczewski, born in 1854; a collection of his paintings can be admired in the local museum. This industrial town, the largest in the voivodeship after Warsaw, is a vital cultural centre with excellent exhibitions and acclaimed theatrical festivals, i.a. featuring plays by Witold Gombrowicz, performed in the Jan Kochanowski Theatre. The oldest local historical monument is an early mediaeval stronghold. Another extant vestige of the past is the town-planning configuration, dating from the *locatio* during the reign of Kazimierz the Great and composed of a pattern of the town walls, the market square and a street network. The few surviving buildings, albeit with time expanded and redesigned and thus no longer stylistically uniform, are also worthy of attention. Fragments of the church of St. Wacław (Wenceslas) originate probably from the thirteenth century, the Late Gothic brick parish church was founded by Kazimierz the Great. The church of the Bernardine monastery also represents the Late Gothic style, and the originally Baroque and later redesigned Piarist collegiate church continues to serve as a school.

Radom, church
of the Holy Trinity

MUSEUMS AND HISTORICAL OBJECTS IN THE REGION OF RADOM

Radom and its nearest vicinity are a region of museums. The extremely interesting Museum of the Radom Village, to the south of the town, is accompanied by an ethnographic park stretching along the road to Szydłowiec. The village of Orońsko contains an important manorial complex from the second half of the nineteenth century; this former property of the outstanding painter Józef Brandt has been adapted for a Centre of Polish Sculpture, which holds plein air exhibitions. A small distance away lies Szydłowiec – one of the greatest landmarks of the voivodeship and a charming town which once belonged to the Szydłowiecki and Radziwiłł families. Steeped in history, it features old buildings: the Late Gothic parish church, whose interior brims with exceptional monuments, a Late Renaissance town hall and a castle which combines the features of the aforementioned styles and now houses a Museum of Folk Instruments. The Jewish cemetery in the eastern part of

169

the town is strewn with matsevahs from the eighteenth and nineteenth century and remains the best preserved object of this type in the voivodeship.

Szydłowiec,
Gothic-
-Renaissance
castle (beginning
of sixteenth
century)

Przysucha

A scenic tour of the region of Radom could end in this small town to the west of Szydłowiec. For many years, Przysucha was inhabited also by Jewish and German communities which had their own market squares. The Jewish square still includes a Classicistic synagogue from the end of the eighteenth century, one of the scarce surviving examples in Poland; other objects of this type were intentionally destroyed by the Nazis. The town of Przysucha was a famous Chassidic centre, and at the turn of the eighteenth century the residence of the "Holy Jew", tsadik Jakow Icchak Rabinowicz, a legendary figure already during his lifetime. Przysucha is also the birthplace of Oskar Kolberg (b. 1814), member of a German family strongly attached to Polishness, a great Polish patriot, a researcher into Polish folk culture and a renowned musicologist whose biography comprises the theme of a local museum. Blessed Władysław of Gielniów, the patron saint of Warsaw, was born in nearby Gielniów in 1440. The archaic words of his Church hymns – the first to be written in Polish – are sung to this day.

How to Visit Mazovia

The only opportunity for seeing true Mazovia is to follow the side and country roads, not crowded highways, frequently enclosed by billboards. Side roads incline the visitor to drive slowly and to savour the lowland landscape. The number of gas stations and roadside bars, restaurants and cafes is adequate. Embarking upon excursions into the local woods it is necessary to keep in mind that the numerous parking lots are, as a rule, unprotected – it is better to leave the car next to a tourist centre, a hotel or a house and, after making suitable arrangements to park, e.g. within a fenced-in farm area.

Hiking Across Mazovia

The most popular, least expensive and healthiest form of tourism is hiking. In Mazovian conditions hiking does not call for special equipment, as long as it is comfortable and suitable for the time of year. There are more than 2 000 kms. of marked trails, and the marking system is identical as in the mountains – the signs are painted along the course, e.g. on trees. Such trails are found in several regions, the greatest number occurring near Warsaw, Płock and in region of Radom. They include trails which are ideal for longer, several day long holidays such as the approx. 170 km. long Bolesław the Wrymouth trail (red signs), leading from Urszulewskie Lake near Sierpc, across Płock and Gostynin to Kutno, or 100 kms. of a forest trail on the Bug (red signs), from Sadowne to Pułtusk, and the 80 km. long landscape trail in the region of Otwock (blue signs), from Glinianki *via* Otwock and Osieck to Garwolin. The majority of the routes were delineated for the purposes of day or weekend trips. The direct environs of Warsaw abound with a thick network of marked trails, making it possible to arrange an excursion on one's own; the routes are of arbitrary length, depending on the willingness and physical prowess of the tourist. The most popular foot trails in the neighbourhood of Warsaw are to be found in riverside terrains or woodlands, especially in protected nature reserves such as the Kampinoski National Park and other assorted landscape parks.

Biking and Skiing in Mazovia

Many of the rural woodland paths and roads create excellent conditions for bikers. It is not recommended, however, to start such excursions in the city – the bicycles should be taken into the countryside, best by car. The dense network of well-marked trails, specifically intended for hiking, is open also for bikers. Some of the trails constitute an excellent opportunity for riding mountain bikes, since the paths are frequently sandy or, depending on the given season of the year periodically muddy; they may also lead across dunes – a rather adventurous undertaking which requires considerable skill. Numerous side or hard-surface roads with small or even scarce traffic are also open to bikers, and are worth recommending to all those fearing more strenuous trips. The further from Warsaw the greater the number of such opportunities.

A layer of snow, which is thick enough to enable comfortable skiing, occurs for a rather brief period of time and substantial wintertime snowfalls are a rarity. Mazovia also does not provide opportunities for Alpine skiing, although the hillocks of the Gielniowski Hump near Szydłów, along the southern edges of the voivodeship, attain a height of 400 metres above sea level, and the differences in levels are sizable. Pleasant moraine rises are to be found in the vicinity of Płock, for instance near Sikórz. The region of Mazovia is excellent for cross-country skiing. Near Warsaw good conditions are to be enjoyed in suburban Pomiechówek where annual skiing races are held.

The Great Surprise of the Region: Narrow-gauge Railways

Trips on vintage narrow-gauge railways, which were introduced at the end of the nineteenth century, are an extremely attractive form of sightseeing in Mazovia. The second half of the nineteenth century was the Golden Age of such trains which served the local brick works, sugar refineries and sawmills, and were used by crowds of city dwellers longing for vacations in the countryside. After 1945, narrow-gauge lines ceased to be fashionable and their exploitation became much too expensive. Fortunately, several lines have survived, and the Warsaw suburban networks continue to serve tourists. They include the Mławska Commuter Railway from Mława to Maków Mazowiecki, the Nasielska Railway from Nasielsk to Pułtusk, the Sochaczewska Railway from Sochaczew to the Kampinoski National Park, the Grójecka line from Piaseczno to Grójec and Nowe Miasto on the Pilica, and the Rogowska line from Rogów to Rawa Mazowiecka and Biała Rawska.

Narrow-gauge railways do not run according to a strict timetable, but tourist excursions are available and the ticket prices are identical to those in train communication as a whole. A special tourist train with a programme either suggested by a particular line or by the client may be booked along a route chosen at will by individuals who are interested in the service. The engine can draw one or several carriages, including a buffet car. The prices vary, and tourists up to the age of 26 pay much lower rates. Information is available and reservations can be made either at the offices of particular lines or at the Commuter Trains board in the central offices in Warsaw. A special Narrow-gauge Railway Museum in Sochaczew features a superior collection of more than a hundred different vehicles: steam engines, carriages and go-devils, the passenger car of the last Polish horse-drawn train, used in Białowieska Forest for carrying Marshal Józef Piłsudski, as well as the hundred year-old club cars of a vintage train which can be booked upon special occasions, and for an equally special price. A small railway Skansen and souvenirs are among the other tourist offerings of Mława.

In Search for a Farmland Landscape

Up to this day, the origin of the name of Mazovia remains undeciphered. One of the suggestions claims that it comes from "maz", "mazać" (to smear, to soil), supposedly given to the population and the region by the inhabitants of neighbouring terrains to describe people "soiled" by work on the land. Undoubtedly, the farming landscape is the most universally encountered vista. The lowlands to the west of Warsaw have been cultivated for over twenty centuries, and farming has developed in the Płock and Ciechanów parts of Mazovia for more than ten centuries. The landscape is composed of several variants: regions where the dominating crops is grain, primarily rye, and large areas occupied by fields growing sugar beet and, traditionally, potatoes. Market gardening thrives along the western boundaries of Warsaw. Large raspberry plantations are to be found near Zakroczym and in the Płońsk region. Strawberries predominate near Warka and along the Vistula in the Garwolin area. The immense fruit orchards near Grójec, Góra Kalwaria and Warka are unique in Europe. A characteristic element of the local landscape are numerous herds of grazing cattle and the horse-drawn wagons and carts used by many farmers.

Rural landscape

MAZOVIAN ATTRACTIONS: FAIRS AND MARKETS

Why not visit a local fair or market? The ancient tradition of such events is enhanced by the fact that we are dealing with living monuments of the past. A century ago, the Mazovian villagers regarded a fair as an opportunity for purchasing all the indispensable and necessary commodities. Such gatherings continue being a considerable tourist attraction, although in view of the universal availability of assorted goods in the shops, their significance is slowly waning. By way of example, let us mention just a few of the numerous fairs and markets held in Mazovia. The annual horse market in Skaryszew near Radom has retained its rank for decades. Jazdów is the site of a celebrated market held every Monday after St. John's Eve, i.e. on 24 June, and every first Monday after Epiphany, i.e. after 6 January, followed by a market held after St. Helen's, i.e. 2 March and after All Souls', that is, 1 November. A locally acclaimed market is held in Myszyniec (the Kurpie region) after St. Martin's, i.e. 12 October. In the past, a given settlement attached great importance to a royal or ducal privilege granting the right to hold markets. In the case of numerous localities, market days remain unchanged for centuries. Some of the most memorable ones are those in Karczew, Maciejowice and Nowe Miasto on the Pilica (Mondays), Błonie, Jazdów, Kałuszyn, Ostrów Mazowiecka, Piaseczno, Pruszków, Siedlce and Wyszków (Tuesdays), Płońsk (poultry, eggs, grain and meat) and Sochaczew (horses – Tuesday after every first and fifteenth day of the month). Wednesday is a market day in Garwolin, Grodzisk Mazowiecki, Jazdów, Mińsk Mazowiecki, Nowy Dwór Mazowiecki, Radzymin and Warka. On Thursdays, such events take place in Grójec (the men gather along the road to Radom, and the women trade in the centre of the town) and Mszczonów (a lavish affair, held after every first and fifteenth day of the month). Piaseczno and Pułtusk organise markets on Fridays.

FOLLOWING THE TRAILS OF FOLKLORE

Certain regions of Mazovia preserved interesting and divergent old customs, costumes and folk art. A fascinating vestige of olden customs are patron saints' feast days and Church holidays, e.g. Palm Sunday in Łyse (the Kurpie region) when the congregation brandishes several metre long Easter palms. Other noteworthy events include the Corpus Christi procession in Kadzidło, Kołbiel, Łęgonice and Obryt, where the local inhabitants wear colourful regional costumes. Beautiful thanksgiving ceremonies connected with the Assumption of the Virgin Mary are held in almost every rural parish. Many villages still contain wooden architecture, whose finest examples are collected in ethnographic parks, e.g. in Sierpc or Radom. Folk art is displayed in museums which also provide information about living folk artists who may be visited in their homes.

One of the vital domains of contemporary folk art is sculpture – the region of Sierpc is populated by an exceptionally large number of outstanding folk sculptors. The likeness of Christ the Sorrowful, regarded as a symbol of Polish folk art,

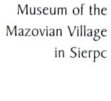
Museum of the Mazovian Village in Sierpc

174

is a frequent motif pursued by the local artists. An enthralling collection of works with this theme is to found in the church in Kadzidło in the Zielone region of Kurpie. The Kurpie residents of Myszyniecka Forest, also known as Zielona Forest, continue cultivating an astonishingly original folk culture kept alive in Łyse, e.g. during the celebrations of Palm Sunday. The traditions of beekeeping and wild beekeeping are revived every last Sunday in August, when the so-called Kurpie Honey Gathering takes place near Myszyniec. Two hundred years ago representatives of the Kurpie population from Zielona Forest appeared in Biała Forest where they produced a different type of folk culture and art. The most beautiful folk embroidery includes the so-called Pułtusk variant, made predominantly in the environs of Pniew. World-famous Mazovian paper cutouts are sold as regional souvenirs. The State Ethnographic Museum in Warsaw features Polish folk art and culture, depicting Mazovia against the background of other parts of the country.

A LAND OF SAINTS AND THE BLESSED

The numerous sanctuaries, holy sites and localities of Mazovia are the destinations of pilgrimages, even those from the most distant regions of Poland. The faithful gather at the Marian sanctuaries in Czerwińsk on the Vistula, Lewiczyn, Miedniewice, Nowe Miasto on the Pilica, Przasnysz, Smardzew, Szymanów and Stara Błotnica. Brodowe Łąki in the Kurpie region and Drogiszka near Ciechanów draw thousands of visitors for the local Church services and saints' feast days connected with the holiday of the Transfiguration of the Lord. Pilgrimages to Prostynia on the Bug are associated with the day of the Holy Trinity, while the feast day of St. Rosalie attracts crowds to a small woodland church near Pułtusk. On the day of St. Roch, the patron saint of farmers, pilgrims make their way to, i.a. Brochów near Kampinoska Forest and Długosiodło in Biała Forest.

Mazovia is a true land of the saints and the blessed venerated by the Catholic Church. Blessed Ładysław of Gielniów, the later patron saint of Warsaw, came from Gielniów near Przysucha. Grójec is the birthplace of Piotr Skarga, the famous preacher from the Vasa era and one of the most outstanding figures in the Catholic Church in Poland. The Franciscan sanctuary in Niepokalanów, connected with St. Maksymilian Kolbe, is one of the most acclaimed cult centres, celebrated not only in the country. Feast days in Rostków near Przasnycz, where St. Stanisław Kostka was born, attract crowds of visitors. The Capuchin monastery in Nowe Miasto on the Pilica, the residence of blessed Father Honorat Koźmiński, features memorabilia connected with his person. Szymanów is renowned for its monastery of the order of the Sisters of the Immaculate Conception of the Holy Virgin Mary, co-founded by blessed Mother Marcelina Darowska. Laski near Warsaw displays souvenirs connected with Mother Elżbieta Czacka, the founder of the local institution for the blind, while Czerwińsk on the Vistula has a parish and missionary museum of the Salesian order.

TRACING DRAMATIC AND PAINFUL HISTORY

Hundreds of Mazovian landmarks resound with battle cries; those stained with the blood of soldiers and innocent civilians shed during the last two centuries years include Maciejowice, where Tadeusz Kościuszko waged his last battle during the Insurrection of 1794, Pułtusk and Ostrołęka, the battlefields of Napoleonic armies in 1809, Iganie near Siedlce and Ostrołęka, where the insurgents of the November Uprising of 1830–1831 waged their main battles, and Radzymin – the

scene of the most renowned clashes from the Polish-Bolshevik war of 1920. Warsaw, Modlin and the region of Sochaczew witnessed dramatic confrontations between Polish troops and the German army in 1939. The Uprising in the Warsaw Ghetto (1943) and the Warsaw Uprising of 1944 became part of world history, while Palmiry in Kampinoska Forest is the site of a cemetery of the victims of Nazi terror. One of the consequences of the second world war was the disappearance of the Jewish community, which for centuries had been part of the history of Mazovia. "The Jewish shtetls of Poland are no more...", wrote Antoni Słonimski in a dramatic poem composed upon learning about the mass-scale annihilation of the Polish Jews. Scarce traces

Cemetery in Palmiry. Here, the Nazis conducted mass-scale executions of the inhabitants of Warsaw

include plaques, monuments, fragments of wooden architecture in the Jewish resort town of Otwock, vestiges of cemeteries in Karczew, Góra Kalwaria and, primarily, Szydłowiec as well as the synagogue in Przysucha and a highly moving monument marking the Nazi death camp in Treblinka.

Wandering Among the Beauty of Nature

Just as a view of the sea seen on the television screen cannot replace the experience of submerging oneself in real waves, so the best film cannot take the place of direct contacts with nature. Undoubtedly, the best of all the varieties of tourism are nature tours; nature study is a source of extraordinary pleasure, albeit it requires patience and perseverance from amateurs of exploring the mysteries of the natural environment. This type of tourism may be pursued on one's own, but it seems worth benefiting from the assistance offered by specialists or more advanced non-professionals. Mazovian didactic centres and their staff supply information and help to all interested visitors who may take this opportunity to become introduced to the mysteries of nature. Such facilities are to be found in the boards of, e.g. the Kampinoski National Park and the following landscape parks: Bolimowski, Brudzeński, Chojnowski, Mazowiecki, Gostynińsko-Włocławski, Kozienicki and Nadbużański.

Expeditions for wild mushrooms and berries are extremely popular. With the exception of the Kampinoski National Park, where picking all woodland fruit is forbidden, every Mazovian forest welcomes visitors. It is indispensable, however, to observe the binding rules; for example, afforestation areas and wild animal reserves are closed. Blueberries are harvested for a month, usually to about 20 June, especially in the vicinity of the railway line between Celestynów and Garwolin and in the area of Łochów and Sadowne. The first half of July is the season for wild raspberries and strawberries, while blackberries, picked in the second half of August, are to be found in almost all woodland complexes, primarily in Bolimowska Forest and the woods around Mszczonów. Certain varieties of fungi appear already in June. The most valued species, such as the boletus, are available already in July, but the true season takes place in September and October. During a good year mushrooms grow everywhere, the most prolific being Zielona Forest near Chorzele, Parciaki, and Myszyniec (the Kurpie region), the woods between Tłuszcz, Stanisławów and Dobre, as well as Bolimowska Forest and the Guzowskie Woods from Skierniewice to Żyrardów, Biała Forest near Popowo, Wyszków, Ostrów Mazowiecka and the Garwolińskie Woods in the area of Wilga and Maciejowice. Professional pickers prefer the area around Radom up to Stromecka Forest and Kozienicka Forest.

The Rivers and Lakes of Mazovia

The extremely attractive canoe trails of Mazovia equal the most popular offers in other parts of Poland. The scenic trail along the Narew from Łomża and Nowogród to Zegrzyńskie Lake accentuates the original landscape merits of one of the largest Polish rivers. Another remarkable trail leads along the Drzewiczka from Odrzywół to Nowe Miasto, and from here across Warka along the Pilica to its outlet in the Vistula, and further on along the side river-beds of the Vistula to Góra Kalwaria. The only obstacles encountered on the exceptionally beautiful trails along the Skrwa Prawa from Sierpc to Płock are mills, both standing objects and fragments of those which had been pulled down. This experience is almost equalled by the trail along the river Wkra. One of the most impressive lowland routes in Poland along the Rawka comprises a canoe trail for sophisticated lovers

The river Bug near Brok

177

of water sports; bristling with obstacles, it includes sudden and narrow meanders, numerous fallen trees, mills and former mill sills, as well as a rapid current. The Liwiec and the Świder are also available, but in the summer both rivers have a low water level and the shallow spots could hinder the trip. Tourist offices and private firms specialise in canoe rental and transportation.

Only some of the rivers provide suitable conditions for bathing, i.a. the Liwiec, the Swider, the Pilica and the Rawka. Certain localities have swimming pools or bathing facilities in local river reservoirs, e.g. in Zalesie Górne near Piaseczno and Maków Mazowiecki near Radom. Popular lakes next to Płock or Sierpc welcome lovers of swimming, boating and leisure in attractive surroundings. Bathing and outdoors recreation are favoured by the natural beaches on the majority of our rivers and and lakes. The Zegrzyńskie Lake, the largest water reservoir of the region, offers excellent conditions for sailing, and its banks are studded with tourist centres and marinas, where the visitor may rent boats.

There is excellent fishing in the closest environs of Warsaw, with numerous accessible and pleasant fishing grounds. The acclaimed Zegrzyńskie Lake, together with the Narew and the Bug flowing into it, is one of the best Central European fishing terrains. Here, visitors come to catch sheatfish and pike-perch, especially at the crossing of the rivers. The regions of Modlin include the Narew and the Wkra as well as the Vistula, where the stretch from Modlin to Płock abounds with sheatfish, pike-perch, barbel and other species; the rich river fauna, including the highly valued vimba, is being restored. The old river beds of the Vistula and the Bug are the home of the sheatfish, the carp, and the tench. Other noteworthy species of Mazovian fish include the crucian, the chub, and the ide. Boatmen in the Gostynińskie Lake District fish for bream. Only in the Pilica did the number of valuable fish decline. Fishing is not foreseen on such rivers as the Rawka and the Świder, which serve as nature reserves.

On Horseback and By horse-drawn Carriages

Such excursions are becoming increasingly popular. Numerous Mazovian stables and riding schools offer lessons and facilities for trips in the closest vicinity. Current information is published in local newspapers and specially issued brochures and guidebooks, available in select bookstores. The best known are the stables in Łąck near Płock, in Dąbrowa Leśna, Zaborów, Korfowe, Kampinos on the edge of the Kampinoski National Park, Stara Miłosna, Świdry Małe and other spots in the region of Otwock, as well as in Paszyn near Nadarzyn and Żółwin next to Podkowa Leśna, Błędów near Pomiechówek, the Zegrzyńskie Lake area, Grabskie Budy and Mogiły in the Bolimowski Landscape Park, and many other localities.

Lechosław Herz

ADDRESSES IN MAZOWIECKIE VOIVODESHIP

I. Voivodeship Authorities

1. Self-Government Administration

Mazowieckie Voivodeship Sejmik – Presidium
00-950 Warszawa, Pl. Bankowy 3/5

President of the Sejmik
Włodzimierz Nieporęt
tel. 620-13-74

Vice-President of the Sejmik
Danuta Grabowska
tel. 694-19-89

Vice-President of the Sejmik
Andrzej Łuszczewski
tel. 623-10-05

Vice-President of the Sejmik
Aleksander Sopliński
tel. (023) 673-03-67 w. 366

Office of the Mazowieckie Voivodeship Sejmik
Director of the Office of the Mazowieckie Voivodeship Sejmik
Danuta Marciniak, tel. 695-66-16

Commissions of the Mazowieckie Voivodeship Sejmik and their chairmen

Agriculture and Rural Terrains
Krzysztof Borkowski

Budget and Finances
Janusz Piechociński

Culture and National Heritage
Jan Parys

Economic Development, Infrastructure and Combating Unemployment
Krzysztof Czeszejko-Sochacki

Education, Sciences and Higher Schools
Krzysztof Dołowy

Health and Physical Culture
Adam Struzik

Law, Self-Government, Public Security and Order
Ryszard Grodzicki

Revision Commission
Marian Rodzeń

Promotion of Mazowiecki Voivodeship and Foreign Cooperation
Jolanta Gontarczyk

Protection of the Natural Environment
Jan Hawrylewicz

Regional Development Strategy and Spatial Administration
Michał Strąk

Social and Family Policy
Ewa Mańkowska

Mazowieckie Voivodeship Board
03-472 Warszawa, ul. Brechta 3, tel. exch. 618-53-00; fax 618-82-07

Voivodeship Marshal	–	Dr. Zbigniew Kuźmiuk	tel. 618-15-77
Vice-Chairman of the Board	–	Jerzy Dobek	tel. 618-85-16
Vice-Chairman of the Board	–	Leszek Mizieliński	tel. 618-34-21
Member of the Board	–	Henryk Kisielewski	tel. 618-66-85
Member of the Board	–	Leszek Kwiatek	tel. 618-59-34

Mazowieckie Voivodeship Marshal's Office

03-472 Warszawa, ul. Brechta 3, tel. exch. 618-53-00, fax 618-82-07

Director of the Marshal's Office
Waldemar Kuliński – tel. 618-96-88

Voivodeship Treasurer
Marek Miesztalski – tel. 618-80-52

Marshal's Office
Director Maria Hołownia – tel. 618-89-46

Bureau of the Sejmik, pl. Bankowy 3/5
Director Danuta Marciniak – tel. 695-65-30

Departments and Groups of the Marshal's Office

Administrative-Economic Group
Andrzej Kuczyński – Director
tel. 618-33-57

Agriculture, Modernisation of Rural Terrains and Protection of the Natural Environment
Romuald Woźniak – Director

Culture and the Protection of Cultural Heritage
Mariusz Chwedczuk – Director
tel. 618-59-55tel. 618-91-76

Health and Social Policy
Marek Lejk – Director
tel. 618-69-67

Land Surveying and Cartography
Al. Jerozolimskie 28
Józef Kalisz – Director
tel. 827-72-54

Organisational-Legal and Staff
Waldemar Kuliński – Director
tel. 618-96-88

Physical Culture and Tourism Group
Krzysztof Książek – Director
tel. 618-49-38

Promotion, Inter-Regional and Foreign Cooperation
Edward Krasowski – Director
tel. 619-72-25

Public Education
Jerzy Polański – Director

Public Roads and Transport
Zygmunt Wielogórski – Director
tel. 619-53-05

Public Security and Defence Group
ul. Floriańska 10
Andrzej Czyż – Director
tel. 818-03-46tel. 618-61-82

Spatial Administration and Regional Development
Maciej Trzaskowski – Director
tel. 618-65-29

Treasury and Finances
Marek Miesztalski – Director
tel. 618-80-52

Delegatures of the Mazowieckie Voivodeship Marshal's Office

Delegature in Ciechanów
Sławomir Morawski – Kierownik Delegatury, ul. 17 Stycznia 7, 06-400 Ciechanów;
tel. (023) 672-68-26

Delegature in Ostrołęka
Marian Krupiński – Kierownik Delegatury, pl. Generała Bema 3, 07-400 Ostrołęka;
tel. (029) 40-84

Delegature in Płock
Krystyna Furmańska – Kierownik Delegatury, ul. 1 Maja 7b, 09-400 Płock;
tel. (024) 262-26-13

Delegature in Radom
Paweł Zawodnik – Kierownik Delegatury, ul. Żeromskiego 53, 26-600 Radom;
tel. (048) 362-57-87

Delegature in Siedlce
Zbigniew Piwoński – Kierownik Delegatury, ul. Piłsudskiego 40, 08-110 Siedlce;
tel. (025) 644-72-23

II. Government Administration

Mazowieckie Voivodeship Office in Warsaw

pl. Bankowy 3/5, 00-950 Warszawa

Voivode
Antoni Pietkiewicz
tel. 695-62-51; fax 620-37-04

I Vice-Voivode
Stanisław Pietrzak
tel. 695-62-75; fax 620-64-15

Vice-Voivode
Dariusz Krajowski-Kukiel
tel. 695-65-45; fax 695-65-53

Director General
tel. 695-62-36; fax 695-65-53

Cabinet of the Voivode
tel. 695-62-44; fax 695-62-22

Press Spokesman for the Voivode
tel. 695-62-72; fax 695-62-22

Administrative-Budget Department
tel. 695-60-15; fax 620-48-10

Financial Department
tel. 695-63-57; fax 620-23-75

Land Surveying and Real Estate Administration Department
tel. 695-60-98; fax 620-29-32

Architecture, Spatial Administration and Regional Development Department
tel. 695-65-10; fax 695-65-11

State Treasury and Ownership Transformations Department
tel. 695-60-29; fax 695-60-71

Promotion and Foreign Cooperation Department
tel. 695-62-16; fax 620-99-40

Organisation and Surveillance Department
tel. 695-60-60; fax 620-33-86

Agriculture and Technical Cooperation Department
tel. 695-60-82; fax 620-24-53

Protection of the Natural Environment Department
tel. 695-67-02; fax 620-45-38

Legal Department
tel. 695-60-70; fax 695-60-71

Social Issues Department
ul. Czerniakowska 44, 00-717 Warszawa
tel. 840-00-94; fax 841-54-87

Civic Issues Department
tel. 695-66-01; fax 620-13-96

Services for the Mazowiecki Voivodeship Office in Warsaw
tel. 695-60-61; fax 695-60-62

Office of the Voivodeship Computer Scientist
tel. 695-68-05; fax 695-62-26

Office for the Protection of Secret Information
tel. 695-66-58

Crisis Management and Civil Devence Department
tel. 695-64-81; fax 695-64-84

Duty Centre of the Voivode
tel. 695-65-53; fax 620-19-40

Delegatures – Branches of the Mazowieckie Voivodeship Office

Ciechanów 06-400, ul. 17-go Stycznia 7, Roman Niesiobędzki; tel. (023) 672-20-51

Ostrołęka 07-400, ul. Gorbatowa 15, Tadeusz Romanowski; tel. (029) 760-24-95

Płock 09-402, ul. Kolegialna 15, Mirosław Milewski; tel. (024) 262-41-68

Radom 26-600, ul. Żeromskiego 53, Ryszard Dyrabik; tel. (048) 362-08-86

Siedlce 08-110, ul. Piłsudskiego 38, Adam Grytner; tel. (025) 644-32-84

IIa. Voivodeship unaffiliated administration organs

Office of School Inspector-General
00-508 Warszawa, Al. Jerozolimskie 32,, tel./fax exch. (022) 826-64-91 do 96

Voivodeship Police Headquarters
26-617 Radom, ul. 11 Listopada 43, tel. (048) 362-23-10

Voivodeship State Fire Brigade Headquarters
00-622 Warszawa, ul. Polna 1, tel. (022) 628-48-07; fax 825-30-01

Voivodeship Sanitary-Epidemological Office
00-875 Warszawa, ul. Żelazna 79, tel. (022) 620-90-01

Inspectorate for the Protection of the Natural Environment
00-024 Warszawa, Al. Jerozolimskie 30, tel. (022) 827-21-44

Inspectorate for the Purchase and Processing of Farm Produce
02-532 Warszawa, ul. Rakowiecka 36, tel. (022) 49-85-87; fax 49-90-78

Voivodeship Pharmaceutics Inspector
00-564 Warszawa, ul. Koszykowa 8, tel./fax (022) 628-28-60

Voivodeship Seed Inspection Inspectorate
05-075 Warszawa, ul. Żółkiewskiego 17, tel. (022) 773-59-08, 773-59-09

Voivodeship Department of the State Service for the Protection of Historical Monuments
00-082 Warszawa, ul. Senatorska 14, tel. (022) 826-57-52

State Trade Inspection Inspectorate
00-015 Warszawa, ul. Sienkiewicza 3, tel. (022) 826-18-30

Building Supervision Inspectorate
00-512 Warszawa, ul. Krucza 38/42, tel. (022) 661-80-10

Mazovian Health Insurance Fund 07R
00-033 Warszawa, ul. Sienkiewicza 3, tel. (022) 827-50-76 do 79

Statistical Office in Warsaw
02-134 Warszawa, ul. 1 Sierpnia 21, tel. (022) 846-30-61

Voivodeship Labour Exchange[*]
01-194 Warszawa, ul. Młynarska 16, tel. (022) 631-22-15

Voivodeship Veterinary Inspectorate
08-100 Siedlce, ul. Kazimierzowska 29, tel. (025) 222-68

Treasury Chamber
00-044 Warszawa, ul. Świętokrzyska 12, tel. (022) 694-55-55

Labour Inspection, Regional Inspectorate
02-013 Warszawa, ul. Lindleya 16, tel. (022) 628-96-99

[*] As of 1 january 2000 labour exchanges will become part of the self-government administration.

III. Poviats – Poviat Starostys

Starostwo powiatu białobrzeskiego
pl. Zygmunta Starego 9, 26–800 Białobrzegi
tel. (048) 13-34-14; fax 13-34-20

Starostwo powiatu ciechanowskiego
ul. 17 Stycznia 7, 06-400 Ciechanów
tel. (023) 672-29-45, 672-23-85;
fax 672-26-55

Starostwo powiatu garwolińskiego
ul. Staszica 15, 08-410 Garwolin
tel. (025) 684-30-10; fax 684-30-10

Starostwo powiatu gostynińskiego
ul. Dmowskiego 13, 09-500 Gostynin
tel. (0418) 89-81; fax 89-85

Starostwo powiatu grodziskiego
ul. Kościuszki 30
05-825 Grodzisk Mazowiecki
tel. (022) 724-18-33; fax 724-30-49

Starostwo powiatu grójeckiego
ul. Piłsudskiego 59, 05-600 Grójec
tel. (048) 664-37-51, 670-44-14;
fax 664-38-78

Starostwo powiatu kozienickiego
ul. Radomska 1, 26-900 Kozienice
tel. (048) 614-38-21; fax 614-33-50

Starostwo powiatu legionowskiego
ul. Sikorskiego 11, 05-120 Legionowo
tel. (022) 774-06-41; fax 774-20-17

Starostwo powiatu lipskiego
Rynek 1, 27-300 Lipsko
tel. (048) 378-11-50; fax 378-11-50

Starostwo powiatu łosickiego
ul. Piłsudskiego 6, 08-206 Łosice
tel. (083) 357-35-41

Starostwo powiatu makowskiego
Rynek 1, 06-200 Maków Mazowiecki
tel./fax (029) 717-12-31

Starostwo powiatu mińskiego
ul. Kościuszki 3, 05-300 Mińsk Mazowiecki
tel. (025) 758-42-05; fax 758-42-05

Starostwo powiatu mławskiego
ul. Reymonta 6, 06-500 Mława
tel. (023) 654-34-09; fax 654-34-09

Starostwo powiatu nowodworskiego
ul. Zakroczymska 30
05-100 Nowy Dwór Mazowiecki
tel. (022) 775-32-58, 775-36-79;
fax 775-36-79

Starostwo powiatu ostrołęckiego
pl. gen. Józefa Bema 5, 07-400 Ostrołęka
tel. (029) 764-32-81; fax 764-36-45

Starostwo powiatu ostrowskiego
ul. 3 Maja 68, 07-300 Ostrów Mazowiecka
tel. (0217) 62-232; fax (48217) 62-232

Starostwo powiatu otwockiego
ul. Górna 11/13, 05-400 Otwock
tel. (022) 779-50-64, 779-50-65;
fax 779-32-95

Starostwo powiatu piaseczyńskiego
ul. Chyliczkowska 14, 05-500 Piaseczno
tel. (022) 757-20-60, 757-20-51;
fax 757-20-51

Starostwo powiatu płockiego
ul. Bielska 59, 09-400 Płock
tel. (024) 262-30-31; fax 262-21-61

Starostwo powiatu płońskiego
ul. Płocka 39, 09-100 Płońsk
tel. (023) 662-40-39; fax 662-38-16

Starostwo powiatu pruszkowskiego
ul. Drzymały 30, 05-800 Pruszków
tel. (022) 758-67-61; fax 758-67-61

Starostwo powiatu przasnyskiego
ul. Św. St. Kostki 5, 06-300 Przasnysz
tel. (0478) 22-70; fax 22-70

Starostwo powiatu przysuskiego
ul. Wojsk Ochrony Pogranicza 10
26-400 Przysucha
tel. (048) 75-25-53, 75-23-52;
fax 75-36-72

Starostwo powiatu pułtuskiego
ul. Białowiejska 5, 06-100 Pułtusk
tel. (023) 692-12-60; fax 692-52-77

Starostwo powiatu radomskiego
ul. Domagalskiego 7, 26-600 Radom
tel. (048) 365-57-40; fax 365-57-40

Starostwo powiatu siedleckiego
ul. Skwer Niepodległości 2, 08-100 Siedlce
tel. (025) 632-20-81; fax 633-95-15

Starostwo powiatu sierpeckiego
ul. Świętokrzyska 2 A, 09-200 Sierpc
tel. (024) 275-46-48; fax 275-48-06

Starostwo powiatu sochaczewskiego
ul. 1 Maja 16, 96-500 Sochaczew
tel. (046) 862-24-27; fax 862-24-27

Starostwo powiatu sokołowskiego
ul. Wolności 24
08-300 Sokołów Podlaski
tel. (0417) 87-70-93; fax 87-31-03

Starostwo powiatu szydłowieckiego
pl. Marii Konopnickiej 7, 26-500 Szydłowiec
tel. (048) 617-10-08; fax 617-10-61

Starostwo powiatu warszawskiego
ul. Koszykowa 6ᴬ, 00-564 Warszawa
tel. (022) 621-18-99; fax 621-50-55

Starostwo powiatu warszawskiego zachodniego
ul. Wolska 167, 01-258 Warszawa
tel. (022) 37-39-49; fax 37-89-90

Starostwo powiatu węgrowskiego
ul. Przemysłowa 5, 07-100 Węgrów
tel. (025) 792-26-17; fax 792-26-17

Starostwo powiatu wołomińskiego
ul. Prądzyńskiego 3, 05-200 Wołomin
tel. (022) 787-43-00; fax 787-42-99

Starostwo powiatu wyszkowskiego
ul. Aleja Róż 2, 07-200 Wyszków
tel. (029) 742-42-70; fax 742-42-70

Starostwo powiatu zwoleńskiego
ul. Jagiełły 4, 26-700 Zwoleń
tel. (048) 676-27-48; fax 676-25-20

Starostwo powiatu żuromińskiego
pl. Piłsudskiego 4, 09-300 Żuromin
tel. (023) 657-47-00, 657-35-00;
fax 657-35-35

Starostwo powiatu żyrardowskiego
ul. Limanowskiego 45, 96-300 Żyrardów
tel. (046) 855-20-21; fax 855-20-21

Municipal Poviats

Ostrołęka
Urząd Miasta
pl. gen. Józefa Bema 1, 07-400 Ostrołęka
tel. (029) 764-68-11, 764-68-21,
764-68-22-; fax 764-39-49

Płock
Urząd Miasta
Stary Rynek 1, 09-400 Płock
tel. (024) 262-51-93, 262-35-52;
fax 268-69-99

Radom
Urząd Miasta
ul. Kilińskiego 24, 26-600 Radom
tel. (048) 362-02-01; fax 362-67-53
www. radom.pl

Siedlce
Urząd Miasta
Skwer Niepodległości 2, 08-110 Siedlce
tel. (025) 632-20-31, 644-51-40;
fax 644-67-49
e-mail: admin@siedlce.um.gov.pl
www.siedlce.um.gov.pl

IV. Gminas – Gmina Offices

Białobrzegi Poviat

Białobrzegi
Urząd Miasta i Gminy
ul. Reymonta 11, 26-800 Białobrzegi
tel. (048) 13-24-72, tel./fax 13-25-72

Promna
Urząd Gminy
26-803 Promna
tel./fax (048) 13-36-28

Radzanów
Urząd Gminy
Radzanów 92ᴬ, 26-807 Radzanów
tel. (048) 13-63-62; fax 13-62-36

Stara Błotnica
Urząd Gminy
Stara Błotnica 46, 26-806 Stara Błotnica
tel. (048) 13-73-12 w. 82

Stromiec
Urząd Gminy
ul. Piaski 4, 26-804 Stromiec
tel. (048) 13-40-21; fax 13-43-08

Wyśmierzyce
Urząd Miasta i Gminy
ul. Mickiewicza 75, 26-811 Wyśmierzyce
tel./fax (048) 13-27-94

Ciechanów Poviat

Ciechanów
Urząd Gminy
ul. Fabryczna 8, 06-400 Ciechanów
tel./fax (023) 672-26-46

Ciechanów
Urząd Miasta
Rynek 6, 06-400 Ciechanów
tel. (023) 672-32-41 do 44; fax 672-29-63
www.ciechanow.pl

Glinojeck
Urząd Miasta i Gminy
ul. Płocka 12, 06-450 Glinojeck
tel. (023) 674-01-11; tel./fax 674-00-17

Gołymin-Ośrodek
Urząd Gminy
ul. Szosa Ciechanowska 8
06-420 Gołymin
tel./fax (023) 671-60-93

Grudusk
Urząd Gminy
ul. Ciechanowska 54, 06-460 Grudusk
tel. (023) 671-50-12; fax 671-50-70

Ojrzeń
Urząd Gminy
ul. Ciechanowska 27, 06-456 Ojrzeń
tel. (023) 671-83-20; tel./fax 671-83-10

Opinogóra Górna
Urząd Gminy
ul. Krasińskiego 4
06-406 Opinogóra Górna
tel./fax (023) 673-61-10, 671-70-24

Regimin
Urząd Gminy
06-461 Regimin
tel./fax (023) 681-17-56

Sońsk
Urząd Gminy
ul. Ciechanowska 16, 06-430 Sońsk
tel. (023) 671-30-32, 671-30-85;
fax 671-30-66

Garwolin Poviat

Borowie
Urząd Gminy
08-412 Borowie
tel. (025) 685-90-70, 685-90-79;
fax 685-90-72

Garwolin
Urząd Gminy
ul. Staszica 14ᴬ, 08-400 Garwolin
tel. (025) 684-35-23; fax 684-39-31

Garwolin
Urząd Miasta
ul. Staszica 15, 08-400 Garwolin
tel. (025) 684-34-23; fax 684-34-66

Górzno
Urząd Gminy
08-404 Górzno
tel. (025) 683-15-12

Łaskarzew
Urząd Gminy
Duży Rynek 32, 08-450 Łaskarzew
tel./fax (025) 684-50-24

Łaskarzew
Urząd Miasta
Duży Rynek 32, 08-450 Łaskarzew
tel. (025) 684-52-50; fax 684-50-97

Maciejowice
Urząd Gminy
Rynek 7, 08-480 Maciejowice
tel./fax (025) 683-20-31

Miastków Kościelny
Urząd Gminy
08-420 Miastków Kościelny
tel./fax (025) 751-12-86

Parysów
Urząd Gminy
ul. Kościuszki 28, 08-441 Parysów
tel./fax (025) 685-53-19

Pilawa
Urząd Miasta i Gminy
al. Wyzwolenia 158, 08-440 Pilawa
tel. (025) 685-61-10; fax 685-60-83

Sobolew
Urząd Gminy
ul. Marzysza 16, 08-460 Sobolew
tel. (025) 682-50-23, 682-51-03;
fax 683-27-36

Trojanów
Urząd Gminy
08-455 Trojanów
tel./fax (025) 682-19-07

Wilga
Urząd Gminy
ul. Warszawska 38, 08-470 Wilga
tel. (025) 685-30-70; fax 685-30-71

185

Żelechów
Urząd Miasta i Gminy
ul. Piłsudskiego 47, 08-430 Żelechów
tel./fax (025) 754-11-44

Gostynin Poviat

Gostynin
Urząd Gminy
pl. Wolności 26, 09-500 Gostynin
tel./fax (024) 235-26-57

Gostynin
Urząd Miasta
pl. Wolności 26, 09-500 Gostynin
tel. (024) 235-24-41; fax 235-30-76

Pacyna
Urząd Gminy
ul. Wyzwolenia 7, 09-541 Pacyna
tel./fax (024) 285-80-54; 285-80-64

Sanniki
Urząd Gminy
ul. Warszawska 169, 09-540 Sanniki
tel./fax (024) 277-68-51

Szczawin Kościelny
Urząd Gminy
09-550 Szczawin Kościelny
tel. (024) 235-13-45 do 47, 235-13-72;
tel./fax 235-13-66

Grodzisk Mazowiecki Poviat

Baranów
Urząd Gminy
96-314 Baranów 54
tel. (046) 856-03-23, 856-03-20;
tel./fax 856-03-17

Grodzisk Mazowiecki
Urząd Miasta
ul. Kościuszki 32a
05-825 Grodzisk Mazowiecki
tel. (022) 755-20-16; fax 755-53-27

Jaktorów
Urząd Gminy
ul. Warszawska 33, 96-313 Jaktorów
tel./fax (046) fax 855-21-88

Milanówek
Urząd Miasta
ul. Kościuszki 45, 05-822 Milanówek
tel. (022) 758-30-61

Podkowa Leśna
Urząd Miasta
ul. Akacjowa 39/41
05-807 Podkowa Leśna
tel./fax (022) 758-98-78

Żabia Wola
Urząd Gminy
ul. Główna 3, 96-321 Żabia Wola
tel. (046) 857-81-81

Grójec Poviat

Belsk Duży
Urząd Gminy
ul. Kozietulskiego 4^A
05-622 Belsk Duży
tel.fax (048) 661-12-81

Błędów
Urząd Gminy
ul. Sadurkowska 13, 05-620 Błędów
tel. (048) 668-00-10, 668-00-94, 668-01-33;
tel./fax 668-06-55

Chynów
Urząd Gminy
05-650 Chynów
tel./fax (048) 661-42-14

Goszczyn
Urząd Gminy
ul. Bądkowska 8, 05-610 Goszczyn
tel./fax (048) 663-22-60

Grójec
Urząd Miasta i Gminy
ul. Piłsudskiego 47, 05-600 Grójec
tel. (048) 664-23-01; fax 664-21-03

Jasieniec
Urząd Gminy
ul. Warecka 42, 05-604 Jasieniec
tel. (048) 661-35-70; fax 661-35-81
e-mail: info@jasieniec.ug.gov.pl

Mogielnica
Urząd Miasta i Gminy
Rynek 1, 05-640 Mogielnica
tel. (048) 663-52-63, 663-53-22;
tel./fax 663-51-49

Nowe Miasto n. Pilicą
Urząd Miasta i Gminy
pl. O.H. Koźmińskiego 1/4
05-645 Nowe Miasto n. Pilicą
tel./fax (048) 674-10-98

Pniewy
Urząd Gminy
05-652 Pniewy
tel./fax (048) 668-64-24

Tarczyn
Urząd Gminy
ul. Rynek 8^A, 05-555 Tarczyn
tel. (048) 727-81-84, 727-70-53;
fax 727-81-91

Warka
Urząd Miasta i Gminy
pl. Czarnieckiego 1, 05-660 Warka
tel./fax (048) 667-20-02, 667-22-28
e-mail: z.administracja@warka.pl

Kozienice Poviat

Garbatka-Letnisko
Urząd Gminy
ul. Kochanowskiego 93
26-930 Garbatka-Letnisko
tel. (048) 621-01-94; fax 621-00-54

Głowaczów
Urząd Gminy
ul. Rynek 35, 26-903 Głowaczów
tel. (048) 623-10-75; fax 623-10-51

Gniewoszów
Urząd Gminy
ul. Lubelska 16, 26-920 Gniewoszów
tel. (048) 621-50-03; fax 621-50-46

Grabów n. Pilicą
Urząd Gminy
ul. Pułaskiego 51
29-902 Grabów n. Pilicą
tel. (048) 662-70-14; fax 662-70-52

Kozienice
Urząd Miasta i Gminy
ul. Parkowa 5, 26-900 Kozienice
tel. (048) 614-21-23, 614-39-92;
tel./fax 614-20-48

Magnuszew
Urząd Gminy
ul. Saperów 26, 26-910 Magnuszew
tel. (048) 621-71-05; tel./fax 621-70-25

Sieciechów
Urząd Gminy
Rynek 16, 26-922 Sieciechów
tel./fax (048) 621-60-08

Legionowo Poviat

Jabłonna
Urząd Gminy
ul. Modlińska 152, 05-110 Jabłonna
tel. (022) 774-38-34; fax 782-43-50
e-mail: info@jablonna.com.pl

Legionowo
Urząd Miasta
ul. J. Piłsudskiego 3
05-120 Legionowo
tel. (022) 774-20-31, 774-28-16;
fax 774-02-32, 784-49-81
e-mail: urzad@legionowo.uw.gov.pl
www.legionowo.um.gov.pl

Nieporęt
Urząd Gminy
pl. Wolności 1, 05-126 Nieporęt
tel. (022) 774-83-21; fax 774-32-57

Serock
Urząd Miasta i Gminy
Rynek 21, 05-140 Serock
tel. (022) 782-74-36; fax 782-74-88

Wieliszew
Urząd Gminy
ul. Modlińska 1, 05-135 Wieliszew
tel./fax (022) 782-20-22, 782-22-32,
782-27-22, 782-27-32
e-mail: info@wieliszew.ug.gov.pl

Lipsko Poviat

Chotcza
Urząd Gminy
27-312 Chotcza
tel. (048) 378-28-55

Ciepielów
Urząd Gminy
ul. Czachowskiego 1, 27–310 Ciepielów
tel. (048) 378-80-06, 378-80-80;
fax 378-80-44

Lipsko
Urząd Miasta i Gminy
Rynek 1, 27-300 Lipsko
tel. (048) 378-01-75; tel./fax 378-00-48

Rzeczniów
Urząd Gminy
27-353 Rzeczniów
tel. (048) 616-70-24, 616-70-41;
fax 616-73-10

Sienno
Urząd Gminy
Rynek 36/40, 27-350 Sienno
tel./fax (048) 378-16-11 w. 18

Solec n. Wisłą
Urząd Gminy
Rynek 1, 27-320 Solec n. Wisłą
tel. (048) 376-12-66; tel./fax 376-12-75

Łosice Poviat

Huszlew
Urząd Gminy
80-206 Huszlew
tel. (083) 358-01-23; fax 358-01-08

Łosice
Urząd Miasta i Gminy
ul. Piłsudskiego 6, 08-200 Łosice
tel. (083) 357-35-42; tel./fax 357-27-01
www.bmb.pl/losice/

Olszanka
Urząd Gminy
08-207 Olszanka
tel. (083) 357-51-23; fax 357-51-83

Platerów
Urząd Gminy
ul. 3 Maja 5, 08-210 Platerów
tel./fax (083) 357-84-47
e-mail: info@platerow.ug.gov.pl

Sarnaki
Urząd Gminy
ul. Joselewicza 3, 08-220 Sarnaki
tel. (083) 359-91-98; fax 359-91-48

Stara Kornica
Urząd Gminy
08-205 Stara Kornica
tel. (083) 358-78-22; fax 358-78-93

Maków Mazowiecki Poviat

Czerwonka
Urząd Gminy
06-232 Czerwonka
tel. (029) 717-95-05, 717-95-21;
fax 717-95-17

Karniewo
Urząd Gminy
06-425 Karniewo
tel. (023) 691-10-13, 691-10-54, 691-11-02;
tel./fax 691-10-73

Krasnosielc
Urząd Gminy
Rynek 39, 06-212 Krasnosielc
tel. (029) 717-50-73; fax 717-50-74

Maków Mazowiecki
Urząd Miasta
ul. Moniuszki 6
06-200 Maków Mazowiecki
tel. (029) 717-12-46; fax 717-15-07

Młynarze
Urząd Gminy
ul. Ostrołęcka 7, 06-231 Młynarze
tel./fax (029) 766-95-92

Płoniawy-Bramura
Urząd Gminy
06-210 Płoniawy-Bramura
tel. (029) 717-80-43; fax 717-80-47

Różan
Urząd Gminy
pl. Obrońców Różana 4, 06-230 Różan
tel. (029) 766-90-05; fax 766-91-02

Rzewnie
Urząd Gminy
06-225 Rzewnie
tel. (029) 761-34-09; tel./fax 761-34-31

Sypniewo
Urząd Gminy
ul. Ostrołęcka 27, 06-216 Sypniewo
tel./fax (029) 717-77-83

Szelków
Urząd Gminy
06-220 Szelków
tel. (029) 717-60-01; fax 717-60-04

Mińsk Mazowiecki Poviat

Cegłów
Urząd Gminy
ul. Kościuszki 2, 05-319 Cegłów
tel. (025) 757-01-88, 758-63-85;
tel./fax 757-01-87

Dębe Wielkie
Urząd Gminy
ul. Strażacka 4, 05-311 Dębe Wielkie
tel./fax (025) 757-77-71

Dobre
Urząd Gminy
ul. Kościuszki 1, 05-307 Dobre
tel./fax (025) 711-90

Halinów
Urząd Gminy
ul. Spółdzielcza 1, 05-074 Halinów
tel. (022) 783-60-20, 783-60-80, 783-61-05;
fax 783-61-07
www.bmb.pl/halinow

Jakubów
Urząd Gminy
05-306 Jakubów
tel. (025) 757-91-90

Kałuszyn
Urząd Miasta i Gminy
ul. Pocztowa 1, 05-310 Kałuszyn
tel. (025) 757-66-18; tel./fax 757-60-26

Latowicz
Urząd Gminy
ul. Rynek 4, 05-334 Latowicz
tel. (025) 752-10-80, 752-10-90

Mińsk Mazowiecki
Urząd Gminy
ul. Kościuszki 3, 05-300 Mińsk Mazowiecki
tel./fax (025) 758-24-89, 758-35-17

Mińsk Mazowiecki
Urząd Miasta
ul. Konstytucji 3 Maja 1
05-300 Mińsk Mazowiecki
tel. (025) 758-20-44; fax 758-40-25

Mrozy
Urząd Gminy
ul. Mickiewicza 35, 05-320 Mrozy
tel. (025) 757-41-90

Siennica
Urząd Gminy
ul. Kołbielska 1, 05-332 Siennica
tel./fax (025) 758-86-25

Stanisławów
Urząd Gminy
Rynek 32, 05-304 Stanisławów
tel./fax (025) 757-50-90
e-mail: info@stanislawow.ug.gov.pl

Sulejówek
Urząd Miasta
ul. Dworcowa 55, 05-070 Sulejówek
tel. (022) 783-11-44; tel./fax 783-12-22

Wesoła
Urząd Miasta
ul. I Praskiego Pułku 21, 05-075 Wesoła
tel./fax (025) 773-57-26

Mława Poviat

Dzierzgowo
Urząd Gminy
ul. Kościuszki 1, 06-520 Dzierzgowo
tel. (023) 655-23-27; fax 655-23-26

Lipowiec Kościelny
Urząd Gminy
06-545 Lipowiec Kościelny
tel./fax (023) 655-50-28, 655-50-29

Mława
Urząd Miasta
Stary Rynek 19, 06-500 Mława
tel. (023) 654-33-82; fax 654-36-52
e-mail: info@mlawa.um.gov.pl
www.mlawa.um.gov.pl

Radzanów
Urząd Gminy
pl. Piłsudskiego 26, 06-540 Radzanów
tel. (023) 653-42-89

Strzegowo
Urząd Gminy
pl. Wolności 32, 06-445 Strzegowo
tel. (023) 679-40-47

Stupsk
Urząd Gminy
ul. Sienkiewicza 10, 06-561 Stupsk
tel. (023) 653-12-54, 653-12-55;
fax 653-10-16

Szreńsk
Urząd Gminy
pl. Kanoniczny 10, 06-550 Szreńsk
tel./fax (023) 653-44-71

Szydłowo
Urząd Gminy
06-516 Szydłowo
tel. (023) 655-40-84; fax 654-93-28

Wieczfnia Kościelna
Urząd Gminy
ul. Kościelna 48,
06-513 Wieczfnia Kościelna
tel./fax (023) 654-00-04

Wiśniewo
Urząd Gminy
06-521 Wiśniewo
tel. (025) 655-70-25; fax 655-72-27

Nowy Dwór Mazowiecki Poviat

Czosnów
Urząd Gminy
ul. Gminna 2, 05-152 Czosnów
tel. (022) 785-02-01; fax 785-00-57

Leoncin
Urząd Gminy
ul. Partyzantów 3, 05-155 Leoncin
tel./fax (022) 785-65-82 do 85, 785-66-00

Nasielsk
Urząd Miasta i Gminy
ul. Kilińskiego 10, 06-130 Nasielsk
tel. (023) 691-26-64, 691-25-74, 691-24-27;
fax 691-24-70

Nowy Dwór Mazowiecki
Urząd Miasta
ul. Zakroczymska 30
05-100 Nowy Dwór Mazowiecki
tel./fax (022) 775-24-52, 775-25-32

Pomiechówek
Urząd Gminy
ul. Szkolna 1^A, 05-180 Pomiechówek
tel. (022) 785-41-85

Zakroczym
Urząd Miasta i Gminy
ul. Warszawska 7, 05-170 Zakroczym
tel. (022) 785-21-45; fax 785-26-22
www.bmb.pl/zakroczym

Ostrołęka Poviat

Baranowo
Urząd Gminy
pl. XXX-lecia 7, 06-320 Baranowo
tel. (029) 761-37-76, 761-37-82;
fax 761-37-93

Czarnia
Urząd Gminy
07-431 Czarnia
tel. 900 w. 17, 18

Czerwin
Urząd Gminy
Plac 1000-lecia 1, 07-407 Czerwin
tel./fax (029) 761-45-93

Goworowo
Urząd Gminy
ul. Szkolna 16ᴬ, 07-440 Goworowo
tel./fax (029) 761-40-43, 761-40-66

Kadzidło
Urząd Gminy
ul. Targowa 4, 07-420 Kadzidło
tel. (029) 761-80-42, 761-80-67;
tel./fax 761-80-16
e-mail: info@kadzidlo.ug.gov.pl

Lelis
Urząd Gminy
07-402 Lelis
tel./fax (029) 761-10-24

Łyse
Urząd Gminy
ul. Ostrołęcka 2, 07-437 Łyse
tel. (029) 772-50-27; fax 772-50-03

Myszyniec
Urząd Miasta i Gminy
pl. Wolności 60, 07-430 Myszyniec
tel./fax (029) 772-11-41

Olszewo-Borki
Urząd Gminy
ul. Broniewskiego 13
07-415 Olszewo-Borki
tel. (029) 761-31-07

Ostrołęka
Urząd Miasta
pl. gen. Józefa Bema 1, 07-400 Ostrołęka
tel. (029) 764-68-11, 764-68-21,
764-68-22-; fax 764-39-49

Rzekuń
Urząd Gminy
ul. Kościuszki 33, 07-411 Rzekuń
tel. (029) 761-73-01, 761-73-02

Troszyn
Urząd Gminy
ul. Słowackiego 13, 07-405 Troszyn
tel. (029) 761-11-70 w. 53

Ostrów Mazowiecka Poviat

Andrzejewo
Urząd Gminy
ul. Warszawska 36, 07-305 Andrzejewo
tel. (086) 271-70-03; fax 271-71-20

Boguty-Pianki
Urząd Gminy
al. Papieża Jana Pawła II 45
18-325 Boguty Pianki
tel. (086) 277-50-03

Brok
Urząd Miasta i Gminy
pl. Kościelny 6, 07-306 Brok
tel. (0217) 57-554; fax 57-596

Małkinia Górna
Urząd Gminy
ul. Przedszkolna 1, 07-320 Małkinia Górna
tel. (0217) 44-80-00, 44-80-01, 55-013,
55-032, 55-115, 55-674; fax 55-118

Nur
Urząd Gminy
ul. Drohiczyńska 2, 18–322 Nur
tel./fax (086) 277-40-75

Ostrów Mazowiecka
Urząd Miasta
ul. 3 Maja 66, 07-300 Ostrów Mazowiecka
tel. (0217) 44-07-50; fax 44-07-60
www.bmb.pl/ostrowmazowiecka

Ostrów Mazowiecka
Urząd Gminy
ul. Sikorskiego 3
07-300 Ostrów Mazowiecka
tel. (0217) 44-06-94; tel./fax 44-05-00

Stary Lubotyń
Urząd Gminy
07-303 Stary Lubotyń
tel. (0217) 44-64-22; fax 44-64-25

Szulborze Wielkie
Urząd Gminy
ul. Romantyczna 6
18-324 Szulborze Wielkie
tel./fax (086) 270-40-84

Wąsewo
Urząd Gminy
ul. Zastawska 13, 07-311 Wąsewo
tel. (0217) 45-80-00
e-mail: info@wasewo.ug.gov.pl

Zaręby Kościelne
Urząd Gminy
ul. Kowalska 14, 18-323 Zaręby Kościelne
tel. (086) 270-60-72; fax 270-62-00

Otwock Poviat

Celestynów
Urząd Gminy
ul. Regucka 3, 05-430 Celestynów
tel. (022) 789-71-19; fax 789-70-11

Józefów
Urząd Miasta
ul. Ks. Kard. Wyszyńskiego 1
05-420 Józefów
tel. (022) 789-49-13, 789-50-14, 789-21-22,
789-23-92; fax 789-51-02

Karczew
Urząd Miasta i Gminy
ul. Warszawska 28, 05-480 Karczew
tel. (022) 779-65-16; 779-60-83;
fax 779-65-36
e-mail: info@karczew.umig.gov.pl

Kołbiel
Urząd Gminy
ul. Kościuszki 23, 05-340 Kołbiel
tel. (025) 757-31-79; tel./fax 757-30-20

Osieck
Urząd Gminy
Rynek 1, 08-445 Osieck
tel. (025) 685-70-26; fax 685-70-90

Otwock
Urząd Miasta
ul. Armii Krajowej 5, 05-400 Otwock
tel. (022) 779-20-01 do 06; fax 779-42-25

Sobienie-Jeziory
Urząd Gminy
ul. Garwolińska 16
08-443 Sobienie-Jeziory
tel. (025) 685-80-90; fax 685-80-92

Wiązowna
Urząd Gminy
ul. Lubelska 59, 05-462 Wiązowna
tel. (022) 789-01-28, 789-01-67, 789-03-62;
fax 789-01-20
e-mail: info@wiazowna.ug.gov.pl

Piaseczno Poviat

Góra Kalwaria
Urząd Miasta i Gminy
ul. 3 Maja 10, 05-530 Góra Kalwaria
tel. (022) 727-34-11 do 13, 727-35-93;
fax 727-13-78, 727-15-93
e-mail: gorakal@mail.gorakal.umig.gov.pl
www.gorakal.umig.gov.pl

Konstancin-Jeziorna
Urząd Miasta i Gminy
ul. Warszawska 32
05-520 Konstancin-Jeziorna
tel. (022) 756-48-10, 756-42-50;
fax 756-48-85

Lesznowola
Urząd Gminy
ul. Gminnej Rady Narodowej 60
05-506 Lesznowola
tel. (022) 757-93-40 do 42; fax 757-92-70
e-mail: gmina@lesznowola.wow.pl
www.lesznowola.waw.pl

Piaseczno
Urząd Miasta i Gminy
ul. Kościuszki 5, 05-500 Piaseczno
tel. (022) 756-70-40 do 43; fax 756-70-49
www.bmb.pl/piaseczno

Prażmów
Urząd Gminy
ul. Główna 57, 05-505 Wola Prażmowska
tel. (022) 727-05-21, 727-05-22;
tel./fax 727-01-77

Płock Poviat

Bielsk
Urząd Gminy
pl. Wolności 6, 09-230 Bielsk
tel. (024) 261-55-05; fax 261-51-89

Bodzanów
Urząd Gminy
09-470 Bodzanów
tel. (024) 260-70-06 ; fax 260-70-83

Brudzeń Duży
Urząd Gminy
09-414 Brudzeń Duży
tel. (024) 260-40-23

Bulkowo
Urząd Gminy
09-454 Bulkowo
tel. (024) 265-20-13

Drobin
Urząd Miasta i Gminy
ul. Piłsudskiego 12, 09-210 Drobin
tel. (024) 260-14-41; fax 260-10-62

Gąbin
Urząd Miasta i Gminy
Stary Rynek 16, 09-530 Gąbin
tel./fax (024) 277-10-75

Łąck
Urząd Gminy
ul. Gostynińska 2, 09-520 Łąck
tel. (022) 261-45-95; tel./fax 262-92-93

191

Mała Wieś
Urząd Gminy
ul. Kochanowskiego 1, 09-460 Mała Wieś
tel./fax (024) 231-40-84

Nowy Duninów
Urząd Gminy
ul. Osiedlowa 1, 09-505 Nowy Duninów
tel. (024) 261-02-36

Płock
Urząd Miasta
Stary Rynek 1, 09-400 Płock
tel. (024) 262-51-93, 262-35-52;
fax 268-69-99

Radzanowo
Urząd Gminy
ul. Płocka 32, 09-451 Radzanowo
tel. (024) 261-34-97; fax 261-34-10

Słubice
Urząd Gminy
ul. Płocka 32, 09-533 Słubice
tel./fax (024) 277-82-10

Słupno
Urząd Gminy
ul. Miszewska 8^A, 09-472 Słupno
tel. (024) 261-29-40, 261-29-77

Stara Biała
Urząd Gminy
09-411 Stara Biała
tel. (024) 261-32-60; fax 365-61-65

Staroźreby
Urząd Gminy
ul. Płocka 18, 09-440 Staroźreby
tel./fax (024) 261-70-65

Wyszogród
Urząd Miasta i Gminy
ul. Rębowska 37, 09-450 Wyszogród
tel. (024) 231-10-20; tel./fax 231-10-24

Płońsk Poviat

Baboszewo
Urząd Gminy
ul. Warszawska 9^A, 09-130 Baboszewo
tel. (023) 661-10-91, 661-10-92;
fax 661-10-71

Czerwińsk n. Wisłą
Urząd Gminy
ul. Władysława Jagiełły 16
09-445 Czerwińsk n. Wisłą
tel. (023) 231-50-75; tel./fax 231-51-99

Dzierzążnia
Urząd Gminy
09-164 Dzierzążnia
tel. (023) 661-19-04; fax 661-19-02

Joniec
Urząd Gminy
09-131 Joniec
tel. (023) 661-60-17; fax 661-63-30

Naruszewo
Urząd Gminy
09-152 Naruszewo
tel. (023) 661-39-07; fax 661-38-72 w. 14

Nowe Miasto
Urząd Gminy
ul. Apteczna 8, 09-120 Nowe Miasto
tel. (023) 661-40-69; fax 661-44-56

Płońsk
Urząd Gminy
ul. 19-go Stycznia 39, 09-100 Płońsk
tel. (023) 662-56-35, 662-21-97;
fax 662-24-26

Płońsk
Urząd Miasta
ul. Płocka 39, 09-100 Płońsk
tel. (023) 662-27-25; fax 662-55-11

Raciąż
Urząd Miasta
pl. Mickiewicza 17, 09-140 Raciąż
tel. (023) 679-11-63; fax 679-10-28

Raciąż
Urząd Gminy
pl. Mickiewicza 17, 09-140 Raciąż
tel. (023) 679-12-80, 679-13-06

Sochocin
Urząd Gminy
pl. Nowotki 9, 09-110 Sochocin
tel./fax (023) 661-80-01

Załuski
Urząd Gminy
09-142 Załuski
tel. (023) 661-95-03

Pruszków Poviat

Brwinów
Urząd Miasta i Gminy
ul. Grodziska 12, 05-840 Brwinów
tel. (022) 729-59-06; fax 729-56-64
www.bmb.pl/brwinow

Michałowice
Urząd Gminy
ul. Raszyńska 34, 05-816 Michałowice
tel./fax (022) 723-81-78

Nadarzyn
Urząd Gminy
ul. Mszczonowska 19, 05-830 Nadarzyn
tel. (022) 729-81-85

Piastów
Urząd Miasta
ul. 11 Listopada 2, 05-820 Piastów
tel. (022) 723-60-70, 723-64-99;
fax 723-10-54

Pruszków
Urząd Miasta
ul. Kraszewskiego 14/16
05-800 Pruszków
tel. (022) 758-64-31; fax 758-66-50
www.pruszkow.gminy.pl

Raszyn
Urząd Gmin
ul. Szkolna 2^A, 05-090 Raszyn
tel. (022) 720-25-90, 720-25-91;
fax 720-30-11
e-mail: raszyn@gmina.raszyn.waw.pl

Przasnysz Poviat

Chorzele
Urząd Miasta i Gminy
ul. Ogrodowa 7, 06-330 Chorzele
tel. (029) 752-59-55 w. 161;
fax 752-59-55 w. 34

Czernice Borowe
Urząd Gminy
ul. Dolna 2, 06-415 Czernice Borowe
tel. (023) 674-62-15; fax 674-60-66

Jednorożec
Urząd Gminy
ul. Odrodzenia 14, 06-323 Jednorożec
tel. (029) 751-33-92, 751-33-94;
fax 751-33-22

Krasne
Urząd Gminy
ul. Mickiewicza 23, 06-408 Krasne
tel. (023) 671-00-17

Krzynowłoga Mała
Urząd Gminy
ul. Kościelna 3, 06-316 Krzynowłoga Mała
tel. (029) 751-27-20; fax 751-27-25

Przasnysz
Urząd Gminy
ul. Św. St. Kostki 5, 06-300 Przasnysz
tel./fax (029) 752-27-09

Przasnysz
Urząd Miasta
ul. Św. St. Kostki 5, 06-300 Przasnysz
tel. (029) 752-22-66; fax 752-22-68

Przysucha Poviat

Borkowice
Urząd Gminy
ul. Ogrodowa 9, 26-422 Borkowice
tel. (048) 75-79-10, 75-79-60;
tel./fax 75-79-23

Gielniów
Urząd Gminy
pl. Wolności 75, 26-434 Gielniów
tel. (048) 75-66-79

Klwów
Urząd Gminy
ul. Opoczyńska 35, 26-415 Klwów
tel. (048) 75-38-31

Odrzywół
Urząd Gminy
ul. Warszawska 53, 26-425 Odrzywół
tel. (041) 75-72-11 w. 36; tel./fax 75-66-78

Potworów
Urząd Gminy
ul. Grabowa 50^A, 26-414 Potworów
tel. (048) 27-31-48; fax 75-14-11 w. 41

Przysucha
Urząd Miasta i Gminy
pl. Kolberga 11, 26-400 Przysucha
tel. (048) 75-22-19; tel./fax 75-21-06

Rusinów
Urząd Gminy
ul. Żeromskiego 4, 26-411 Rusinów
tel. (048) 75-12-11 w. 23; fax 75-66-76

Wieniawa
Urząd Gminy
ul. Kochanowskiego 88, 26-432 Wieniawa
tel. (048) 75-71-11 w. 1; fax 75-23-22

Pułtusk Poviat

Gzy
Urząd Gminy
06-126 Gzy
tel. (023) 691-31-22, 691-31-67

Obryte
Urząd Gminy
07-215 Obryte
tel. (023) 692-11-56

Pokrzywnica
Urząd Gminy
06-121 Pokrzywnica
tel. (023) 691-07-21; fax 691-05-55

Pułtusk
Urząd Miasta i Gminy
ul. Rynek-Ratusz 41, 06-100 Pułtusk
tel. (023) 692-82-41, 692-03-91;
fax 692-42-96

Świercze
Urząd Gminy
ul. Pułtuska 47, 06-150 Świercze
tel. (029) 691-22-91

Winnica
Urząd Gminy
06-120 Winnica
tel. (023) 691-40-21, 691-40-92;
fax 691-40-25

Zatory
Urząd Gminy
07-217 Zatory
tel. (029) 742-72-42

Radom Poviat

Gózd
Urząd Gminy
ul. Radomska 7, 26-634 Gózd
tel. (048) 320-20-65; tel./fax 320-20-97

Iłża
Urząd Miasta i Gminy
ul. Rynek 11, 27-100 Iłża
tel. (048) 16-31-35; fax 16-33-00
e-mail: info@ilza.unig.gov.pl
www.ilza.unig.gov.pl

Jastrzębia
Urząd Gminy
26-631 Jastrzębia
tel. (048) 610-68-23; fax 610-68-25

Jedlińsk
Urząd Gminy
ul. Warecka 19, 26-660 Jedlińsk
tel./fax (048) 321-30-21

Jedlnia-Letnisko
Urząd Gminy
ul. Radomska 43, 26-630 Jedlnia-Letnisko
tel. (048) 322-10-56; fax 322-20-86

Kowala-Stępocina
Urząd Gminy
26-624 Kowala Stępocina
tel. (048) 610-17-15; fax 610-17-60

Pionki
Urząd Gminy
ul. Zwycięstwa 6, 26-670 Pionki
tel. (048) 612-15-14; fax 612-12-34

Pionki
Urząd Miasta
ul. Kolejowa 97, 26-670 Pionki
tel. (048) 612-33-96; fax 612-53-48

Przytyk
Urząd Gminy
ul. Zachęta 57, 26-650 Przytyk
tel. (048) 618-00-95; fax 618-00-87

Radom
Urząd Miasta
ul. Kilińskiego 24, 26-600 Radom
tel. (048) 362-02-01; fax 362-67-53
www. radom.pl

Skaryszew
Urząd Miasta i Gminy
ul. Słowackiego 59, 26-640 Skaryszew
tel./fax (048) 610-30-89

Wierzbica
Urząd Gminy
ul. Kościuszki 73, 26-680 Wierzbica
tel. (048) 18-20-70; tel./fax 18-20-15

Wolanów
Urząd Gminy
ul. Radomska 20, 26-625 Wolanów
tel./fax (048) 618-60-51

Zakrzew
Urząd Gminy
26-652 Zakrzew
tel. (048) 610-51-22; fax 610-51-43

Siedlce Poviat

Domanice
Urząd Gminy
08-113 Domanice
tel./fax (025) 642-43-52

Korczew
Urząd Gminy
ul. Ks. Brzóski 20^A, 08-108 Korczew
tel./fax (025) 631-20-22

Kotuń
Urząd Gminy
ul. Siedlecka 56^C, 08-130 Kotuń
tel. (025) 641-43-15, 641-43-83;
fax 632-78-30

Mokobody
Urząd Gminy
pl. Chreptowicza 25, 08-124 Mokobody
tel./fax (025) 641-13-15

Mordy
Urząd Miasta i Gminy
ul. J. Kilińskiego 9, 08-140 Mordy
tel. (025) 641-54-02; tel./fax 641-54-26

Paprotnia
Urząd Gminy
ul. 3 Maja 2, 08-107 Paprotnia
tel. (025) 631-21-22; tel./fax 631-21-10

Przesmyki
Urząd Gminy
ul. 11 Listopada 13, 08-109 Przesmyki
tel. (025) 641-23-82, 641-23-87;
fax 642-23-22

Siedlce
Urząd Miasta
Skwer Niepodległości 2, 08-110 Siedlce
tel. (025) 632-20-31, 644-51-40;
fax 644-67-49
e-mail: admin@siedlce.um.gov.pl
www.siedlce.um.gov.pl

Siedlce
Urząd Gminy
ul. Kościuszki 7, 08-110 Siedlce
tel./fax (025) 632-77-31

Skórzec
Urząd Gminy
ul. Siedlecka 5, 08-114 Skórzec
tel./fax (025) 631-28-91

Suchożebry
Urząd Gminy
ul. A. Ogińskiej 11, 08-125 Suchożebry
tel./fax (025) 631-25-15

Wiśniew
Urząd Gminy
ul. Siedlecka 13, 08-112 Wiśniew
tel. (025) 641-73-23; tel./fax 641-73-13

Wodynie
Urząd Gminy
08-117 Wodynie
tel. (025) 631-26-23; fax 631-26-81
e-mail: info@wodynie.ug.gov.pl

Zbuczyn Poduchowny
Urząd Gminy
ul. Terespolska 13
08-106 Zbuczyn Poduchowny
tel./fax (025) 411-63-90

Sierpc Poviat

Gozdowo
Urząd Gminy
ul. Gozdawy 19, 09-213 Gozdowo
tel./fax (024) 276-21-12

Mochowo
Urząd Gminy
09-214 Mochowo
tel. (024) 276-31-78

Rościszewo
Urząd Gminy
ul. Jana Pawła II 19, 09-204 Rościszewo
tel. (024) 275-39-90; tel./fax 275-57-79

Sierpc
Urząd Gminy
ul. Biskupa Floriana 4, 09-200 Sierpc
tel. (024) 275-57-01; fax 275-66-01

Sierpc
Urząd Miasta
ul. Piastowska 11^A, 09-200 Sierpc
tel. (024) 275-27-03; tel./fax 275-13-68
e-mail: info@sierpc.um.gov.pl
www.sierpc.um.gov.pl

Szczutowo
Urząd Gminy
ul. Lipowa 5^A, 09-227 Szczutowo
tel. (024) 276-71-67; fax 276-71-96

Zawidz
Urząd Gminy
ul. Mazowiecka 24
09-226 Zawidz
tel. (024) 276-61-01; fax 276-61-44

Sochaczew Poviat

Brochów
Urząd Gminy
05-089 Tułowice
tel./fax (022) 725-70-03, 725-70-51

Iłów
Urząd Gminy
ul. Płocka 2, 09-520 Iłów
tel./fax (024) 277-42-22
e-mail: info@ilow.ug.pl
www.ilow.ug.pl

Młodzieszyn
Urząd Gminy
ul. Wyszogrodzka 25, 96-512 Młodzieszyn
tel. (046) 861-64-55; tel./fax 861-68-13

Nowa Sucha
Urząd Gminy
96-513 Nowa Sucha
tel./fax (046) 861-20-51
e-mail: info@nowas.ug.gov.pl
www.nowas.ug.gov.pl

Rybno
Urząd Gminy
ul. Długa 19, 96-514 Rybno
tel./fax (046) 861-14-38

Sochaczew
Urząd Gminy
ul. 1 Maja 16, 96-500 Sochaczew
tel. (046) 862-29-21

Sochaczew
Urząd Miasta
ul. 1 Maja 16, 96-500 Sochaczew
tel. (046) 862-22-35; fax 862-26-02

Teresin
Urząd Gminy
ul. Zielona 20, 96-515 Teresin
tel. (046) 861-38-15 do 17

Sokołów Podlaski Poviat

Bielany
Urząd Gminy
ul. Słoneczna 2, 08-311 Bielany
tel. (0417) 87-80-11; fax 87-80-13

Ceranów
Urząd Gminy
08-322 Ceranów
tel./fax (0417) 87-07-79

Jabłonna Lacka
Urząd Gminy
ul. Klonowa 14, 08-304 Jabłonna Lacka
tel. (0417) 87-10-23; fax 87-11-49

Kosów Lacki
Urząd Gminy
ul. Kolejowa 1, 08-330 Kosów Lacki
tel. (0417) 87-91-05; fax 87-90-38

Repki
Urząd Gminy
ul. Parkowa 7, 08-307 Repki
tel. (0417) 87-50-23, 87-50-29;
fax 87-50-66

Sabnie
Urząd Gminy
ul. Główna 73, 08-331 Sabnie
tel. (0417) 87-41-90; fax 87-41-50

Sokołów Podlaski
Urząd Gminy
ul. Piękna 2, 08-300 Sokołów Podlaski
tel. (0417) 26-10; fax 87-73-50

Sokołów Podlaski
Urząd Miasta
ul. Wolności 21, 08-300 Sokołów Podlaski
tel. (0417) 87-26-21; fax 87-25-78

Sterdyń
Urząd Gminy
ul. Kościuszki 6, 08-320 Sterdyń
tel./fax (0417) 87-00-04

Szydłowiec Poviat

Chlewiska
Urząd Gminy
ul. Czychowskiego 49, 26-510 Chlewiska
tel./fax (048) 617-52-02

Jastrząb
Urząd Gminy
pl. Niepodległości 1, 26-502 Jastrząb
tel. (048) 628-40-15 w. 21; fax 628-42-87

Mirów
Urząd Gminy
26-503 Mirów
tel. (048) 628-39-12; fax 628-39-89

Orońsko
Urząd Gminy
ul. Szkolna 8, 26-681 Orońsko
tel. (048) 618-40-12; fax 618-40-67
e-mail: info@oronsko.ug.gov.pl

Szydłowiec
Urząd Miasta i Gminy
Rynek Wielki 1, 26-500 Szydłowiec
tel. (048) 617-12-53, 617-10-16;
fax 617-05-10

Warsaw Poviat

Warszawa-Bemowo
Urząd Gminy
ul. Powstańców Śląskich 67^C
01-355 Warszawa
tel. (022) 533-75-00; fax 665-62-60

Warszawa-Białołęka
Urząd Gminy
ul. Modlińska 197, 03-122 Warszawa
tel. (022) 676-66-03; fax 619-36-92
www.bialoleka.waw.pl

Warszawa-Bielany
Urząd Gminy
ul. Przybyszewskiego 70/72
01-824 Warszawa
tel./fax (022) 669-10-27; fax 663-08-60,
669-19-91
e-mail: gmina@bielany.waw.pl
www.bielany.waw.pl

Warszawa-Centrum
Urząd Gminy
ul. Niecała 2, 00-098 Warszawa
tel. (022) 827-77-70; fax 826-81-25

- **Warszawa-Mokotów**
Urząd Dzielnicy
ul. Rakowiecka 25/27, 02-517 Warszawa
tel. (022) 849-81-61, 849-47-24,
849-50-51; fax 848-71-71
www.mokotow.waw.pl

- **Warszawa-Ochota**
Urząd Dzielnicy
ul. Grójecka 17^A, 02-021 Warszawa
tel. (022) 822-20-21 do 28; fax 659-80-08

- **Warszawa-Praga Południe**
Urząd Dzielnicy
ul. Grochowska 274, 03-841 Warszawa
tel. (022) 612-47-12, 810-54-63;
fax 810-69-99

- **Warszawa-Praga Północ**
Urząd Dzielnicy
ul. ks. Kłopotowskiego 15
03-708 Warszawa
tel. (022) 619-86-72, 619-00-41;
fax 619-16-05

- **Warszawa-Śródmieście**
Urząd Dzielnicy
ul. Nowogrodzka 43, 00-691 Warszawa
tel. (022) 628-35-71, 621-32-11;
fax 628-15-22

- **Warszawa-Wola**
Urząd Dzielnicy
al. Solidarności 90, 01-003 Warszawa
tel. (022) 838-90-83, 838-80-31;
fax 838-89-81

- **Warszawa-Żoliborz**
Urząd Dzielnicy
ul. Słowackiego 6/8, 01-627 Warszawa
tel. (022) 39-98-81, 39-95-21;
fax 39-90-03

Warszawa-Rembertów
Urząd Gminy
al. Sztandarów 2, 04-423 Warszawa
tel. (022) 673-40-34, 673-40-35;
fax 673-52-05

Warszawa-Targówek
Urząd Gminy
ul. Kondratowicza 20, 03-285 Warszawa
tel. (022) 675-30-66; fax 675-22-43
www.targowek.waw.pl

Warszawa-Ursus
Urząd Gminy
ul. Sosnowskiego 16, 02-495 Warszawa
tel. (022) 662-77-72, 662-70-02, 667-92-69;
fax 662-63-97

Warszawa-Ursynów
Urząd Gminy
ul. Lanciego 14, 02-792 Warszawa
tel. (022) 649-40-85, 644-79-79;
fax 648-42-60
e-mail: ursynow@wonet.com.pl

Warszawa-Wawer
Urząd Gminy
ul. Żegańska 19, 04-713 Warszawa
tel. (022) 613-38-87; fax 613-38-92

Warszawa-Wilanów
Urząd Gminy
ul. St. Kostki Potockiego 11
02-958 Warszawa
tel. (022) 642-60-01; fax 642-76-43

Warszawa-Włochy
Urząd Gminy
al. Krakowska 110/114, 02-256 Warszawa
tel. (022) 846-63-30, 846-79-25;
fax 650-14-03

Western Warsaw Poviat

Błonie
Urząd Miasta i Gminy
Rynek 6, 05-870 Błonie
tel. (022) 725-30-04, 725-45-55;
fax 725-30-67

Izabelin
Urząd Gminy
ul. 3 Maja 42, 05-080 Izabelin
tel. (022) 722-80-05; fax 722-80-06

Kampinos
Urząd Gminy
ul. Niepokalanowska 3, 05-085 Kampinos
tel. (022) 725-00-40; fax 725-04-44

Leszno
Urząd Gminy
al. Wojska Polskiego 21, 05-084 Leszno
tel. (022) 725-80-05, 725-90-35;
fax 725-85-52

Łomianki
Urząd Miasta i Gminy
ul. Warszawska 115, 05-092 Łomianki
tel. (022) 751-10-01; fax 751-11-35
e-mail: info@lomianki.unig.gov.pl

Ożarów Mazowiecki
Urząd Miasta i Gminy
ul. Kolejowa 2, 05-850 Ożarów Mazowiecki
tel. (022) 722-22-07; fax 722-18-87

Stare Babice
Urząd Gminy
Rynek 32, 05-082 Stare Babice
tel. (022) 722-95-81; fax 722-90-21
e-mail: babice-stare@sos.com.pl
www.babice-stare.waw.pl

Węgrów Poviat

Grębków
Urząd Gminy
07-110 Grębków 37
tel./fax (025) 793-00-77

Korytnica
Urząd Gminy
ul. Szkolna 1, 07-120 Korytnica
tel. (025) 661-22-84; fax 661-22-60

Liw
Urząd Gminy
ul. Mickiewicza 2, 07-100 Węgrów
tel./fax (025) 792-28-21

Łochów
Urząd Gminy
al. Pokoju 75, 07-130 Łochów
tel. (025) 675-12-42; tel./fax 675-12-35

Miedzna
Urząd Gminy
pl. 11 Listopada 4, 07-106 Miedzna
tel. (025) 691-83-27; tel./fax 691-83-28

Sadowne
Urząd Gminy
ul. Kościuszki 3, 07-140 Sadowne
tel. (025) 675-33-08; fax 675-33-13

Stoczek
Urząd Gminy
ul. Kosowska 5, 07-104 Stoczek
tel. (025) 691-90-20; tel./fax 691-90-25

Węgrów
Urząd Miasta
Rynek Mariacki 16, 07-100 Węgrów
tel. (025) 792-23-26; fax 792-25-23

Wierzbno
Urząd Gminy
07-111 Wierzbno 90
tel. (025) 793-44-95;fax 793-45-72

Wołomin Poviat

Dąbrówka
Urząd Gminy
ul. Kościuszki 14, 05-252 Dąbrówka
tel. (029) 757-80-02, 757-80-03;
fax 757-82-20

Jadów
Urząd Gminy
ul. Świerczewskiego 17, 05-280 Jadów
tel. (025) 675-40-44; fax 675-43-84

Klembów
Urząd Gminy
05-205 Klembów
tel. (029) 799-93-90; tel./fax 757-39-92

Kobyłka
Urząd Miasta
ul. Wołomińska 1, 05-203 Kobyłka
tel. (022) 786-33-28; fax 786-31-11

Marki
Urząd Miasta
al. Piłsudskiego 95, 05-270 Marki
tel. (022) 781-10-03, 781-11-02;
fax 781-13-78

Poświętne
Urząd Gminy
ul. Krótka 1, 05-326 Poświętne
tel. (025) 776-70-21; fax 752-03-90

Radzymin
Urząd Miasta i Gminy
pl. Kościuszki 2, 05-250 Radzymin
tel. (025) 786-62-92; fax 786-51-95
e-mail: info@radzymin.unig.gov.pl

Strachówka
Urząd Gminy
ul. Norwida 6, 05-282 Strachówka
tel. (025) 675-60-26

Tłuszcz
Urząd Miasta i Gminy
ul. Warszawska 10, 05-240 Tłuszcz
tel./fax (029) 757-30-16

Wołomin
Urząd Miasta i Gminy
ul. Ogrodowa 4, 05-200 Wołomin
tel. (022) 787-64-81 do 90; fax 787-65-14
e-mail: unwol@medianet.com.pl

Ząbki
Urząd Miasta
ul. Wojska Polskiego 10, 05-091 Ząbki
tel. (022) 781-68-14 do 17; fax 781-68-13

Zielonka
Urząd Miasta
ul. Lipowa 5, 05-220 Zielonka
tel. (022) 781-99-60; fax 781-99-89

Wyszków Poviat

Brańszczyk
Urząd Gminy
ul. Jana Pawła II 45, 07-221 Brańszczyk
tel./fax (029) 679-40-40
e-mail: info@branszczyk.ug.gov.pl

Długosiodło
Urząd Gminy
ul. Kościuszki 2, 07-210 Długosiodło
tel. (0217) 620-73 w. 512

Rząśnik
Urząd Gminy
ul. Jesionowa 3, 07-205 Rząśnik
tel./fax (029) 742-19-90

Somianka
Urząd Gminy
07-203 Somianka
tel. (029) 742-18-90; tel./fax 742-18-96

Wyszków
Urząd Miasta i Gminy
al. Róż 2, 07-200 Wyszków
tel./fax (029) 742-40-20
e-mail: ugwyszk@btsnet.com.pl
www.bmb.pl/wyszkow

Zabrodzie
Urząd Gminy
07-230 Zabrodzie
tel. (029) 757-12-28; tel./fax 757-12-61

Zwoleń Poviat

Kazanów
Urząd Gminy
pl. Partyzantów 28, 26-713 Kazanów
tel. (048) 676-60-55, 676-60-66;
fax 676-60-33

Policzna
Urząd Gminy
ul. Prusa 11, 26-907 Policzna
tel. (048) 677-00-39; fax 677-00-51

Przyłęk
Urząd Gminy
26-704 Przyłęk
tel. (048) 677-30-16, 677-30-18, 677-30-19;
fax 677-30-01

Tczów
Urząd Gminy
26-706 Tczów
tel. (048) 676-80-22; tel./fax 676-80-23

Zwoleń
Urząd Miasta i Gminy
pl. Kochanowskiego 1, 26-700 Zwoleń
tel. (048) 676-22-10; tel./fax 676-27-26

Żuromin Poviat

Bieżuń
Urząd Miasta i Gminy
ul. Warszawska 1, 09-320 Bieżuń
tel. (023) 657-80-56

Kuczbork Osada
Urząd Gminy
ul. Mickiewicza 7, 09-310 Kuczbork Osada
tel./fax (023) 657-62-59

Lubowidz
Urząd Gminy
ul. Leśna 11, 09-304 Lubowidz
tel. (023) 658-20-78

Lutocin
Urząd Gminy
ul. Poniatowskiego 1, 09-317 Lutocin
tel./fax (023) 657-45-19

Siemiątkowo Koziebrodzkie
Urząd Gminy
09-135 Siemiątkowo Koziebrodzkie
tel. (023) 679-24-89

Żuromin
Urząd Miasta i Gminy
pl. Piłsudskiego 3, 09-300 Żuromin
tel. (023) 657-25-58; fax 657-25-40

Żyrardów Poviat

Mszczonów
Urząd Miasta i Gminy
ul. Grójecka 45, 96-320 Mszczonów
tel./fax (046) 857-17-64, 857-17-68,
857-16-89, 857-30-00

Puszcza Mariańska
Urząd Gminy
96-122 Puszcza Mariańska
tel. (046) 831-81-51, 831-81-69;
fax 831-81-18

Radziejowice
Urząd Gminy
ul. Kubickiego 10, 96-325 Radziejowice
tel. (046) 857-71-20, 857-71-71;
fax 857-71-22

Wiskitki
Urząd Gminy
ul. Kościuszki 1, 96-315 Wiskitki
tel. (046) 855-47-58, 856-72-12, 856-72-16,
856-72-84; fax 855-41-54

Żyrardów
Urząd Miasta
pl. Jana Pawła II 1, 96-300 Żyrardów
tel. centrala (046) 855-30-34;
tel./fax 855-37-82
e-mail: promocja@zyrardow.pl
www.zyrardow.pl

V. Cultural Institutions in Mazowieckie Voivodeship

Theatres

Warsaw

Ateneum Theatre
ul. Jaracza 2, tel. 625-73-30

Dramatyczny Theatre
Pałac Kultury i Nauki,
Pl. Defilad 1, tel. 656-68-44

Jewish Theatre
pl. Grzybowski 12/16, tel. 620-70-25

**Komedia Theatre
– Northern Centre of Art**
ul. Słowackiego 19a, tel. 833-68-80

Kwadrat Theatre
Czackiego 15/17, tel. 826-23-89

Mały Theatre
ul. Marszałkowska 122, tel. 827-50-22

National Theatre
pl. Teatralny 3, tel. 692-06-10

Na Woli Theatre
ul. Kasprzaka 22, tel. 632-24-78

Nowy Theatre
ul. Puławska 37/39, tel. 849-35-51

Ochoty Theatre
ul. Reja 9, tel. 825-85-44

Polski Theatre
ul. Karasia 2, tel. 826-79-92

Polski Theatre – Scena Kameralna
ul. Foksal 16, tel. 826-49-18

Powszechny Theatre
ul. Zamoyskiego 20, tel. 818-25-16

Rampa Theatre
ul. Kołowa 20, tel. 679-05-35, 679-89-76

"Roma" Music Hall
ul. Nowogrodzka 49, tel. 628-03-60

Rozmaitości Theatre
Marszałkowska 8, tel. 629-02-20

Scena Prezentacje Theatre
ul. Żelazna 51/53, tel. 620-82-88

Studio Theatre
Pałac Kultury i Nauki,
Pl. Defilad 1, tel. 620-21-02

Studio-Buffo Theatre
ul. Konopnickiej 6, tel. 625-47-09

Syrena Theatre
Riviera Remont, ul. Waryńskiego 12,
tel. 660-98-75

Tothe Lachmann „Poza" Videotheatre
Pałac Szustra, ul. Morskie Oko 2,
tel. 849-68-56, 825-32-34

Wielki Theatre – National Opera
pl. Teatralny 1, tel. 826-32-88

Współczesny Theatre
ul. Mokotowska 13, tel. 825-59-79

Warsaw Chamber Opera
al. Solidarności 76b, tel. 831-22-40

Płock

J. Szaniawski Theatre
pl. Nowy Rynek 11, tel. (024) 262-60-71

Radom

**Jan Kochanowski
Powszechny Theatre**
pl. Jagielloński 15, tel. 362-79-27

Museums

Warsaw

John Paul II Collection
pl. Bankowy 1, tel. 620-27-25

Royal Łazienki
ul. Agrykola 1, tel. 621-62-41

Archeological Museum
ul. Długa 52, tel. 831-15-37

Museum of Asia and Pacific
ul. Solec 24

Maria Dąbrowska Museum
ul. Polna 40 m. 31, tel. 25-31-13

Xawery Dunikowski Museum
Pałac Królikarnia, ul. Puławska 113a,
tel. 843-15-86

Extension X of Citadel Museum
ul. Skazańców 25, tel. 39-12-68

Etnographic Museum
ul. Kredytowa 1, tel. 827-76-41

Museum of Evolution PAN
Pałac Kultury i Nauki,
Pl. Defilad 1, Pałac Młodzieży,
tel. 656-66-37

Fryderyk Chopin Museum
Zamek Ostrogskich, ul. Okólnik 1,
tel. 826-59-35

Museum of Geology
ul. Rakowiecka 4, tel. 849-53-51

**History of Polish Peasant
Movement Museum**
al. Wilanowska 204, tel. 843-38-76

Historical Museum of Warsaw
Rynek Starego Miasta 42, tel. 635-16-25

Museum of the Iwaszkiewiczs in Stawiska
Podkowa Leśna, ul. Gołębia 1,
tel. 758-93-63

Museum of Caricature
ul. Kozia 11, tel. 827-88-95

Katyń Museum
ul. Powsińska 13, tel. 842-66-11

Museum of the Railways
ul. Towarowa 1, tel. 620-04-80

**Adam Mickiewicz Museum
of Literature**
Rynek Starego Miasta 20, tel. 831-76-91

Museum of Hunting and Horseriding
ul. Szwoleżerów 9

National Museum
al. Jerozolimskie 3, tel. 621-10-31

Museum of Independence
al. Solidarności 62, tel. 826-90-91

**I.J. Paderewski and Polish
Emmigration Museum**
ul. Szwoleżerów 9, tel. 622-64-34

**Royal Paper Mill Museum
in Jeziorna**
Konstancin-Jeziorna, ul. Mirkowska 45,
tel. 754-83-88

Pawiak Prison Museum
ul. Dzielna 24, tel. 831-13-17

Poster Museum
Wilanów, ul. S.K. Potockiego 10/16,
tel. 842-26-06

Museum of Industry
ul. Żelazna 51/53, tel. 620-47-92

Museum of Sports and Tourism
ul. Wawelska 5, tel. 825-04-07

Museum of Technology
Pałac Kultury i Nauki,
Pl. Defilad 1, tel. 656-67-47

Museum of Warsaw University
Pałac Kazimierzowski,
ul. Krakowskie Przedmieście 26/28,
tel. 620-03-81

Museum of Strife and Martyrdom
al. Szucha 25, tel. 629-49-19

Museum of the Polish Army
al. Jerozolimskie 3, tel. 629-52-71

Museum of Wola
ul. Srebrna 12, tel. 624-38-79

Museum of the Earth PAN
al. Na Skarpie 20/26, tel. 629-80-63

Museum in Wilanów
ul. S.K. Potockiego 10/16, tel. 841-07-95

Royal Castle
pl. Zamkowy 4, tel. 657-21-70,
fax 657-21-70

Ciechanów

Art Gallery 'Galeria C'
ul. Pułtuska 20 A, tel. 672-48-44

Museum of Mazovian Gentry
ul. Warszawska 61, tel. 672-55-87

Castle of Mazovian Dukes
ul. Zamkowa, tel. 672-40-64

Mława

Museum of Zawkrze Land
ul. 3 Maja, tel. (023) 654-33-48

Ostrołęka

Museum of Kurpie Culture
pl. Bema, tel. 764-35-00, 764-54-43

Płock

Diocese Museum
ul. Tumska 3 A, tel. 262-26-23

Museum of Mazovia
ul. Tumska 2, tel. 262-44-91, 92, 93

Płock Art Gallery
ul. Nowy Rynek 11, tel. 262-89-82

Pruszków

Museum of Ancient Mazovian Metallurgy
Pruszków, pl. Jana Pawła II 2,
tel. 758-72-66

Pułtusk

Regional Museum
Rynek, 06-100 Pułtusk,
tel. (023) 692-51-32

Radom

Museum of Scouting
ul. Jana i Jędrzeja Śniadeckich 2,
26-610 Radom, tel. (048) 667-22-67

Regional Museum
ul. Szydłowiecka 30, 26-612 Radom,
tel. (048) 331-59-28

Sierpc

Museum of the Mazovian Village – Skansen
ul. Narutowicza 64, tel. 275-28-83

Różne

Museum of Small Towns
Stary Rynek 19, 09-320 Bieżuń

J. Kochanowski Museum
26-908 Czarnolas, tel. (048) 677-20-05

Museum of Romanticism
06-406 Opinogóra, tel. (023) 671-70-25

O. Kolberg Museum
– Oddział Muzeum Ludowych
Instrumentów Muzycznych
al. WOP 11, 26-400 Przysucha,
tel. (048) 75-22-48

Museum of Folk Musical Instruments
ul. J. Sowińskiego 2, 26-500 Szydłowiec,
tel. (048) 617-17-89, 617-17-88

Museum of Warka History
ul. K. Pułaskiego 12, 05-660 Warka,
tel. (048) 667-24-41

Kazimierz Pułaski Museum
05-660 Winiary, tel. (048) 667-22-67

VI. Significant Cultural Centres in Mazowieckie Voivodeship

Białobrzegi Poviat

Ośrodek Kultury
05-127 Białobrzegi
tel. (022)

Miejsko-Gminny Ośrodek Kultury
ul. Kościelna 31, 26-800 Białobrzegi
tel. (048) 13-23-70

Gminny Ośrodek Kultury
ul. Mławska 4, 06-540 Radzanów
tel. (082) 18

Ciechanów Poviat

Miejsko-Gminny Ośrodek Kultury
ul. Targowa 6, 06-450 Glinojeck
tel. (023) 249

Gminny Ośrodek Kultury i Sportu
pl. Grunwaldzki 4, 06-460 Grudusk
tel. (023) 71-50-33

Gminny Ośrodek Kultury
ul. C.K. Norwida 2, 06-460 Opinogóra
tel. (023) 71-70-38

Garwolin Poviat

Gminny Ośrodek Kultury
08-412 Borowie
tel. (0248) 116-12

Ośrodek Kultury
ul. Nadwodna 1, 08-400 Garwolin
tel. (0248) 20-51, 24-21, 24-08

Gminny Ośrodek Kultury
Rynek 2, 08-480 Maciejowice
tel. (025) 104

Wiejski Dom Ludowy
08-450 Łaskarzew

Dom Pracy Twórczej
08-450 Łaskarzew
tel. (025) 45-120

Gminny Ośrodek Kultury
ul. Borowska 1, 08-441 Parysów
tel. (0248) 11-366

Miejsko-Gminny Ośrodek Kultury
08-440 Pilawa
tel. (0248) 11-064

Gminny Ośrodek Kultury
08-470 Wilga
tel. (0248) 13-562

Miejsko-Gminny Ośrodek Kultury
ul. R. Traugutta 5, 08-430 Żelechów
tel. 160

Gostynin Poviat

Dom Kultury
ul. 18 Stycznia 2, 09-500 Gostynin
tel. (024) 73-34-47

Gminny Ośrodek Kultury
ul. Wyzwolenia 7, 09-541 Pacyna
tel. (024) 85-80-56, 85-80-54

Gminny Ośrodek Kultury
ul. Warszawska 11, 09-540 Sanniki
tel. 170

Grodzisk Mazowiecki Poviat

Ośrodek Kultury Gminy
ul. J. Kilińskiego 9
05-825 Grodzisk Mazowiecki
tel. (022) 725-33-47

Miejski Ośrodek Kultury
ul. Kościelna 3, 05-822 Milanówek
tel. (0-22) 758-32-34

„Koło-Podkowa" – Ośrodek Kultury
ul. Świerkowa 1, 05-807 Podkowa Leśna
tel. (022) 758-94-41

Grójec Poviat

Centrum Kultury Regionalnej
ul. J. Piłsudskiego 1, 05-600 Grójec
tel. (0488) 64-23-06

Miejsko-Gminny Ośrodek Kultury
pl. Poświętne 11, 05-640 Mogielnica
tel. (0-48) c. 68-31-11 w. 44

Regionalny Ośrodek Kultury
ul. Ks. Oszkiela, 05-555 Tarczyn
tel. (0-22) 727-71-96

Ośrodek Kultury, Sportu i Wypoczynku „Warka"
ul. Warszawska 27, 05-660 Warka
tel. (0488) 72-421, fax 72-783

Kozienice Poviat

Dom Kultury
ul. 1 Maja 8, 26-900 Kozienice
tel. (048) 14-26-25

Gminny Ośrodek Kultury
ul. Saperów 30, 26-910 Magnuszew
tel. (048) 14-70-41 w. 97

Legionowo Poviat

Ogrodniczy Dom Kultury
ul. Modlińska 102, 05-110 Jabłonna
tel. (0-22) 782-47-37

Wojskowy Ośrodek Kultury „Legionowo"
ul. Zegrzyńska 1, 05-119 Legionowo
tel. (0-22) 680-64-12

Miejski Ośrodek Kultury
ul. K.c. Norwida 10, 05-120 Legionowo
tel. (022) 744-44-74

Ośrodek Kultury
05-126 Nieporęt
tel. (022) 774-63-22

Ośrodek Kultury
ul. Kościelna 22, 05-126 Nieporęt
tel. (022) 774-86-22

Ośrodek Kultury
pl. Wolności 7, 05-126 Nieporęt
tel. (022) 774-83-26

Ośrodek Kultury, Kultury Fizycznej i Rekreacji
ul. Pułtuska 47, 05-140 Serock
tel. (022) 782-73-50

Lipsko Poviat

Lipskie Centrum Kultury
Rynek 2, 27-300 Lipsko
tel. (048) 378-01-31, 378-01-84

Gminny Ośrodek Kultury
Rynek 17, 27-350 Sienno
tel. (048) c. 78-16-11 w. 62

Gminny Ośrodek Kultury
pl. Bolesława Śmiałego 6, 27-320 Solec
tel. (048) c. 78-12-11 w. 315

Maków Mazowiecki Poviat

Gminny Ośrodek Kultury
07-425 Czerwonka
tel. (029) c. 17-30-12, 17-23-00

Gminny Ośrodek Kultury
06-425 Karniewo
tel. (0238) 110-13

Gminny Ośrodek Kultury
Rynek, 06-212 Krasnosielc
tel. (029) 17-25-00

Miejski Dom Kultury
ul. S. Moniuszki 2
06-200 Maków Mazowiecki
tel. (029) 17-12-72

Gminny Ośrodek Upowszechniania Kultury im. Marszałka Józefa Piłsudskiego
ul. A. Mickiewicza 1, 06-230 Różan
tel. (029) 66-90-42

Gminny Ośrodek Kultury
ul. Ostrołęcka 24, 06-216 Sypniewo
tel. (029) 61-77-76

Gminny Ośrodek Kultury
06-220 Szelków
tel. (029) 17-24-00

Mińsk Mazowiecki Poviat

Gminny Ośrodek Kultury
05-307 Dobre
tel. (025) 71-520

Dom Kultury
ul. Warszawska 45, 05-310 Kałuszyn
tel. (025) 76-210

Miejski Dom Kultury
ul. Warszawska 173
05-300 Mińsk Mazowiecki
tel. (0256) 39-17, 52-08

Gminny Ośrodek Kultury
Rynek 32, 05-304 Stanisławów
tel. (025) 67-05-07

Miejski Ośrodek Kultury
ul. S. Starzyńskiego 21, 05-440 Wesoła
tel. (022) 773-95-06

Mława Poviat

Miejski Dom Kultury
Stary Rynek 13, 06-500 Mława
tel. (023) 54-35-85

Gminny Ośrodek Kultury
06-550 Szreńsk
tel. 122

Nowy Dwór Mazowiecki Poviat

Gminny Ośrodek Kultury
ul. Partyzantów 1, 05-153 Leoncin
tel. (022) c. 785-65-82 w. 27, 14

Gminny Ośrodek Kultury
ul. J. Kilińskiego 1, 05-180 Pomiechówek
tel. (022) 785-41-55

Dom Kultury
ul. K. Koźmińskiego 39
05-170 Zakroczym
tel. (022) 785-21-89

Ostrołęka Poviat

Gminny Ośrodek Kulturalno-Oświatowy
07-402 Lelis
tel. (029) 61-10-77

Gminny Ośrodek Kultury
ul. Kościelna 19, 07-437 Łyse
tel. (029) 47

Gminny Ośrodek Kultury
ul. Przedszkolna 3, 07-320 Małkinia
tel. (0217) 55-062

Gminny Ośrodek Kultury
pl. Wolności 48, 07-430 Myszyniec
tel. (029) 147

Nowodworski Ośrodek Kultury
ul. Mazowiecka 8
05-100 Nowy Dwór Mazowiecki
tel. 775-33-84

Centrum Kultury
ul. Szkolna 6, 07-405 Troszyn
tel. (029) c. 61-11-70

Ostrów Mazowiecka Poviat

Miejski Dom Kultury
ul. 3 Maja 50, 07-300 Ostrów Mazowiecka
tel. (0217) 62-703

Gminne Centrum Kultury Sportu i Rekreacji
ul. Zastawska 13, 07-311 Wąsewo
tel. (0217) 61-592

Otwock Poviat

Gminny Ośrodek Kultury
ul. Regucka 4, 05-170 Celestynów
tel. (022) 789-71-02

Miejski Ośrodek Kultury
ul. Kardynała S. Wyszyńskiego 1
05-420 Józefów
tel. (022) 789-20-26

Klub Osiedlowy „Grota" Spółdzielni Mieszkaniowej „Otwock"
ul. S. Grota-Roweckiego 2
05-480 Karczew
tel. (022) 779-63-90

Miejsko-Gminny Ośrodek Kultury
ul. Świderska 27, 05-480 Karczew
tel. (022) 779-65-17

Klub Kultury
ul. Pilawska 23, 08-445 Osieck
tel. (022) 779-16-97

Klub Dziecięcy „Batory”
ul. Stefana Batorego 34, 05-400 Otwock
tel. (022) 779-50-97

Klub „Proton”
ul. J. Poniatowskiego 1, 05-400 Otwock
tel. (022) 779-59-77

Miejski Ośrodek Kultury
ul. Warszawska 11/13, 05-400 Otwock
tel. (022) 779-26-61

Młodzieżowy Dom Kultury
ul. J. Poniatowskiego 10, 05-400 Otwock
tel. (022) 779-33-57

Gminny Ośrodek Kultury
ul. Kościelna 21, 05-462 Wiązowna
tel. (022) 789-01-46, 789-03-48

Piaseczno Poviat

Ośrodek Kultury
ul. Rybie 8, 05-530 Góra Kalwaria
tel. (022) 757-35-39

Ośrodek Kultury
ul. Oborska 2, 05-510 Konstancin Jeziorna
tel. (022) 756-40-46

Gminny Ośrodek Kultury, Czytelnictwa i Rekreacji
ul. Gminnej Rady Narodowej 60
05-506 Lesznowola
tel. (0-22) c. 757-93-40 do 42 w. 12

Miejsko-Gminny Ośrodek Kultury
ul. T. Kościuszki 49, 05-500 Piaseczno
tel. (022) 756-76-00

Płock Poviat

Gminny Ośrodek Kultury
09-420 Bielsk
tel. (024) 61-55-74

Miejsko-Gminny Ośrodek Kultury
ul. Tylna 1, 09-210 Drobin
tel. (024) 61-57-00

Miejsko-Gminny Ośrodek Kultury
Stary Rynek 14, 09-530 Gąbin
tel. (024) 10-30-77

Gminny Ośrodek Kultury
ul. Szkolna 3, 09-451 Radzanowo
tel. (024) 61-34-84

Gminny Ośrodek Kultury
ul. B. Głowackiego 2, 09-440 Staroźreby

Płońsk Poviat

Gminny Ośrodek Kultury
ul. Warszawska 3
09-445 Czerwińsk n. Wisłą
tel. 115, 76

Gminny Ośrodek Kultury
09-120 Nowe Miasto
tel. (023) 311

Miejskie Centrum Kultury
ul. Płocka 50, 09-100 Płońsk
tel. (023) 62-22-32, 62-27-02

Gminny Ośrodek Kultury
pl. M. Nowotki 8 A, 09-110 Sochocin
tel. (023) 61-80-01

Pruszków Poviat

Dom Kultury – Filia Ośrodka Kultury
05-870 Błonie
tel. (022) 725-33-47

Miejsko-Gminny Ośrodek Kultury
ul. J. Wilsona 2, 05-840 Brwinów
tel. (022) 729-59-34

Miejski Ośrodek Kultury
ul. Warszawska 24, 05-820 Piastów
tel. (022) 723-65-50

Dom Kultury Kolejarza
ul. B. Prusa 8, 05-800 Pruszków
tel. (022) 758-69-43

Miejski Ośrodek Kultury
ul. Poprzeczna 5, 05-800 Pruszków
tel. (022) c. 728-39-40 , 42 i 44

Młodzieżowy Dom Kultury
ul. T. Kościuszki 41, 05-800 Pruszków
tel. (022) 758-81-28

Gminny Ośrodek Kultury
ul. Szkolna 2 A, 05-090 Raszyn
tel. (022) 756-09-87

Przasnysz Poviat

Ośrodek Upowszechniania Kultury
ul. Żabia 1, 06-330 Chorzele
tel. (0478) 189

Miejski Dom Kultury
ul. 3 Maja 16, 06-300 Przasnysz
tel. (0478) 32-20

205

Przysucha Poviat

Gminny Ośrodek Kultury
ul. Szkolna 1, 26-434 Gielniów
tel. (048) c. 75-15-11 w. 57

Dom Kultury
ul. Radomska 9, 26-400 Przysucha
tel. (048) 75-24-73, 75-23-81

Gminny Ośrodek Kultury
26-432 Wieniawa
tel. (048) c. 75-71-11 w. 62

Pułtusk Poviat

Miejski Dom Kultury
pl. Teatralny 4, 06-100 Pułtusk
tel. (023) 83-421

Radom Poviat

Dom Kultury
ul. Garbarska 5, 27-100 Iłża
tel. (048) 16-31-08

Gminny Ośrodek Kultury
ul. Warszawska 2, 26-660 Jedlińsk
tel. (048) 321-30-52

Ośrodek Upowszechniania Kultury „Kasyno"
ul. Zakładowa 7, 26-940 Pionki
tel. (048) 12-20-24

Miejski Ośrodek Kultury
ul. Radomska 1, 26-940 Pionki
tel. (048) 12-51-25; fax 12-52-25

Dom Kultury „Amfiteatr"
ul. Parkowa 1, 26-600 Radom
tel. (048) 42-968

Dom Kultury „Idalin"
ul. Bluszczowa 4/8, 26-600 Radom
tel. (048) 52-717

Dom Kultury „Obozisko"
ul. Śniadeckich 2, 26-600 Radom
tel. (048) 44-207

Klub Środowisk Twórczych „Łaźnia"
ul. St. Żeromskiego 56, 26-600 Radom
tel. (048) 362-18-87; fax 360-17-18

S.c. Centrum Kultury „Południe"
ul. Czarnoleska 17, 26-600 Radom
tel. (048) 31-82-11

Miejskie Centrum Kultury i Informacji Międzynarodowej
ul. R. Traugutta 31/32, 26-600 Radom
tel. (048) 360-17-27; fax 360-17-27

Miejsko-Gminny Ośrodek Kultury
ul. J. Słowackiego 5, 26-640 Skaryszew
tel. (048) 610-30-29

Młodzieżowy Dom Kultury
ul. I. Daszyńskiego 5, 26-600 Radom
tel. (048) 360-62-02

Gminny Dom Kultury
Osiedle bl. 27, 26-520 Wierzbica
tel. (048) 18-20-33

Gminny Ośrodek Kultury
ul. Opoczyńska 9, 26-625 Wolanów
tel. (048) c. 10-42-11 w. 65

Siedlce Poviat

Klub Młodzieży
ul. Siedlecka 82, 08-130 Kotuń
tel. (0-25) 41-43-63

Gminny Ośrodek Kultury
ul. 1 Maja 1, 08-109 Przesmyki
tel. (025) 12-317; fax 12-322

Centrum Kultury i Sztuki
ul. Bpa I. Świrskiego 31, 08-100 Siedlce
tel. (025) 44-68-00; fax 44-56-46

Gminny Ośrodek Kultury
08-119 Siedlce
tel. (025) 44-36-91

Gminny Ośrodek Kultury
ul. Batalionów Chłopskich 2
08-112 Wiśniew
tel. (025) 41-73-11

Gminny Ośrodek Kultury
ul. Terespolska 1
08-106 Zbuczyn Poduchowny
tel. (025) 641-61-61

Sierpc Poviat

Dom Kultury
ul. Piastowska 37, 09-200 Sierpc
tel. (024) 75-24-93

Sochaczew Poviat

Gminny Ośrodek Kultury
05-910 Iłów
tel. (024) 77-41-87

Sokołów Podlaski Poviat

Gminny Ośrodek Kultury
ul. Kubusia Puchatka
08-304 Jabłonna Lacka
tel. (0417) 87-10-36

Gminny Ośrodek Kultury
ul. Słoneczna 2, 08-330 Kosów Lacki
tel. 157 i 57

Gminny Ośrodek Kultury
ul. Strażacka 5, 08-307 Repki
tel. (0417) 87-50-80

Gminny Ośrodek Kultury
ul. Lipowa 2, 08-320 Sterdyń
tel. (025) 87-02-65

Szydłowiec Poviat

Dom Pracy Twórczej „Reymontówka"
08-130 Chlewiska
tel. (025) 41-43-19

Ośrodek Kultury
ul. T. Kościuszki 209, 26-500 Szydłowec
tel. (048) 17-15-38

Szydłowiecki Ośrodek Kultury
ul. Gen. J. Sowińskiego 2
26-500 Szydłowiec
tel. (048) 17-02-96, 17-19-51

Warsaw Poviat

Bielański Ośrodek Kultury
ul. C. Goldoniego 1, 01-913 Warszawa
tel. (022) 34-65-47

Centrum Amerykańskie
ul. Senatorska 13/15, 00-071 Warszawa
tel. (022) 26-21-17; fax 26-06-62

Centrum Sztuki Współczesnej
al. Ujazdowskie 6, 00-461 Warszawa
tel. (022) c. 628-12-71; fax 628-95-50

Dom Kultury – Włochy
ul. Bolesława Chrobrego 27
02-479 Warszawa
tel. (022) 863-73-23; fax 863-92-69

Dom Kultury „Kadr"
ul. Gotarda 16, 02-683 Warszawa
tel. (022) 43-88-81

Dom Kultury „Rakowiec"
ul. Wiślicka 8, 02-114 Warszawa
tel. (022) 23-66-97, 23-66-72

Dom Kultury „Świt"
ul. P. Wysockiego 11, 03-371 Warszawa
tel. (022) 11-01-05, 11-11-09

Dom Kultury „Wygoda"
ul. Koniecpolska 14, 04-267 Warszawa
(022) 12-06-33

Dom Kultury „Zacisze"
ul. Blokowa 1, 03-641 Warszawa
tel. (022) 679-84-69; fax 679-98-60

**Dom Kultury Przedsiębiorstwa Usług
Socjalnych i Mieszkaniowych**
ul. E. Ciołka 16, 01-402 Warszawa
(022) c. 36-02-41 w. 243, 245

Dom Wojska Polskiego
ul. S. Banacha 2, 02-097 Warszawa
tel. (022) 23-50-08

**Dzielnicowe Centrum Promocji Kultury
Dzielnicy Praga-Południe Gminy
Warszawa Centrum**
ul. Grochowska 274, 04-844 Warszawa
tel. (022) c. 612-47-12 w. 25

**Dzielnicowy Dom Kultury – Centrum
Edukacyjno-Kulturalne „Łowicka"**
ul. Łowicka 21, 02-502 Warszawa
tel. (022) 45-56-75, 45-50-62;
fax 45-56-75

Dzielnicowy Dom Kultury Nauczyciela
ul. Działdowska 6, 01-184 Warszawa
tel. (022) 632-31-91, 632-31-96

**Dzielnicowy Ośrodek Kultury Wola
im. S. Żeromskiego**
ul. Obozowa 85, 01-425 Warszawa
tel. (022) 36-22-15, 36-44-72

Klub „Chomiczówka"
ul. Pabla Nerudy 1, 01-926 Warszawa
tel. (022) 669-74-18

Klub „Helios"
ul. Wspólna Droga 13, 04-345 Warszawa
tel. (022) 610-75-31

Klub „Ikar"
ul. Orlego Lotu 6, 03-982 Warszawa
tel. (022) 671-26-59

Klub „Iskra"
ul. Brygady Pościgowej 6
03-984 Warszawa
tel. (022) 681-70-06

Klub „Kuźnia"
ul. Ząbkowska 42, 03-735 Warszawa
tel. (022) 18-58-59, 619-42-67

Klub „Nad Jeziorkiem"
ul. Ostrzycka 2/4, 04-035 Warszawa
tel. (022) 13-09-64, 10-07-64

Klub „Orion"
ul. Egipska 7, 03-977 Warszawa
tel. (022) 672-02-30

Klub „Panorama"
ul. Górnośląska 1, 00-443 Warszawa
tel. (022) 629-22-23

Klub „Relax"
ul. Witolińska 2 A, 04-185 Warszawa
tel. (022)13-78-71

Klub Księgarza
Rynek Starego Miasta 22
00-272 Warszawa
tel. (022) 636-25-97

Klub Nauczyciela
ul. Radomska 13/21, 02-325 Warszawa
tel. (022) 23-37-56

Liceum Francuskie – Centrum Kultury „Rene Gościme"
ul. Walecznych 4/6, 03-916 Warszawa
tel. (022) 617-62-31

Młodzieżowy Dom Kultury
ul. H.Ch. Andersena 4, 01-911 Warszawa
tel. (022) 35-98-45

Młodzieżowy Dom Kultury
ul. Białobrzeska 19, 02-364 Warszawa
tel. (022) 22-28-95

Młodzieżowy Dom Kultury
ul. Puławska 97, 02-595 Warszawa
tel. (022) 45-51-21

Młodzieżowy Dom Kultury „Bielany"
ul. Cegłowska 39, 01-809 Warszawa
tel. (022) 34-13-47

Młodzieżowy Dom Kultury im. W. Broniewskiego
ul. Łazienkowska 7, 00-449 Warszawa
tel. (022) 629-47-10, 621-68-32

Mokotowski Klub Nauczyciela
ul. A. Odyńca 57, 00-644 Warszawa
tel. (022) 44-45-77

Ośrodek Edukacji Kulturalnej „Sadyba"
ul. Korczyńska 6, 02-934 Warszawa
tel. (022) 42-27-93; fax 642-59-08

Ośrodek Kultury „Arsus"
ul. Traktorzystów 14, 02-495 Warszawa
tel. (022) 667-34-54; fax 662-76-26

Ośrodek Kultury Ochoty
ul. Grójecka 75, 02-094 Warszawa
tel. (022) 22-48-70, 22-74-36;
fax 22-93-17

Pałac Młodzieży
Pałac Kultury i Sztuki
ul. Świętokrzyska, 00-901Warszawa
tel. (022) 620-33-63

Spółdzielczy Dom Kultury „Kamionek"
ul. Kinowa 19, 04-030 Warszawa
tel. (022) 10-14-57, 13-53-28;
fax 10-52-50

Staromiejski Dom Kultury
Rynek Starego Miasta 2
00-272 Warszawa
tel. (022) 831-23-75, 831-17-15;
fax 831-99-31

Stołeczne Centrum Edukacji Kulturalnej
ul. Jezuicka 4, 00-281 Warszawa
tel. (022) 831-37-62, 831-53-93;
fax 831-33-35

Stołeczny Klub Garnizonowy
al. Niepodległości 141, 02-570 Warszawa
tel. (022) 49-48-58

Śródmiejski Klub
ul. Hoża 41, 00-681 Warszawa
tel. (022) 621-95-32; fax 31-99-31

Zespół Wolskich Placówek Edukacji Kulturalnej
ul. J. Brożka 1ᴬ, 01-442 Warszawa
tel. (022) 36-13-13

Western Warsaw Poviat

Ośrodek Kultury „Poniatówka"
ul. C. Norwida 1, 05-870 Błonie
tel. (022) 725-43-26

Gminny Ośrodek Kultury i Sportu
ul. Szkolna 10, 05-084 Leszno
tel. (022) 725-80-91

Dom Kultury
ul. Wiejska 12 ᴬ, 05-092 Łomianki
tel. (022) 751-35-02

Ośrodek Kultury „Uśmiech"
ul. Konotopska 6
05-850 Ożarów Mazowiecki
tel. (022) 722-14-45

Węgrów Poviat

Gminny Ośrodek Kultury
pl. Wolności 4, 07-106 Miedzna
tel. (0258)12-576

Miejski i Gminny Ośrodek Kultury
ul. 1 Maja 22, 07-130 Łochów
tel. (025) 12-16-75

Miejsko-Gminny Ośrodek Kultury i Wypoczynku
ul. J. Piłsudskiego 21
21-450 Stoczek Łukowski
tel. (025) 797-00-54

Węgrowski Ośrodek Kultury
ul. A. Mickiewicza 4 A, 07-100 Węgrów
tel. (0258) 49-14

Wołomin Poviat

Gminny Ośrodek Kultury
ul. K. Świerczewskiego 17, 07-160 Jadów
tel. (025) 75-10-88, 75-14-59,
c. 75-10-89 w. 107, 47

Centrum Kultury
05-205 Klembów
tel. (022) 776-71-60

Miejski Ośrodek Kultury
ul. J. Fałata 4 A, 05-230 Kobyłka
tel. (022) 786-13-73, 786-20-73

Marecki Ośrodek Kultury
ul. Fabryczna 2, 05-270 Marki
tel. (022) 781-14-06

Miejsko-Gminny Ośrodek Kultury
ul. Komunalna 2, 05-250 Radzymin
tel. (022) 786-52-99

Centrum Kultury
ul. Szkolna 1, 05-240 Tłuszcz
tel. (0216) 73-134

Miejski Dom Kultury
ul. Mariańska 7, 05-200 Wołomin
tel. (022) c. 776-34-81 w. 173

Miejski Ośrodek Kultury
ul. J. Słowackiego 10, 05-091 Ząbki
tel. (022) 781-64-30, 781-64-30

Miejski Ośrodek Kultury
ul. Literacka 20, 05-220 Zielonka
tel. (022) 781-04-18; fax 781-04-18

Wyszków Poviat

Gminne Centrum Kultury i Informacji
ul. I armii Wojska Polskiego
07-221 Brańszczyk
tel. (0216) 21-490; fax 21-490

Gminny Ośrodek Kultury
07-203 Somianka
tel. (0216) 12-860

Dom Kultury
ul. Prosta 7, 07-200 Wyszków
tel. (0216) 24-448, 23-555;
fax 24-448

Gminne Centrum Kultury
07-230 Zabrodzie
tel. (0216) 71-254

Gminny Ośrodek Kultury
ul. Dąbrowszczaków 4
07-210 Długosiodło
tel. 140

Zwoleń Poviat

Dom Kultury
ul. Puławska 6, 26-700 Zwoleń
tel. (048) 676-27-85

Żuromin Poviat

Miejsko-Gminny Ośrodek Kultury
ul. Mławska 5, 09-320 Bieżuń
tel. 4

Żuromińskie Centrum Kultury i Sportu
pl. J. Piłsudskiego 1, 09-300 Żuromin
tel. (023) 57-27-99, 57-27-97

Note on Sources and Bibliography

The fundamental part of this presentation of the voivodeship of Mazovia was written in September–October 1999. Available statistics thus pertained primarily to the year 1998 and referred to voivodeships in accordance with th binding territorial divisione then. A special publication issued by the Main Statistical Office (GUS) *Polska w nowym podziale terytorialnym*, which attempted to overcome this problem, appeared in 1998 and contained data from 1997, aggregated at the level of the new voivodeships (in numerous cases dating from 1996). The authors of this work, concerned with topicality, endeavoured to use the latest data, in particular by referring to data supplied by the Main Statistical Office in Warsaw, the results of the research conducted in the Institute of Economic Sciences at the Polish Academy of Sciences and the Institute of Studies into Market Economy, the Local Data Base at GUS, the REGON system data, data supplied by the State Agency for Foreign Investments, and own calculations. Upon select occasions, they resorted to information obtained from government and self-government administrative units and even enterprises. Sources of quantitative data are indicated in footnotes below suitable tables, and in those cases when this practice was omitted, due to necessary abbreviations or the incidental nature of the references, they are based on universally available GUS data. In select situations, despite topical fragmentary data at our disposal, it was necessary to resign from their presentation for the sake of comparing the characteristics of particular analysis units.

In the chapter on poviats, an important role was played by the development potential index, constructed and applied by the Centre for Development Studies. The index in question takes into consideration the following criteria: a) economic activity (the number of private firms and the rate of their increase, the level of employment, and the size of the economic sector); b) civic activity (the member of non-profit organisations, attendance at latest self-government elections); the emigration balance in 1998); d) the quality of the infrastructure (telecommunication, state of roads); e) self-government investments calculated per capita in the course of the last five years. The applied point system is as follows: low potential (to 2 points), middle potential (2–4 points), high potential (more than 4 points). A detailed presentation of sources to the chapter on the history of Mazovia would demand several pages. The same is true of the chapter on Mazovian natural environment, society and culture. The editors thus resolved that a popular publication such as ours can and even should resign from footnotes, commentaries and methodological explanations characteristic for scientific monographs. In the bibliography, we were compelled to restrict ourselves to listing the most significant works, both popular and relatively easily accessible. The establishment of the addresses and telephone numbers of self-government administration offices encountered certain unexpected obstacles. We thus resorted to data contained in *Gospodarczy atlas Polski 1999* (CD version, obtained through the intermediary of the Marshal's Office), which in many cases we were able to bring up to date.

Basic Literature

Biuletyn Statystyczny Województwa Mazowieckiego 1999, nr 7–9.

Dymek B., *Mazowsze do 1247 r. (zarys dziejów)*, Warszawa 1995.

Dymek B., *Udzielne księstwo mazowieckie 1247–1381 (zarys dziejów)*, Warszawa 1996.

Dziemianowicz W., „Struktura gospodarcza województwa" (in:) K. Gawlikowska-Hueckel (ed.), *Województwo mazowieckie*, Instytut Badań nad Gospodarką Rynkową (dalej IBnGR), seria Regiony Polski, Gdańsk–Warszawa 1999.

Gawlikowska-Hueckel K., D. Sobczak, *Atrakcyjność inwestycyjna województw*, IBnGR, Gdańsk 1999.

Geysztor A., H. Samsonowicz (eds.), *Dzieje Mazowsza do 1526 roku*, Warszawa 1994.

Gieysztorowa I., A. Zahorski, *Cztery wieki Mazowsza. Szkice z dziejów 1526–1914*, Warszawa 1968.

Glinka T., M. Kamiński, M. Piasecki, K. Przygoda, A. Walenciak, *Mazowsze Północne. Przewodnik*, Warszawa 1998.

Kociszewski A., *Mazowsze w epoce napoleońskiej*, Ciechanów 1976.

Kondracki J., *Regionalizacja fizyczno-geograficzna Polski*, Wydawnictwo Naukowe PWN, Warszawa 1998.

Mały rocznik statystyczny 1999, GUS, Warszawa 1999.

Mazowsze w dwudziestoleciu międzywojennym (w granicach województwa warszawskiego), Warszawa 1998.

Nawrot A., *Bilans instytucji wspierania biznesu w Polsce. Raport wstępny*, IBnGR, Gdańsk 1999.

Orłowski W.M., E. Saganowska, L. Zienkowski, *Szacunek produktu krajowego brutto według 16 województw za 1996 i 1997 rok. (Metoda uproszczona)*, Zakład Badań Statystyczno-Ekonomicznych GUS i PAN, seria: Z Prac Zakładu Badań Statystyczno-Ekonomicznych, Zeszyt 262, Warszawa 1998.

Pazyra S., *Geneza i rozwój miast mazowieckich*, Warszawa 1959.

Polska w nowym podziale terytorialnym, GUS, Warszawa 1998.

Problemy regionu warszawskiego, t. V: *Mazowsze, kształtowanie struktur przestrzennych*, Szkoła Główna Handlowa. Instytut Gospodarstwa Społecznego, Warszawa 1989.

„Rocznik Mazowiecki", t. I–X, Warszawa 1967–1998.

Rowiński J. M. Wigier, *Rolnictwo*, (in:) K. Gawlikowska-Hueckel (ed.), *Województwo mazowieckie*, IBnGR, seria Regiony Polski, Gdańsk–Warszawa 1999.

Skrok Z., *Mazowsze nieznane*, Warszawa 1999.

Stan środowiska w województwie mazowieckim, Raport Wojewódzkiego Inspektoratu Ochrony Środowiska w Warszawie, Warszawa 1999.

Swianiewicz P., W. Dziemianowicz, *Atrakcyjność inwestycyjna miast. II ranking*, IBnGR, Warszawa 1999.

Szymańska A., „Rynek pracy" (in:) K. Gawlikowska-Hueckel (ed.), *Województwo mazowieckie*, IBnGR, seria Regiony Polski, Gdańsk–Warszawa 1999.

Warszawa i Mazowsze, t. 1 i 2: *Rozważania nad dziejami*, Warszawa 1978–1998.

Warszawa i Mazowsze, t. 3: *Materiały do dziejów*, Warszawa 1999.

Warszawskie. Rozwój województwa w Polsce Ludowej, Warszawa 1972.

Zarycki T., *Nowa przestrzeń polityczna Polski*, EUROREG, Warszawa 1997.

Index of Localities

215